Betty Crocker

cookbook
for
women

The Complete Guide to
Women's Health and Wellness
at Every Stage of Life

BICENTENNIAL
1807
WILEY
2007
BICENTENNIAL

Wiley Publishing, Inc.

A heartfelt thanks to the numerous women who provided insightful quotes and shared the things that work in their quest to stay well every day.

Library of Congress Cataloging-in-Publication Data:

Betty Crocker cookbook for women : the complete guide to women's health and wellness at every stage of life / Betty Crocker editors.

    p. cm.

    Includes index.

    ISBN: 978-0-471-99797-9 (cloth)

    1. Women—Nutrition. 2. Women—Health and hygiene. 3. Cookery. I. Crocker, Betty.

    TX361.W55B48 2007

    641.5--dc22

                       2006036936

Manufactured in the United States of America

10 9 8 7 6 5 4 3

General Mills

Director, Book and Online Publishing: Kim Walter

Manager, Cookbook Publishing: Lois Tlusty

Senior Editor: Cheri Olerud

Recipe Development and Testing: Betty Crocker Kitchens

Photography: General Mills Photography Studios and Image Library

Photographer: Val Bourassa

Food Stylists: Carol Eirones and Susan Brosious

Wiley Publishing, Inc.

Publisher: Natalie Chapman

Executive Editor: Anne Ficklen

Senior Production Editor: Angela Riley

Cover Design: Suzanne Sunwoo

Interior Design and Layout: Mauna Eichner and Lee Fukui

Photography Art Direction: Sue Schultz

Manufacturing Manager: Kevin Watt

Our Betty Crocker Kitchens seal guarantees success in your kitchen. Every recipe has been tested in America's Most Trusted Kitchens™ to meet our high standards of reliability, easy preparation and great taste.

Find more great ideas and shop for name-brand housewares at:

BettyCrocker.com

Dear Friend,

Betty Crocker cares about you . . . and all women. You may be newly married or married for a long time, you may be a thirty-something with or without a family, a working woman in your fifties or sixties, or a busy grandmother in your seventies. You may live in an apartment, house or condo, in a small town or a large city. You may represent any culture or faith on earth.

Different? In many ways, yes. But one common thing is shared . . . you are all women. This book can help you discover how to live a contented and healthy life whatever life stage you are in.

In this cookbook, a woman's life has been divided into decades and includes recipes, health and fitness tips, and practical cooking ideas to help you live a fun-filled life whatever age you happen to be now. Use the stages as a guide— remember great tips are included in every decade.

Betty wants you to know . . . living a healthier life is an important first step toward living a happier life.

To Your Health!

Betty Crocker

Contents

Ages and Stages of Life

Recipe for a Happy Life

If there is one thing you can share with your girlfriends, it's this:

Women, at any age, are complex and amazing creatures!

As women, you nurture and encourage those you love. You support the people who need you and are the voice of reason when someone needs advice.

You have power over the most complex and yet, the simplest things. You can remove a band-aid with ease, find lost car keys in seconds, add three more guests to the dinner table with little notice, while also putting in a long day at work.

But sometimes, it all catches up and you wonder, "Who does the simple things for *me*? When is it *my* turn? What keeps me going?"

Well, this book is just for you. It's about your health, your relationships, your needs and wishes. Taking the time to do for yourself is just as important as doing for those you love.

Create a recipe for a happy life, no matter what your age, by using this book as a guide to help you be well-fed, fit, positive and healthy.

Read the Directions . . . Yet Be Willing to Try New Spices

How do you cook up a healthy, well-balanced life? Physically, health means you feel *well*. And mentally that means you think *well*, that you feel calm and content with yourself. Health is more than fitness . . . it is all the good things you can do for you. Eating well and being active are part of it. Relationships and friendships, spending time in activities you love, are all part of a healthy life.

Health is about more than counting calories. It's about accepting yourself, loving yourself and being positive for yourself as well as others.

Staying-Well Secrets at Every Age

How do you stay healthy in body and mind? As you go through the sections, you'll notice a decade-by-decade approach to your body's lifetime of changing health needs. Before that, you'll want to know that there are a few secrets to staying well that apply to every age.

When your life seems a little (or even a lot) out of balance, take the time to do the things that make you feel good and keep you going. What are the secrets, the important positive habits that smart women of every age work into their everyday routines?

1. **Be Active**—Almost a prescription to feeling better, being active can help you relax, clear your mind, help you sleep better, keep your spirits "up" and may even prevent you from getting sick. No matter what your age, it's never too late to start, and even a few minutes a day is better than none at all. See Exercise to Stay Healthy, page 182.

2. **Eat Good Food**—Fruits, veggies, whole grains and foods moderate in fat and sodium will do you well. The chart, Eat More of These Essential Foods, page 35, will help you select the right foods and give you everyday hints to use them.

3. **Relax**—Spend a few minutes every day journaling, gardening, meditating, knitting, reading or just resting—anything that helps you relax while you reap the benefits of feeling good. Being more relaxed will also help you sleep better. To get started, read Reduce Your Stress, page 158.

The Recipe Calls for Fun

Recipe for A Happy Life

SERVES: ONE

If you feel your best, you'll be able to enjoy your life at every stage and others will notice. Just like laughter, you'll be infectious and fun to be around.

THE RECIPE:

1 cup Acceptance

1 cup Positive Attitude

1 cup Moxie (Shy People May Substitute: Quietly Just Do the Things You Want to Do)

1 cup Healthy Outlook

1 cup Optimism

1 cup Activity for a Full Life

Mix well and serve up every day. Goes well with favorite foods, friends and family.

RECIPE NOTE:

Flavor will vary from day to day.

---

4. **Harness Humor**—Keep a sense of humor during difficult situations. Stress management experts recommend laughter to release pent-up feelings and help keep perspective, it also appears to have actual physical effects that reduce stress hormone levels.

5. **Call Your Gal Pals**—Talk with a friend to help you handle stress and make decisions to more easily conquer life's challenges. A friend may see your situation differently and offer a creative solution. You can vent your anger or frustration, and feel better afterward. Maybe she'll share a similar experience—she can tell you what worked for her. Problems seem less challenging when you can share them with others.

6. **Get a Full Night's Sleep**—Sleep helps reset your body's natural energy and provides a time for both body and mind to rest. Experts recommend seven to nine hours of sleep per night to maintain a healthy body and a happy spirit.

No matter what age you are, it's important to know the challenges you're likely to face. Live life to the fullest as you journey through it.

As you read through the stages, try not to focus on the things you might have done when you were younger. Just chalk it up to experience and realize that it's never too late to exercise, eat well and reap the benefits those healthy habits deliver. The time to start is now . . .

The 20s can be marvelous, but it's also a time of many transitions. After all, 20-somethings are making the final bridge to adulthood and there are lots of choices and decisions to be made.

An old adage said that life was over at 40, but there are plenty of fit and fantastic 40-year-olds to prove that's just not true. And at 60 and 70, life offers tremendous opportunities, including volunteering, perhaps a job change, more free time, travel, retirement or grandkids that inspire life to begin all over again, in new and different ways.

At every age, life is what you make it.

AGES AND STAGES:

The 20s

In Your 20s:
Not a Teen Anymore

"Though I am a young woman, I'm trying to develop habits that will do well for me as I get older. I try to eat right and I exercise every day."

Amity D., age 25, promotion planner and active runner

The 20s are the first decade of true independence, and life seems to have endless potential. Women in their 20s will likely encounter many new joys—a first "real" job, the excitement of a new home or location, many new relationships, and maybe, marriage. It's exciting, but can feel stressful at times, too. Mom or Dad aren't there to cook balanced meals anymore

and the time you had for sports or for just hanging around when you were in high school or college seems to have disappeared.

In your 20s, make time for building long-term friendships and to keep in contact with your friends. Some of the joy of good health comes from sharing with others—roommates, friends or a new spouse or partner. In fact, pairing up with a new buddy for a long run once a week, taking a cooking class or the occasional spa visit go a long way toward creating healthy habits and friendships that support each other for a lifetime.

In your 20s, you'll want to establish healthy habits that can stay with you through life. Healthful eating, regular exercise and getting enough sleep all affect health now and for the decades to come. Don't start smoking and—if you smoke—this is the time to quit. Smoking's long-term health effects are widely known, yet the short-term ones are nasty, too. Yellowed teeth, bad breath and premature wrinkles around your eyes and lips are just a few of the unattractive extras.

Challenge Yourself to Healthy Habits Now

The Challenge: It's tough to eat right when you're on the go all day.

The Solution: Keep healthy snacks at your desk or in your car. Try:

➤ Fruits. Grapes, bananas, peaches, berries, apples, pears, clementines. Many fruits are filled with vitamins A and C and all supply fiber and phytonutrients.

➤ Vegetables. Baby carrots, edamame (soybeans in pods), green pepper and celery sticks can be purchased in "to go" packs. Many vegetables are filled with vitamins A and C and all supply fiber and phytonutrients.

➤ Cereal bars. Look for whole-grain bars with at least 3 grams of fiber.

➤ Low-fat popcorn. A great low-fat snack and a whole grain!

➤ Pretzels. Mix them with popcorn, cereal and a handful of nuts.

➤ Yogurts or string cheese. They're portable and loaded with calcium.

➤ Cracker snacks. Low-fat, whole-grain crackers and a slice of reduced-fat cheese are easy to pack into a lunch sack. An added plus: Whole-grain crackers contain B vitamins and phytonutrients.

➤ Dried fruits. A small amount of raisins, apricots, peaches, or dates.

➤ Nuts. A handful of walnuts, almonds, peanuts.

The Challenge: A deli or restaurant is much easier and faster than cooking. Can I find healthy food here?

The Solution: Healthy food choices can be made at the deli or take-out. A few good ones:

COFFEE COUNTER CHOICES

You can't do without your morning coffee but you forgot to grab breakfast. Dough-nuts, crème-filled confections and greasy, but yummy, fried breads beckon you to take them to work with you.

What's a girl to do?

Know your healthy choices so you can start your day the right way, even on the run. Choose yogurt, biscotti, nuts, trail mix, or select a low-fat baked item. Selections with whole grains (like a whole wheat bagel or whole wheat bread) are great choices. While lattes and chais are about 300 calories each, order it with skim milk which has many fewer calories and is loaded with calcium. Don't skip breakfast and don't feel guilty—just enjoy the healthier choice instead.

10 Essential Items for a Healthy Pantry

What can you keep on hand for healthy eating and cooking when you are on the go? Try stocking your pantry with:

- Canned beans: baked, pinto, black, chickpeas, soybeans

- Whole grains: quick-cooking whole wheat couscous and pasta, brown rice, barley and bulgur wheat, old-fashioned oatmeal

- Ready-to-eat whole-grain cereals

- Canned water-packed tuna

- Dried fruits: cranberries, raisins, apricots, bananas

- Canned water-packed fruits

- Canola oil or olive oil

- Peanut butter

- Yogurt

- Baby carrots

➤ Buy a rotisserie chicken and pair with a cornmeal muffin and side dishes like rice, baked beans or low-fat cole slaw.

➤ Order an appetizer (don't pick a fried one) and a side vegetable to make your meal.

➤ Go through the salad and vegetable bar at a grocery store. Add a low-calorie dressing or oil-based dressing on the side.

➤ Buy sliced turkey, roast beef or ham, put on slices of whole wheat bread and grab an apple or other fruit for dessert.

➤ At a restaurant, ask the server for low-calorie items. Find out whether items can be ordered steamed.

Choose menu items that contain fruits or vegetables and drink skim milk.

The Challenge: Energy drinks and bars promise energy and nutrition. Do they deliver?

The Solution: Great lower-calorie alternatives to the energy bars and drinks are fruits, vegetables and low-fat yogurt. Look for bars and drinks that contain:

➤ Whole-grain cereal or granola bars with a combination of protein, fat (no more than 3 grams of fat) and carbohydrates. One hundred to 200 calories is a good amount for a snack.

➤ Whole-grain granola bars may be higher in vitamins, minerals and fiber than regular bars.

➤ Many energy drinks provide electrolytes like sodium and potassium lost during exercise. Read the nutrition information on the label to be sure. Water is the best thirst quencher.

➤ If made from yogurt or milk, smoothies contain calcium and the nutrients from the fruit, including vitamins A and C.

The Challenge: Premenstrual syndrome (PMS) may increase food cravings, and cause a surge in appetite and fluid retention.

The Solution: Try eating foods that may help improve PMS symptoms.

➤ Vitamin D, folate and fiber may help improve PMS symptoms. Fortified whole-grain cereals with 4 or more grams of fiber, fat-free dairy foods and dark-green leafy vegetables are good sources of these nutrients.

➤ Try a multivitamin that includes 400 micrograms of folic acid.

➤ Cut back on salt, caffeine and alcohol.

➤ Drink lots of water.

➤ Find an exercise that works for you before, during and after your monthly period, like brisk walking.

GREAT WORKOUTS FOR 20-SOMETHINGS

In your 20s, try new workout options and find exercises you can do with a friend or in limited amounts of time. Join a gym to meet other people or find an exercise group. Weight-bearing exercises like walking or running are good because they help build bone density.

- Running or walking with a friend
- Kickboxing
- Rock climbing
- Hiking or biking
- A spinning class (biking)
- Interval training

The 30s

In Your 30s: When Is There Time for Me?

"I have to remind myself to take care of me so I am up to caring for my 2-year-old twins. I love volleyball, because it's social, active and I have fun with other adults."

Renae P., 39-year-old mother of twins and full-time administrative assistant

In your 30s, many new choices wait at your door. Are you ready for marriage or a partner? What about children? Grad school? A new job? All these choices and the oh-too-adult decisions are a challenge after the "It's all about me" 20s. The 30s are often filled with a sense of "What happened to me?" and "What's next?" A career choice with more responsibility, the time-challenge of deeper relationships and family mean less time to work out or even eat right. Career women and work-at-home moms face similar challenges without even knowing it: There's just no time for "me" let alone the large group of people who seem to depend on you for deadlines, dinner or carpool.

This is the decade to call a truce with yourself. Recognize that girlfriends and family are a key ingredient to your health. Schedule a walk with friends you rarely get to see. Gather up other moms for a roll 'n stroll two days a week with the kids. In short, gal, treat yourself to some "me" time again.

Find the Time for All the Challenges in Your Life

The Challenge: Stress, from work, home, or both, can affect your eating habits and how well certain nutrients are absorbed in your body.

The Solution: Take care of yourself, along with the others in your life.

➤ Eat regular meals.

➤ Choose foods high in vitamin C to strengthen your immune system, such as oranges, bell peppers, papayas, grapefruits, broccoli, kiwifruits, strawberries, tomatoes and cantaloupes.

➤ Drink lots of water and decaffeinated beverages (without added sugar) to stay hydrated.

➤ Be active—regular physical activity is a great stress reliever.

➤ Get enough sleep. Try to go to bed at the same time and get up at the same time every day.

➤ Take at least a few minutes each day to relax.

Five Ways to Make a Meal Healthy:

Use a nonstick spray, vegetable juice or broth for sautéing foods. If you use fat, try oil instead of butter and use as little as possible.

Choose romaine, spinach or dark-green leafy lettuce—they are filled with folic acid, vitamin C, beta-carotene (vitamin A) and potassium.

Eat the skin on fruits, potatoes and other veggies—it increases the fiber content.

Choose whole grains. Buy breads and pastas made with whole grains and rice that contains more fiber and disease-fighting phytochemicals.

Serve a fruit and a vegetable at every meal.

The Challenge: You are planning for a healthy pregnancy.

The Solution: Eat right for baby-to-be. Try:

➤ Enriched whole grains and ready-to-eat cereals, dark green leafy vegetables like spinach, beans and lentils are good sources of folic acid. This vitamin helps reduce the risk for certain types of birth defects.

➤ Check with your doctor to see if you need a prenatal supplement that supplies prenatal and pregnancy nutrients.

➤ Get about three daily servings of dairy and focus on low-fat or fat-free milk, yogurt and cheese.

➤ Stay active: go for a brisk walk, swim or do some type of exercise every day.

The Challenge: You want to get back into shape mentally and physically after having a baby.

The Solution: Breast-feeding increases the need for calories and post-partum healing adds extra stress. To take care of you and your baby:

➤ Eat 300 to 400 extra calories to replace the calories burned during breast-feeding.

➤ Physical activity is a good way to get back into shape, physically and mentally, but get your doctor's okay first.

➤ Continue to get enough dairy to supply you and your baby.

➤ Ask your doctor about continuing your prenatal multivitamin.

➤ Get enough sleep (it may seem impossible at times, but make it a priority) and nap when the baby naps—the house can wait!

The Challenge: Making good food choices is tough. Fast foods and snacks are convenient but can be high in calories and low in nutrients.

The Solution: Learn the healthy food choices at your favorite fast food places.

➤ Best low-calorie choices at the drive-through: chili, baked potato (no toppings or use salsa as a low-fat topping), grilled chicken, regular hamburger, skim milk, salads with low-fat or fat-free dressing, small yogurt parfaits, roast beef sandwiches. Submarine sandwiches made with lean meats and veggies and very little dressing are also good choices, as long as they're made with lean meats and just a bit of cheese.

➤ For quick trips in the car:

    ➤ Keep portable fresh fruit (apple, banana, orange or grapes) or a bag of dried fruit ready—they're big on vitamins and antioxidants.

    ➤ Stash a box of whole-grain cereal bars in the car. Look for varieties that offer 10 or more vitamins and minerals and at least 3 grams of fiber.

    ➤ Carry calcium-fortified juice, skim milk boxes and bottled water with you.

TIME OUT FOR A WORKOUT

It's tough to make time for fitness when everyone seems to want your time. Try these busy, mom-friendly tips:

- Look for a place to exercise that has child care for the kids or trade off kid-sitting with a friend or neighbor.

- Make your baby or toddler a part of your exercise routine.

- Connect with other women or moms. Try a social sport like golf, tennis, volleyball or aerobic dance.

- Low-impact dance classes, swimming, Pilates or any core-based exercise can help you regain pre-baby stomach fitness.

- Buy exercise tapes or DVDs that you can follow at home while the kids sleep or play.

The 30s are a time when bone loss is likely to begin, so weight-bearing exercises like walking, running and dancing are good choices. It's also a good time to begin strength-training or lifting weights to make your metabolism more efficient.

The Challenge: How to control your weight while cooking for your family.

The Solution: Kids need fat calories, you don't need as many!

- ➤ Stock the kitchen with fruits, veggies, whole-grain breads and cereals that provide many vitamins and minerals without an overabundance of calories.

- ➤ Snack on veggies and fruits if you're hungry while preparing dinner: Grapes, celery or carrots are good ones because they contain lots of water that help fill you up.

- ➤ Plan meals weekly. Serve one meal for the entire family—include at least one item on the menu you know everyone likes.

- ➤ Cue in to portion sizes. Check out page 239.

- ➤ Prepare only the amount of food your kids will eat.

- ➤ Let the kids decide how much they eat and store leftovers for a lunch or another meal.

- ➤ Don't eat the food left on the kids' plates.

- ➤ Look for every opportunity to be active: run after the kids at the playground, take a walk with the kids in the stroller.

The 40s

Fabulous and 40: A Time to De-stress

"Yoga is the perfect exercise. I get strength, flexibility and balance all in one workout. Besides, it's a great stress-reliever and has helped me relax."

Stacy P., 43-year-old mother of two school-age children

Forty and fabulous sums up this decade. You may be more confident with yourself: who you are, where you are in your life and who you are spending your life with. Prioritize the things that are important to you and focus on them.

Children are growing and demanding your time in a new way, your career may be fairly well established and most women feel comfortable at this point with family and friends. Or, you may be experiencing devastating life events for the first time, like job downsizing, divorce or even the death of someone close to you.

Juggling career and family continues to be a challenge and while most of us can handle occasional stressors, such as what comes first, work or family, the demanding partner or the demanding boss without personal ill consequences, long-term stressors are not good for your health. You're more likely to become injured under stress and the risk of long-term health problems like heart disease goes up. Try to work in things that make you feel good and help you relax or even feel that you are pampering yourself—like calling a friend, treating your-self to a manicure or a spa day, or just finding a quiet place to read a book once in awhile. Determine your stressors and figure out the best ways for you to counteract them. See Reduce Your Stress, page 158.

For many women, the 40s are family years. Taking charge and making work-family decisions—whether you work full-time, part-time, or choose to be a work-at-home mom—will add to your pleasure and comfort level at this busy time. You may also be caring for an aging parent, adding more to the stress (and stress-eating) equation. Remember: take time for you.

Fabulous Challenges for Change

The Challenge: How to lose weight without going on a fad diet.

The Solution: Follow these healthy tips:

➤ Eat a sensible diet moderate in fat and high in carbohydrates. Weight loss may take a bit longer but will be longer lasting.

- ➤ Include good fats such as canola or olive oil in moderate amounts. Otherwise, calories add up!

- ➤ Eat breakfast every day.

- ➤ Eat more veggies and fruit every day.

- ➤ Cut back on portions. See page 239. One place you don't want to cut is vegetable portions!

- ➤ Increase your activity, about one hour of brisk walking or other activity daily. If you can't take the time all at once, break it up into smaller parts during the day.

- ➤ Set goals and track your progress by keeping a food and exercise log.

- ➤ Learn how to manage stress. See Reduce Your Stress, page 158.

- ➤ Motivate and reward yourself with things other than food: a new outfit, a new hairdo, a day at the spa, finishing that great book.

- ➤ Rather than entirely depriving yourself of treats, allow yourself a small chocolate (or other treat) a day.

ARE THERE ANTI-AGING FOODS?

Anti-aging foods aren't miracle cures . . . they can't change the age on your driver's license, BUT they can add years to your life and a spring to your step. Include these foods for potential anti-aging benefits.

- • Water—Aids nearly every function of your body. Aim for 6 to 8 glasses daily.

- • Fish—Choose ones high in omega-3 fatty acids such as salmon, tuna and mackerel.

- • Fruits—Contain combinations of vitamins A and C and antioxidants. Try oranges, grapefruits, cantaloupes, apricots, papayas and mangoes, berries, prunes and pomegranates.

- • Vegetables—The darker the color, the better, because they contain more nutrients. Choose dark green lettuces, broccoli, peppers and carrots.

- • Yogurt—Eat non-fat or low-fat yogurt and milk products to pump up the calcium. Choose dairy foods fortified with vitamin D for a real bone health boost!

- • Ready-to-Eat Whole-Grain Cereals—They supply essential nutrients that are important for good overall health.

Fabulous Means Fit or "No One Told Me I'd Have to Actually Work to Stay in Shape."

Yes, Ms. 40-something, your metabolism is slowing down and it is harder to get in (and stay in) shape. What's the secret?

- Rev up metabolism and build muscle with strength-building activities like weight lifting and resistance training. Muscle burns more energy than fat! Check with your local Y, health club, bookstore or library for guidance and books.

- Stick with aerobic exercises, like walking, swimming and working out, for 30 minutes every day minimum. Sixty minutes is optimal to maintain weight and 90 minutes every day is necessary to lose weight.

- Find ways to be active every day. Go for a walk when waiting for someone, take the stairs, park your car farther away than usual from the store when running errands.

- Make an appointment for physical activity. Enter it into your PDA or calendar and treat it like an important meeting.

- Find a buddy to partner up with to stay on track with exercising.

The Challenge: Dipping estrogen levels change nutrition needs and a woman's health status.

The Solution: Adjust your 40s diet to improve your health.

- ➤ Add extra calcium to postpone bone loss. Select four calcium-rich foods each day, like skim milk and reduced-fat cheese, yogurt, calcium-fortified juice, tofu and soymilk with added calcium.

- ➤ Eat less saturated and trans fat. Use canola or olive oil to help lower risk for heart disease.

- ➤ Eat 1 1/2 cups fruit and 2 1/2 to 3 cups vegetables, including green leafy and orange vegetables, every day. Divide it up into half-cup servings—two in the morning, one for midmorning snack, three at lunch and three for dinner. Most have no fat and are a good source of fiber.

- ➤ Choose whole grains. Eat three servings of whole-grain foods each day—cereal at breakfast, whole-grain bread at lunch, brown rice or whole wheat pasta for dinner.

The Challenge: As you get closer to 50, symptoms of peri-menopause or menopause may begin.

The Solution: Symptoms may ease up with a few changes in what you eat:

➤ Include soybeans. Use pre-cooked, canned soybeans in salads and casseroles. They contain phytoestrogens (naturally occurring substances that mimic estrogen activity).

➤ Add soy products like low-fat soymilk on your cereal and in recipes.

➤ Snack on edamame (soybeans in pods) or 1/2 cup of roasted soy nuts.

➤ Substitute diced extra-firm tofu for meat in sautés and casseroles.

The 50s

Fit to Be 50

"I've learned that it takes both healthy eating and exercise to keep my weight down. They go hand in hand."

Cathy P., 50-year-old cardiovascular nurse who works out every morning

You may be 50 but you are certainly NOT over the hill. In fact, the 50s can be pretty glorious. Your children may be in their teens or grown and you might find time to devote more attention to yourself and your health needs now.

For many women, the 50s are the decade when *a lot* of body changes take place. As your estrogen levels decline, and menopause nears, major changes are in store for your body.

As your body transitions into menopause (typically lasts about five years), you may notice physical and emotional changes that can be the result of hormonal changes: irregular menstrual periods, hot flashes, vaginal dryness, urinary tract infections, night sweats, insomnia, headaches, forgetfulness, anxiety, irritability and diminished concentration. Fluctuating estrogen levels during the transition (not to mention interrupted sleep) can cause emotional highs and lows, irritability and mood swings.

Your body shape and energy levels may also change. Your metabolism slows down in each life stage, and may get even more sluggish in this decade. Your body's lean muscle mass is also changing: it gradually turns to fat as you age, unless you make it a point to stay active.

The good news is that all it takes is a little more muscle and a little more attention to what you eat to maintain your good health and fitness. Focus on exercise that builds and maintains muscle—muscle burns calories more efficiently. Light weight lifting and other weight-bearing exercises are perfect additions to a 50-something exercise workout. This is a great decade to become intimate with your body mass index or BMI. This measurement of weight as it relates to height provides a quick assessment of normal, overweight or obesity levels. It can serve as a guide to see if you are maintaining a healthy weight.

The 50s are a time when your women-friends may become an even more important element of your life. Changes in your family—kids off to college, the long-term care or possible death of parents—can be a challenge at times. Find friends and groups to share your feelings and learn from others how to handle the major changes that may come your way in your 50s.

Getting Better As You Get Older

The Challenge: Menopause and diminishing estrogen levels increase the risk of osteoporosis and heart disease.

The Solution: Protect your heart health and avoid bone loss with what you eat and how you work out.

10 Power-House Foods

These 10 under-appreciated power-house foods are packed with nutrients. Try:

- Beans—Big on fiber, they also contain protein, iron and phytonutrients, which may help prevent heart disease.

- Red bell peppers—Add these to your diet for a days' worth of vitamin C and half the recommended days' worth of beta-carotene plus other antioxidants that may protect your eyes.

- Sweet potatoes—Tasty and rich in potassium and fiber, also a major source of antioxidants, beta-carotene (vitamin A) and vitamin C.

- Grapes—Who knew? They offer potent flavonoids, special types of phytochemicals that may aid heart health and protect the body from harmful substances.

- Wild rice—It's a good source of protein, some B vitamins, folic acid, magnesium and zinc.

- Blueberries—They're rich in polyphenols, a family of phytochemicals that may aid brain health.

- Peanut butter—High in monounsaturated fat, peanut butter may lower heart disease risk by lowering blood cholesterol and triglycerides.

- Yogurt—Yogurt is among the richest food sources of calcium and is easier to digest for women who get discomfort from the lactose (milk sugar) in milk.

- Barley—Rich in soluble fiber, barley contains a nutrient that may lower heart disease risk when included in a low-fat diet.

- Lettuce—Its high water content makes a green salad dampen your appetite so you eat less during the meal.

➤ Choose at least four servings of foods that are rich in calcium, vitamin D and magnesium, nutrients found mostly in dairy products. About 1200 mg. of calcium is the amount to aim for now.

➤ Some doctors recommend a vitamin D supplement since it can be tough to get enough from food and sunlight alone.

➤ Choose fortified, whole-grain cereals, rich in folic acid and vitamin B12.

➤ Eat salmon, mackerel or tuna, rich in omega-3 fatty acids, at least once a week.

➤ Eat foods high in antioxidants, vitamins and minerals to prevent the damage of healthy cells—fruits and veggies, especially blueberries, strawberries and spinach, whole-grain foods like cereals, breads, brown rice, whole wheat pasta and beans.

➤ Find ways to be active, especially with weight-bearing exercises, every day. For more, see Keep Your Bones Strong, page 84.

WALK AWAY

If a girlfriend said that you could delay aging, control your weight, feel happier and less anxious, sleep better, and ward off illnesses like heart disease, cancer, high blood pressure and diabetes by *walking*, would you believe her?

It's true. All these benefits can be yours by simply taking a 30-minute walk every day. Walking at a brisk pace for three or more hours a week can reduce the risk for coronary heart disease by 35%. As you age walking can become more difficult—many seniors go to physical therapy "walking school" after a fall or bone break—so training your walking muscles for later in life is also an important part of the anti-aging process.

The Challenge: How can I eat fewer calories yet still meet daily nutrition needs?

The Solution: Eat more nutrient-rich foods that are lower in calories and fats.

➤ Start the day with ready-to-eat whole-grain cereals that are fortified with essential vitamins and minerals or oatmeal with raisins.

➤ Include at least nine one-half cup portions of any fruit or vegetable per day. They contain vitamins, minerals, fiber and disease-fighting phytochemicals.

➤ Take a look at your portion sizes. See page 239.

➤ Rely on lean meats, chicken or fish and legumes for protein, iron, zinc and B vitamins.

➤ Enjoy three daily servings of non-fat yogurt or milk; they're a top source of calcium, vitamin D, magnesium and potassium.

➤ Build your meals and snacks on foods that are low in calories and high in nutrients—vegetables, fruits, fat-free dairy items and whole grains.

➤ Use fats and sugars sparingly, and only where they make a flavor difference, for example, a small pat of butter on a baked potato.

➤ Eat small amounts of treats and high-fat foods.

BEAR YOUR WEIGHT

Top exercises for 50-somethings include weight-bearing exercises for bone density, like walking or dancing. Balance is an often-forgotten part of fitness that can be lost if it's not used—it's more noticeable after age 50. Yoga, ballet or other strength classes that focus on balance are important at this time, if not before. Depending on your fitness level, you might try:

• Pilates and Yoga

• Water Aerobics

• Brisk Daily Walking

• Skiing

• Ballroom and Square Dance

• Weight Training

• Stationary Bike or Elliptical Trainer

The 60s

60: Young at Heart and Mind

"Now that my son is grown, I have more time to travel, volunteer, spend time with my family and friends while working full-time. The great thing about life is you can fit everything in, sooner or later."

Lois T., editor, world traveler and active 62-year-old

The 60s can be highly rewarding, a time to look back at the road traveled so far and take pride in the miles covered. Children are on their own, careers are coming to a conclusion and family and friends are a well-established part of your life. You may have grandchildren, and spend time traveling to see them, or spend time seeing the world. Perhaps you've downsized or moved to "that special place" year-round. The 60s are a stage when many things you've wished to do and see all your life can come true. There are so many joyous reasons to hop out of bed every day, with or without a routine.

Aging is natural. Research shows that how you feel about getting older plays an important part in how you age. Think young and you will feel young! People who feel positively about aging may actually live longer than those who don't and are more likely to take control and responsibility for their health. In a recent study, more than half of the women in their 60s believe that these are the best years of their lives or even that their best years are still to come. That's the power and re-sulting good health of positive thinking! Maintaining good health and taking care of yourself are great ways to stay young at heart. The 60s are the perfect time to focus on the inner psychological voice that tells you there's still a lot of magic and opportunity in your life! That's not to say there won't be challenges—they are a reality at every age. But a positive attitude and a healthy outlook go a long way toward creating a healthy life.

Small Changes Reap Big Benefits

The Challenge: Medication can interfere with the way nutrients are used in your body.

The Solution: Learn about medications and their interactions.

> ➤ Keep your doctor updated with the multivitamin supplements you use and any over-the-counter

How to Identify Healthy Menu Terms

Look for these terms when ordering off the menu:

- Baked
- Broiled
- Charbroiled
- Poached
- Steamed
- Boiled
- Braised
- Grilled
- Roasted

medicines you take, such as aspirin, ibuprofen, cold medicine, etc.

➤ Ask the pharmacist if your medicine can react with certain foods.

➤ Unless advised by your doctor, steer clear of multivitamins that provide more than 100% of the Daily Value of any vitamin or mineral.

The Challenge: Travel and increased dining out can mean overeating and added weight.

The Solution: Keep an eye on portions in restaurants. When dining out, ask:

➤ "How large is the portion?" before you order.

➤ If you can order a half-size or smaller portion.

➤ To have sauces and salad dressings placed on the side.

➤ To have foods prepared with little or no fat.

➤ For a take-home container when your meal comes. Put half the portion in it right away to take home for another meal.

➤ If you can pair an appetizer with a side salad or vegetable instead of a full meal.

➤ To share a meal or dessert.

➤ To have the bread basket removed (avoids the temptation and the calories).

➤ For beverages that work with your eating plan— remember that alcohol calories add up (beer, wine, mixed drinks).

The Challenge: Low tolerance for certain foods, like milk or spicy foods, may pop up, you may experience indigestion, heartburn or constipation.

The Solution: Alter your eating habits to accommodate these changes.

➤ Try smaller amounts of the foods that cause problems.

➤ Experiment with foods to see what works and what doesn't for you.

➤ Stay up for two hours after you eat.

➤ Try yogurt with active cultures; you may tolerate it easier than milk.

➤ Look for milk and dairy products treated with lactase, an enzyme that breaks down lactose (milk sugar). Or try lactase tablets that can be taken immediately before drinking milk.

➤ Aim for about 22 grams of fiber a day to avoid constipation. One cup of a whole-grain cereal provides 4 to 10 grams, fruits and veggies offer about 2 to 4 grams and beans and legumes contain 5 to 10 grams in one-half cup.

➤ Drink lots of water to help move foods effortlessly through your intestines.

COMBINE YOUR EXERCISE FOR TOTAL FITNESS

In your 60s, it is important to do **endurance exercise** like walking or jogging, **strength exercise** like weight-training, flexibility and **balance exercise** like yoga or tai chi.

TOP EXERCISES FOR 60-SOMETHINGS

- Walking

- Tennis

- Golf

- Cross-Training (Swim, bike and jog)

- Snowshoeing

- Tai Chi or Yoga

The 70s and 80s

The 70s, 80s and Beyond: Stay Connected, Stay Active

"It's taken some time, but I've finally learned to laugh at myself. And you know what, life is much more fun now!"
Cordy F., active 87-year-old, great-grandmother

The 70s, 80s and beyond are likely a time to enjoy the people and places around you. What that means is staying healthy, alert and active enough to enjoy all that life has to offer. Family and friends are a major part of life now. Their interaction is key to your health and vitality, and you still have so much to share with and offer others, too, in terms of your wisdom and the things you've learned along the way. Sending e-mails or cards to friends, making phone calls to family and keeping in touch by visits is a great gift to others and a great resource to you. Happy and healthy means enjoying others and the things you do with or for them. If you're up to it, invite a friend, grandchild or great-grandchild over.

Sure, as we age, different things happen to our bodies and you will notice a physical difference in these decades. Your body has a harder time absorbing nutrients from food and you may become deficient in iron, vitamin B12 or vitamin D. Talk to your doctor about a daily multivitamin and, while you need to protect your skin from sunburn, it's a good idea to get some sun exposure every day. (Avoid the peak sun exposure hours of 11:00 a.m. to 3:00 p.m. every day, however.)

Try to keep your mind sharp by challenging it every day. Some memory loss is perfectly normal, so don't fret about it. (After all, you misplaced things in your 20s too, didn't you?) Regular exercise, reading the newspaper or magazines, playing games and interacting with friends and family are easy, fun ways to keep your brain sharp and active. This is the perfect time to develop a passion or hobby, something to look forward to every day. You might also consider keeping a journal, or trying a new hobby or volunteer opportunity. Taking the effort to reach out is sometimes all it takes—your efforts will be rewarded. Maybe you could consider a pet—having a pet to care for can reduce blood pressure and create a general sense of well-being and companionship.

Your bones may be a little more fragile now. That's a great reason to keep up exercise like walking and weight-lifting with small hand-held weights. Exercise can also help maintain and improve your bone density and balance, keep you alert, help keep you from falling and help you sleep better.

Stay Active, Stay Connected

The Challenge: How do I stay involved and active?

The Solution: Stay informed of local, world, friend and family happenings.

- ➤ Read the newspaper and magazines to stay updated.

- ➤ Take a class or get involved in community activities.

- ➤ Do crossword puzzles and word games, play card games.

- ➤ Talk to someone every day: at the supermarket, a neighbor or family member.

- ➤ Get dressed, comb your hair and put on a little lipstick and blush; it will help you look (and feel) better.

- ➤ Smile and say hello to someone in the post office, store or when you are out walking. Who knows? It may make their day brighter, too.

- ➤ Volunteer at a local charity or community organization—it will do you as much good as it does others.

The Challenge: Your sense of taste may change over time, which can affect your appetite and interest in eating.

The Solution: Eat foods rich in nutrients and natural flavor enhancers.

- ➤ Zinc is closely linked to sense of taste. Meat, fish and poultry are great sources of zinc; whole-grain foods also contain some zinc.

- ➤ Add spices, herbs, vinegar and lemon to enhance the flavor of food. Or top with salsa, chutneys or mustards.

- ➤ Be gentle with the salt shaker. Some salt may bring out the taste in food, but too much sodium can push up blood pressure.

The Challenge: Nutrient shortages of key vitamins become more common.

The Solution: Get your vitamins and minerals! How?

- ➤ Talk with your doctor about taking a multivitamin for certain nutrients.

- ➤ Include fortified whole-grain cereals and lean meats, like beef and chicken, to get B12, milk and fortified dairy products and juices to get vitamin D and calcium.

The Challenge: Meeting your nutrition needs is difficult when you cook less often or eat by yourself.

The Solution: Try new ways to make mealtime interesting.

- ➤ Get involved in social groups to make new connections. Events often revolve around a meal.

- ➤ Buddy up with a neighbor and share cooking duties—set a regular date for dining.

- ➤ Purchase fresh, ready-to-eat foods, such as sliced, diced and washed lettuces, fruits and veggies.

- ➤ Cook more food at one time so you have leftovers and freeze for later use.

Top Exercises for 70, 80 and Beyond

It's still important to stay active, stay with an endurance exercise like swimming or walking, light weight-lifting, flexibility and balance activities like yoga or tai chi.

- Walking
- Swimming

- Water Aerobics
- Light Weight Training

- Chair Yoga and Pilates
- Tai Chi and Qigong

For All Ages and Stages

Life Choices

Life is about making choices. Choose to live a healthier life. Here is a road map from the Centers for Disease Control on the best choices:

➤ Every day—Eat healthfully, maintain a healthy weight, be active, avoid smoking, manage stress, control your risks, protect yourself, be good to yourself.

➤ Every week—Review your goals and your progress toward your goals, keep up the good work.

➤ Every month—Do a breast self-exam, prepare for emergencies, plan ahead, reflect on your progress and think about your goals for the next month.

➤ Every year—Get routine exams and medical screenings, have a happy and healthy birthday.

More than Good Nutrition

Recently a 103-year-old woman attended her first Green Bay Packers football game. She had been a huge fan for years but had never actually been to Lambeau Field in Wisconsin to experience the cold, snowy outdoor stadium or hear the roaring crowds.

"She's 103!" you might think, "She shouldn't be outdoors in the middle of winter!" But people who live to ripe, old ages often have something besides good health that urges them on toward long lives. They have a positive attitude, and long relationships with family and friends.

Ask yourself, when life throws you a curve ball, do you bounce back or do you fall apart? People with resilience harness inner strengths and tend to rebound more quickly from a setback or one of life's many day-to-day challenges. "Learned optimism" is a skill you can develop just like any other; all it takes is the right mind-set and a few tips:

➤ Look at the positive side.

➤ Be proud of your achievements.

➤ Take time to grieve through a loss or change.

➤ Keep moving forward, but be patient with detours along the way.

➤ Look for the learning that comes with challenges.

➤ Set goals that are realistic and achievable.

➤ Don't overreact to problems.

➤ Believe in yourself.

➤ Live with no regrets. Don't postpone the things that you want to do now.

Benefits of optimism:

➤ Better health

➤ Less depression

➤ Ability to overcome challenges

➤ Successful attainment of goals

➤ More positive efforts

Joys and Stressors Along the Way

There will be many joys and stressors woven into your personal journey. Ideally, joys will outweigh stressors. Yes, some of the same things that are joys may also be stressors. A newborn baby is the most wonderful thing. You're thrilled, yet now you realize the extra time and attention the baby takes, the sleepless nights and change in your old routine.

Similarly, when a child is grown and moves away from home, you're bound to have mixed feelings: relief, sadness or worry, but you may also be extremely proud of that new adult and happy with the job you've done as a parent. Likewise, if you're a member of the sandwich generation, you have the joys and stressors that caring for an aging parent brings.

Part of being a woman is forming strong bonds and lasting relationships. Throughout a woman's life, relationships have great impact. The choices you make have a great impact on the rest of your life. Whatever choices you've made, working through them and being comfortable with where you are in a relationship now, is important.

Next, separate stressors from health habits. The best way to handle a challenge is to isolate it and tackle it head-on. Overeating, stopping exercise, smoking or drinking may feel like short-term solutions, but in the long run, they make coping with stress more difficult.

Eat Today with Tomorrow in Mind

You can significantly influence your health by making a few lifestyle changes. Enjoy the lively taste of good-for-you foods, the energy you get from physical activity and the happiness

WAIST MANAGEMENT

Although weight loss may be possible on almost any type of diet, a balanced approach to weight loss makes the most nutrition sense because you're more likely to stick with it if it's something you can maintain for a lifetime. A few tried-and-true weight loss secrets:

It's all about calories. As long as you burn more calories than you eat, the pounds will come off. Keep in mind that most fad diets really are low-calorie diets in disguise.

It's all about portion size. Bigger portions mean more calories and more trouble maintaining weight. An easy way to shed pounds is to eat less by cutting portion size. Add vegetables as a way to eat more food without too many calories.

Weight loss helps you feel better. Losing weight can boost your self esteem, improve your body image, provide more energy and give you a better quality of life. And who doesn't love to shop for new (and smaller-sized) clothes?

that comes from knowing you are doing your best to be happy and healthy. The foods we eat are made up of three major nutrients, each with its own important function:

- **Protein** builds and repairs muscles, skin and other structural parts of the body. Every organ in the body is made from protein.

  - Good sources—lean meats, poultry, fish; legumes, including soybeans; non-fat and low-fat dairy products

- **Carbohydrate** supplies energy for every activity, large or small. Even when you're sleeping, carbohydrate fuels ongoing body functions. Fiber, found in many carbohydrate foods, helps maintain a healthy digestive tract and soluble fiber can be good for your heart.

  - Good sources—whole-grain and other grain foods; fruits and vegetables; legumes

- **Fat** supplies ingredients the body needs to make hormones, keep skin healthy and support the nervous system. Different types of fats have different health benefits.

  - Good sources—olive, canola, and other vegetable oils; nuts; avocados

Small Steps Pay Off Big

As you make lifestyle changes, you don't have to tackle everything at once. First, try for a smaller change that you can stick with, then once you have that new habit mastered, a month or six weeks later, go on to tackle the next one. Here are some pointers:

- **Eat breakfast**—Breakfast eaters have better brain function in the morning, and their overall diets are healthier, too. The news is even better if you eat cereal—frequent cereal eaters tend to have a healthier body weight.

- **Eat three meals (or more!)**—Your body functions best when it has a steady supply of energy and nutrients over the course of the day. Just be sure that you don't increase your total calories for the day as you transition to smaller meals and snacks throughout the day.

- **Savor plant foods**—Plant foods are the star of the Dietary Guidelines for Americans, and play a featured role in guidelines on preventing cancer, heart disease and diabetes. Fruits, vegetables, grains and legumes are packed with health-promoting benefits, deliver a lot of nutrition without too many calories and are filling and satisfying.

- **Eat brightly colored veggies and fruits**—Each color "family"—red, green, white, yellow/orange and blue/purple—dishes up its own recipe of vitamins, minerals, and phytochemicals, plant compounds that boost health and help the body ward off disease.

- **Fill up on fluids**—Water and other calorie-free fluids help cool your body, keep it functioning normally and aid in getting rid of waste. Drink fluids often during the day, and the next time you feel tired and cranky between meals, try drinking water or another beverage. You may just be thirsty.

Ask the Doctor

Q&A's

WITH DR. RITA REDBERG

Dr. Rita Redberg, cardiologist with the University of California, San Francisco, answers women's frequently asked questions:

Q. "Heart disease runs in my family; how do I know if I am likely to get it?"

A. One way to tell is to know your personal risk factors. Some risk factors are simply a matter of circumstance and cannot be controlled, but knowing about them can help you make decisions that can influence your health. These factors include:

> **Increased Age.** Age is a major risk factor. Heart disease is rare in women who are less than 55 years old, and becomes more common in women than men by age 70.

> **Family History.** If one or both of your parents had heart problems at an early age (less than age 55 for your mother, less than age 45 for your father) you are more likely to develop heart disease than women with no family history of the disease. African-American and Hispanic women have a higher incidence of heart disease than do Caucasian women.

Where you can make a powerful difference is by changing your lifestyle habits and working hard to reduce the risk factors you can control. ***Smoking is the number 1 preventable cause of heart disease:*** don't smoke or stop smoking, eat healthy, manage your weight and be physically active every day. How you live your life now can make a major difference in what happens to your heart later. Reducing one risk factor can improve your heart health in many ways. Exercise regularly, for example, and you may be able to lower your blood pressure, reduce your weight and improve your cholesterol.

Q. "My girlfriends talk about soy foods and soy supplements; can they really help protect my heart?"

A. You might try them—some of them taste great. Research suggests that when women replace some of the animal-protein foods they normally eat with about 25 grams of soy protein daily from soy foods, their blood cholesterol levels tend to drop. Tofu, soymilk, yogurt and soy-based meat substitutes are excellent sources of low-fat, high-quality protein and they deliver a fair amount of fiber, omega-3 fatty acids and calcium. Soy foods also contain isoflavones, hormone-like substances that may have heart-protective and cancer-preventing effects. What's more, using soy foods as occasional meat substitutes can help you lower your intake of saturated fat—and that alone will help your heart. It's best to get your soy from soy foods, not supplements.

Q. "What's the best way to lose weight?"

A. As tempting as it sounds to "lose 10 pounds in one week" experts agree that slow, steady weight loss—one to two pounds per week—is the safest and most lasting strategy. The best diet isn't a diet that you "go on" or "go off," but an everyday way of living. If you make gradual changes, your body will slowly adapt to new behaviors and improved, sustainable habits. If you haven't already, increase your amount or level of activity. Exercise helps people lose weight more easily and keep it off longer than adjusting what you eat alone.

Q. "How do I get my daily physical activity, I don't have time to go to the gym?"

A. Being active every day is pivotal to good health and so important to fit into your lifestyle. If you can't spare a big block of time, squeeze in smaller sessions every day. Walking is an ideal exercise for your bones, heart and overall aerobic workout and most everyone can do it, anytime, anywhere. If you exercise with friends or family, you are more likely to continue. Housework counts, too, as long as it's active. When grocery shopping and running errands, park as far away as possible and walk to your appointment. Or, play with the kids, if you have them! You can increase the frequency and intensity of your activity as your fitness improves. For more on exercise, see page 182.

Q. "What about vitamins or dietary supplements?"

A. Your best diet is one that includes fruits, vegetables and whole grains as part of a low-fat diet. No studies have shown that vitamins or dietary supplements can give the same health benefits as eating well. Take the money you would spend on vitamins or dietary supplements and get a facial or a massage or go to the spa. You'll feel better.

Q. "Some of my friends take an aspirin a day to reduce their risk of heart attack. Is this a good thing for everyone to do?"

A. The American Heart Association does recommend aspirin for patients who've had a heart attack, unstable angina, ischemic stroke (caused by blood clots) or transient ischemic attacks (TIA's or "little strokes"). This is based on clinical trials showing that aspirin helps prevent the recurrence of heart attack, hospitalization for recurrent angina, second strokes, etc. Studies show that aspirin also helps prevent these events from occurring in people at high risk. The risks for aspirin therapy vary for each person, so I recommend consulting your physician first before just taking aspirin on your own.

In Your Kitchen

You can make a big difference in reducing fat, calories and cholesterol and adding flavor when you select and cook the most healthy foods. Here's how:

Cut down on the total amount of fat and saturated fat. When you use fat, think liquid and use canola or olive oil rather than solid butter, shortening or margarine.

Cook without adding fat—braise, steam, poach or bake. Grilling, broiling and using a table-top grill are also good because they allow fat to drip off.

Read food labels to compare sodium levels. Pick no-salt-added or low-sodium broths or other foods when you need to cut back. Don't add salt at the table and don't cook potatoes, pasta or rice in salted water. Season the foods you prepare with herbs, spices and juices, rather than salt.

Boost the amount of potassium you eat to balance out the sodium. Fit in foods that deliver potassium, including sweet potatoes, bananas, soybeans, peaches, tuna, beans, spinach and tomatoes.

If you'd like to reduce cholesterol, you can use egg whites and egg substitutes instead of whole eggs. Also increase the cholesterol-lowering foods like oats, barley and other grains. Eat more oats and barley; they are proven to help reduce blood cholesterol levels.

Eat more colorful foods, like vegetables and fruits. For fruits and vegetables, selecting a colorful array means that they are higher in vitamins, minerals and phytonutrients.

Add legumes and beans to soups, stews and stir-fries to increase your fiber.

A Note about the Recipes

Dairy: Skim milk is used whenever milk is called for, as an easy way to cut fat. Depending on the fat and calorie content of each dish, reduced-fat cream cheese and sour cream are used because the flavor and reduction of fat was a good compromise. If you are used to using fat-free ingredients, you may try them instead.

Eggs: Because eggs contain many nutrients, they are called for first, but you are given a choice of egg whites or egg substitute, if you prefer to reduce cholesterol—the recipes work well with any of the three.

Fats: Canola and olive oils are called for throughout the book, chosen for their heart-wise and health-wise benefits—they are great fats to use for stir-frying, cooking and some baking. Because butter yields a tender product and gives unparalleled flavor to baked goods, you'll see butter in a few recipes (although at a much lower level than in many cookbooks).

What to Eat

The Big Five: Nutrients Women Miss, and Foods that Contain Them

Nutrient	Job	Best sources
Calcium	Builds and maintains bones; helps regulate blood pressure; conducts nerve impulses	Low-fat and fat-free milk and yogurt; cheese; leafy greens; canned fish with bones; salmon; fortified juice; soy products; fortified breakfast cereal
Vitamin D	Helps calcium be absorbed	Milk; fatty fish; egg yolks; fortified yogurt, juice, soy products, breakfast cereal; skin exposure to sunlight
Folic acid	Builds red blood cells; helps prevent the most common birth defects; aids heart health	Leafy, green vegetables; orange juice; legumes; fortified whole-grain cereal; multivitamin supplement
Magnesium	Involved in hundreds of enzyme and energy reactions in the body	Leafy, green vegetables; nuts; seeds; whole grains; legumes; chocolate
Iron	Carries oxygen in red blood cells	Red meat; legumes; tofu; dried fruits; fortified breakfast cereal

Eat More of These Essential Foods

For best overall health, nutritionists suggest that women eat more of essential foods.

Eat more	Examples	Good choices because	Creative ways to use
Breakfast cereals	Ready-to-eat breakfast cereals	Low in calories Provide key nutrients Linked to a better body weight	Add to pretzels, popcorn, nuts and dried fruit to make snack mix Crush and add to baked goods. See recipes (Cranberry-Orange Bread, page 52, Cranberry-Pecan Granola, page 55 and On-the-Go Apple Breakfast Bars, page 59)

Fish	Halibut, sole, cod, snapper, tilapia and other lower fat fish
	
	Salmon, trout, tuna and other higher fat fish that contain omega-3 fatty acids
		High protein, low in fat
		
		May Help:
		    lower blood pressure
		    reduce inflammation
		    prevent plaque build-up in arteries
			Combine with pasta (Salmon-Pasta Toss, page 118)
			
			Mix with light mayo, seasonings for sandwiches, salads
			
			Pair with seafood in a stew

Fruits	Citrus, melons, pears, peaches, plums, bananas, apples, berries, grapes	High in vitamin C and/or A Contain phytonutrients that lower cancer risk	Toss with a light dressing as a side salad Strawberry-Orange–Poppy Seed Salad, page 200 Whip into a smoothie Cut into chunks and freeze for a refreshing snack
Lean meats	Lean cuts of beef (loin, round, rib eye), pork (tenderloin, loin, rib chop), chicken and turkey without skin	High in protein Low in fat and calories Contain iron to carry oxygen in blood	Cut into chunks for kabobs (see Beef Kabobs with Edamame Succotash, page 142) Slice thin and place atop Caesar salad

Eat more	Examples	Good choices because	Creative ways to use
Beans; legumes	Peas, lentils, kidney beans, garbanzos and other dried and canned beans	Rich in soluble fiber to lower risk of heart disease, diabetes Meatless source of iron and zinc Packed with phytonutrients	Combine with beef or pork in chili (Sirloin Three-Bean Chili, page 101) Puree cooked or canned legumes, add broth and season for a quick soup Fill pita with beans, assorted veggies, dressing
Milk and yogurt	Fat-free and low-fat milk and yogurt, containing calcium and vitamin D	Build and protect bones to help prevent osteoporosis Helps keep blood pressure under control May lower body weight, less body fat Low-fat dairy may help prevent breast cancer	Make your own latte with warmed milk, strong coffee Add yogurt to a fruit smoothie Make oatmeal and other hot cereal with milk instead of water
Nuts	Almonds, cashews, walnuts, pecans, hazelnuts, peanuts, nut butters	As part of a low fat diet, reduce total and LDL "bad" cholesterol Filled with heart-healthy monounsaturated fat Provide fiber, phytonutrients, vitamins and minerals	Top noodles with a peanut sauce and serve hot or cold (Noodles and Peanut Sauce Salad Bowl, page 168) Try almond or cashew butter in a sandwich Top vegetable and fruit salads with nuts
Soy	Edamame (soybeans), soymilk, tofu, textured soy protein, soy nuts	May help lower blood cholesterol May help lower blood pressure and reduce plaque in arteries May help strengthen bones Good source of complete protein	Use in place of beef or chicken in a main dish (see Tofu Stroganoff on Wild Rice, page 181) Serve steamed edamame as an appetizer Substitute soymilk for cow's milk in recipes
Veggies	Spinach, romaine lettuce; carrots, sweet potatoes; red pepper, beets, other red vegetables; broccoli, cauliflower, potatoes	Supply vitamins A and/or C Phytonutrients fight cancer, heart disease, age-related eye problems High in nutrients; low in calories	Use as pizza topping (Chilly Garden Pizza, page 66) Roast, puree and season for an appetizer spread (Roasted Carrot and Herb Spread, page 70) Wash, cut and refrigerate in a sealed container for a quick snack
Water	Tap water, bottled water, sparkling water, seltzer, calorie-free beverages	Essential for healthy skin, joints, eyes Flushes out waste products	Flavor sparkling water with a splash of fruit juice Freeze a bottle of water (leave room for the water to expand) for a day-long supply of ice-cold water
Whole grains	Whole-grain breads, cereals, and pasta; brown rice; quinoa; oats; popcorn	Lowered risk of heart disease, obesity, diabetes Supply fiber, folic acid (if fortified), phytonutrients, antioxidants	Use less common grains in salads (Mediterranean Quinoa Salad, page 166) Heat leftover grains with milk, sweetener, raisins for hot breakfast cereal Enjoy whole wheat pasta with your favorite tomato sauce For Grains recipes, see pages 166–187

Recommended intake for adult women based on USDA MyPyramid
Calorie Range for Women

Age	Sedentary	Active
19–30	2000	2400
31–50	1800	2200
51+	1600	2200

Sedentary is light physical activity typical of day-to-day life. Active is physical activity equivalent to walking more than 3 miles per day at 3 or 4 miles per hour in addition to light physical activity of day-to-day life.

➤ Daily Nutrition Guidelines for adult women based on USDA MyPyramid

➤ Total Fat: 20% to 35% of total calories

➤ Saturated Fat: Less than 10% of total calories

➤ Cholesterol: Less than 300 mg.

➤ Sodium: Less than 2300 mg.

➤ Potassium: 4700 mg.

➤ Calcium: 1000 to 1300 mg.

➤ Total Carbohydrates: Around 45% to 65% of total calories

➤ Protein: 10% to 35% of total calories

➤ Dietary Fiber: 22 to 28 grams

Begin with Breakfast

1

Wake up your taste buds with an array of colorful choices

Orange Pancakes with Raspberry Sauce

PREP TIME: 30 Minutes   **START TO FINISH:** 30 Minutes   **8 SERVINGS** (two 4-inch pancakes and 2 tablespoons sauce each)

NOTE FROM DR. R
These pancakes are a good source of calcium. Adding low-fat milk, yogurt or buttermilk to recipes is an ideal way to get more calcium. Experts recommend at least 3 servings of low-fat or fat-free dairy foods daily—your bones will thank you!

SAUCE

3 tablespoons sugar

1 tablespoon cornstarch

2/3 cup orange juice

1 box (10 oz) frozen raspberries in syrup, thawed, undrained

PANCAKES

2 eggs

1 1/2 cups fat-free (skim) milk

1/4 cup canola oil

2 cups all-purpose flour

2 tablespoons sugar

2 teaspoons baking powder

2 teaspoons grated orange peel

1 teaspoon vanilla

1/4 teaspoon salt

1. In 1-quart saucepan, mix 3 tablespoons sugar and the cornstarch. Stir in orange juice and raspberries. Cook over medium heat, stirring constantly, until mixture thickens and boils. Boil and stir 1 minute. Remove from heat.

2. Heat griddle or 12-inch skillet over medium heat or to 375°F. Grease griddle with canola oil if necessary (or spray with cooking spray before heating).

3. In large bowl, beat eggs with wire whisk until well beaten. Beat in remaining pancake ingredients just until smooth.

4. For each pancake, pour slightly less than 1/4 cup batter from cup or pitcher onto hot griddle. Cook pancakes 1 to 2 minutes or until bubbly on top, puffed and dry around edges. Turn and cook other sides 1 to 2 minutes or until golden brown. Serve with sauce.

1 Serving: Calories 290 (Calories from Fat 80); Total Fat 9g (Saturated Fat 1g; Trans Fat 0g; Omega-3 0.5g); Cholesterol 55mg; Sodium 230mg; Total Carbohydrate 47g (Dietary Fiber 3g; Sugars 20g); Protein 7g   **% Daily Value:** Potassium 6%; Vitamin A 4%; Vitamin C 10%; Calcium 15%; Iron 10%; Folic Acid 15%   **Exchanges:** 2 Starch, 1 Other Carbohydrate, 1 1/2 Fat   **Carbohydrate Choices:** 3

Whole-Grain Strawberry Pancakes

PREP TIME: 30 Minutes **START TO FINISH:** 30 Minutes **7 SERVINGS** (two 3 1/2-inch pancakes, 1/4 cup sliced strawberries and 2 tablespoons syrup each)

1 1/2 cups whole wheat flour

3 tablespoons sugar

1 teaspoon baking powder

1/2 teaspoon baking soda

1/2 teaspoon salt

3 eggs

1 container (6 oz) vanilla low-fat yogurt

3/4 cup water

3 tablespoons canola oil

1 3/4 cups sliced fresh strawberries

1 cup strawberry syrup, warmed

1. Heat griddle or 12-inch skillet over medium heat or to 375°F. Grease griddle with canola oil if necessary (or spray with cooking spray before heating).

2. In large bowl, mix flour, sugar, baking powder, baking soda and salt; set aside. In medium bowl, beat eggs, yogurt, water and oil with wire whisk until well blended. Pour egg mixture all at once into flour mixture; stir until moistened.

3. For each pancake, pour slightly less than 1/4 cup batter from cup or pitcher onto hot griddle. Cook pancakes 1 to 2 minutes or until bubbly on top, puffed and dry around edges. Turn and cook other sides 1 to 2 minutes or until golden brown. Top each serving (2 pancakes) with 1/4 cup sliced strawberries and about 2 tablespoons syrup.

"Every day starts with a 30-minute walk. The walk has now become a habit, and the day feels incomplete without it." —Nanci D.

BETTY'S TIP
Besides adding a whole grain, the whole wheat flour adds a nutty flavor and wholesome texture to these great-tasting pancakes. If you are new to whole grains, you can start by using 3/4 cup whole wheat and 3/4 cup all-purpose flour until you get used to the new flavor and texture.

1 Serving: Calories 380 (Calories from Fat 80); Total Fat 9g (Saturated Fat 1.5g; Trans Fat 0g; Omega-3 0.5g); Cholesterol 90mg; Sodium 430mg; Total Carbohydrate 68g (Dietary Fiber 4g; Sugars 29g); Protein 8g % Daily Value: Potassium 7%; Vitamin A 4%; Vitamin C 20%; Calcium 10%; Iron 8%; Folic Acid 8% **Exchanges:** 2 1/2 Starch, 2 Other Carbohydrate, 1 1/2 Fat **Carbohydrate Choices:** 4 1/2

Puffy Oven Pancake with Berries

PREP TIME: 10 Minutes   **START TO FINISH:** 40 Minutes   **4 SERVINGS** (1/4 of pancake and about 1/2 cup berries each)

2 tablespoons butter or margarine
3 eggs or 6 egg whites
1/2 cup all-purpose flour
1/2 cup fat-free (skim) milk
1/4 teaspoon salt
2 1/2 cups assorted fresh berries
Powdered sugar, if desired

BETTY'S TIP
If you'd like to reduce the amount of cholesterol in any of the recipes that contain eggs, you can use an egg product substitute or egg whites; 1/4 cup egg product or 2 egg whites is equivalent to 1 whole egg.

1. Heat oven to 400°F. In 9-inch glass pie plate, melt butter in oven; brush butter over bottom and side of pie plate.

2. In medium bowl, beat eggs slightly with wire whisk or hand beater. Beat in flour, milk and salt just until mixed (do not overbeat). Pour into pie plate.

3. Bake 25 to 30 minutes or until puffy and deep golden brown. Serve pancake immediately topped with berries. Sprinkle with powdered sugar.

1 Serving: Calories 220 (Calories from Fat 90); Total Fat 10g (Saturated Fat 5g; Trans Fat 0g; Omega-3 0g); Cholesterol 175mg; Sodium 250mg; Total Carbohydrate 24g (Dietary Fiber 3g; Sugars 8g); Protein 8g   **% Daily Value:** Potassium 6%; Vitamin A 10%; Vitamin C 25%; Calcium 8%; Iron 8%; Folic Acid 15%   **Exchanges:** 1 Starch, 1/2 Other Carbohydrate, 1/2 Medium-Fat Meat, 1 1/2 Fat   **Carbohydrate Choices:** 1 1/2

Puffy Oven Pancake with Berries

Buckwheat Pancakes with Butter-Pecan Syrup

PREP TIME: 25 Minutes   **START TO FINISH:** 25 Minutes   **5 SERVINGS** (2 pancakes and about 2 tablespoons syrup each)

SYRUP
1 tablespoon butter or margarine
3 tablespoons chopped pecans
1/2 cup maple-flavored syrup

PANCAKES
1 egg
1/2 cup buckwheat flour
1/2 cup whole wheat flour
1 cup fat-free (skim) milk
1 tablespoon sugar
2 tablespoons canola oil
3 teaspoons baking powder
1/2 teaspoon salt
Whole bran or wheat germ, if desired

NOTE FROM DR. R
The current thinking on weight loss and management is not to deprive yourself of the foods you like, but to have them less often or to have small bits of them once in a while. As long as your overall diet is moderate in fat and calories, you'll still be able to fit in the foods you love.

1. In 1-quart saucepan, melt butter over medium heat. Cook pecans in butter, stirring frequently, until browned. Stir in syrup; heat until hot. Remove from heat.

2. In medium bowl, beat egg with hand beater until fluffy. Beat in remaining pancake ingredients except bran just until smooth.

3. Heat griddle or 12-inch skillet over medium heat or to 375°F. Grease griddle with canola oil if necessary (or spray with cooking spray before heating).

4. For each pancake, pour about 3 tablespoons batter from cup or pitcher onto hot griddle. Cook pancakes until puffed and dry around edges. Sprinkle each pancake with 1 teaspoon bran. Turn and cook other sides until golden brown. Serve with syrup.

"I know I need to splurge once in a while to keep *myself on track."*   —Amity D.

1 Serving: Calories 330 (Calories from Fat 110); Total Fat 12g (Saturated Fat 2.5g; Trans Fat 0g; Omega-3 0.5g); Cholesterol 50mg; Sodium 620mg; Total Carbohydrate 49g (Dietary Fiber 3g; Sugars 17g); Protein 6g   **% Daily Value:** Potassium 6%; Vitamin A 4%; Vitamin C 0%; Calcium 25%; Iron 8%; Folic Acid 4%   **Exchanges:** 2 Starch, 1 Other Carbohydrate, 2 Fat **Carbohydrate Choices:** 3

Berry French Toast Bake

PREP TIME: 20 Minutes   **START TO FINISH:** 1 Hour 45 Minutes   **10 SERVINGS**

FRENCH TOAST BAKE

1/2 cup all-purpose flour

1 1/2 cups fat-free (skim) milk or soymilk

1/4 cup sugar

2 teaspoons vanilla

1/4 teaspoon salt

6 eggs or 12 egg whites

1 loaf (1 lb) soft French bread,
cut into 1-inch cubes (8 cups)

1 1/2 cups frozen unsweetened mixed berries
(from two 14-oz bags)

SAUCE

1/2 cup sugar

1 1/2 teaspoons cornstarch

2 tablespoons orange juice

1 cup frozen unsweetened mixed berries

1 1/2 cups fresh strawberries, cut in half

1. Grease bottom and sides of 13 × 9-inch (3-quart) glass baking dish with butter. In large bowl, beat flour, milk, 1/4 cup sugar, the vanilla, salt and eggs with wire whisk until smooth. Stir in bread and 1 1/2 cups mixed berries. Spoon into baking dish. Cover tightly and refrigerate at least 1 hour but no longer than 24 hours.

2. Heat oven to 400°F. Uncover bread mixture. Bake 25 to 35 minutes or until golden brown and knife inserted in center comes out clean.

3. Meanwhile, in 1 1/2-quart saucepan, stir together 1/2 cup sugar and the cornstarch. Stir in orange juice until smooth. Stir in 1 cup mixed berries; heat to boiling over medium heat, stirring constantly. Cook about 4 minutes, stirring constantly, until slightly thickened; remove from heat. Just before serving, stir in strawberry halves. Serve warm over French toast bake.

"I exercise every weekday morning at the same time. This really jump-starts my day."   —Val B.

NOTE FROM DR. R
Eating berries is a flavorful way to eat more fruits each day. The dietary guidelines recommend eating about 2 cups of fruit daily. And berries contain a unique set of vitamins, minerals and health-helping benefits.

1 Serving: Calories 310 (Calories from Fat 45); Total Fat 5g (Saturated Fat 1.5g; Trans Fat 0g; Omega-3 0g); Cholesterol 130mg; Sodium 380mg; Total Carbohydrate 54g (Dietary Fiber 5g; Sugars 23g); Protein 10g   **% Daily Value:** Potassium 8%; Vitamin A 6%; Vitamin C 20%; Calcium 10%; Iron 15%; Folic Acid 30%   **Exchanges:** 2 Starch, 1/2 Fruit, 1 Other Carbohydrate, 1/2 Medium-Fat Meat, 1/2 Fat   **Carbohydrate Choices:** 3 1/2

Whole Wheat Waffles with Honey-Peanut Butter Drizzle

PREP TIME: 35 Minutes   **START TO FINISH:** 35 Minutes   **8 SERVINGS** (2 waffle squares, 1 1/2 tablespoons syrup and 1 tablespoon granola each)

WAFFLES
2 eggs or 4 egg whites
1 cup whole wheat flour
1 cup all-purpose flour
2 cups buttermilk
1 tablespoon sugar
3 tablespoons canola oil
2 teaspoons baking powder
1/4 teaspoon salt
1/2 cup low-fat granola

DRIZZLE
1/2 cup honey
1/4 cup creamy peanut butter

BETTY'S TIP:
Besides being low in fat because it's made with skim milk, buttermilk is a powerful ingredient to use in baking because it adds a terrific dairy flavor and gives a moist baked good. You'll love these easy waffles!

1. Heat waffle iron; brush with canola oil if necessary (or spray with cooking spray before heating). In medium bowl, beat eggs with fork or wire whisk until foamy. Beat in remaining waffle ingredients except granola just until smooth.

2. Pour about 1 cup batter from cup or pitcher onto center of hot waffle iron. (Check manufacturer's directions for recommended amount of batter.) Close lid of waffle iron.

3. Bake about 5 minutes or until steaming stops. Carefully remove waffle. Repeat with remaining batter.

4. Meanwhile, in small microwavable bowl, mix honey and peanut butter. Microwave uncovered on High 40 to 60 seconds or until warm; stir until smooth. Drizzle over waffles. Sprinkle with granola.

1 Serving: Calories 240 (Calories from Fat 70); Total Fat 8g (Saturated Fat 1.5g; Trans Fat 0g; Omega-3 0g); Cholesterol 35mg; Sodium 220mg; Total Carbohydrate 34g (Dietary Fiber 2g; Sugars 16g); Protein 7g   **% Daily Value:** Potassium 5%; Vitamin A 2%; Vitamin C 0%; Calcium 10%; Iron 8%; Folic Acid 8%   **Exchanges:** 1 Starch, 1 Other Carbohydrate, 1/2 High-Fat Meat, 1 Fat   **Carbohydrate Choices:** 2

Whole Wheat Waffles with Honey-Peanut Butter Drizzle

Potato, Egg and Sausage Frittata

PREP TIME: 30 Minutes **START TO FINISH:** 30 Minutes **4 SERVINGS**

4 eggs or 8 egg whites
1/4 cup fat-free (skim) milk
1 teaspoon olive oil
1 1/2 cups frozen country-style shredded hash brown potatoes (from 30-oz bag)
4 frozen soy-protein breakfast sausage links (from 8-oz box), cut into eighths
1/4 teaspoon salt
1/8 teaspoon dried basil leaves
1/8 teaspoon dried oregano leaves
1 cup chopped plum (Roma) tomatoes (3 medium)
1/2 cup shredded mozzarella and Asiago cheese blend with garlic (2 oz)
Freshly ground pepper, if desired

BETTY'S TIP

If you haven't tried the newest soy products lately, you're in for a pleasant surprise. Soy sausage is a tasty alternative to higher-fat regular sausage and an easy addition to this fresh-tasting frittata.

1. In small bowl, beat eggs and milk with fork or wire whisk until well blended; set aside.

2. Coat 10-inch nonstick skillet with oil; heat over medium heat. Cook potatoes and breakfast links in oil 6 to 8 minutes, stirring occasionally, until potatoes are golden brown.

3. Pour egg mixture over potato mixture. Cook uncovered over medium-low heat about 5 minutes; as mixture begins to set on bottom and side, gently lift cooked portions with spatula so that thin, uncooked portion can flow to bottom. Cook until eggs are thickened throughout but still moist; avoid constant stirring.

4. Sprinkle with salt, basil, oregano, tomatoes and cheese. Reduce heat to low. Cover; cook about 5 minutes or until center is set and cheese is melted. Sprinkle with pepper.

1 Serving: Calories 250 (Calories from Fat 110); Total Fat 12g (Saturated Fat 4.5g; Trans Fat 0g; Omega-3 0g); Cholesterol 220mg; Sodium 570mg; Total Carbohydrate 20g (Dietary Fiber 2g; Sugars 3g); Protein 17g **% Daily Value:** Potassium 15%; Vitamin A 15%; Vitamin C 10%; Calcium 15%; Iron 10%; Folic Acid 10% **Exchanges:** 1 1/2 Starch, 2 Medium-Fat Meat **Carbohydrate Choices:** 1

Potato, Egg and Sausage Frittata

Lox and Cream Cheese Scramble

PREP TIME: 20 Minutes **START TO FINISH:** 20 Minutes **4 SERVINGS**

1 teaspoon canola oil

8 eggs or 16 egg whites

1/4 teaspoon dried dill weed

1/4 teaspoon salt

2 medium green onions, chopped (2 tablespoons)

3 oz salmon lox, chopped

2 tablespoons reduced-fat cream cheese (Neufchâtel)

Reduced-fat sour cream, if desired

Capers, if desired

NOTE FROM DR. R
The salmon adds extra color and flavor as well as nutrition to this egg scramble. To reduce the amount of cholesterol in this recipe, use egg substitute instead of eggs.

1. Coat 12-inch nonstick skillet with oil; heat over medium heat. In large bowl, beat eggs, dill weed and salt with fork or wire whisk until well blended. Pour egg mixture into skillet. Cook uncovered 4 minutes; as mixture begins to set on bottom and side, gently lift cooked portions with spatula so that thin, uncooked portion can flow to bottom. Avoid constant stirring.

2. Gently stir in onions and lox. Drop cream cheese by teaspoonfuls onto mixture. Cook 4 to 5 minutes, stirring gently, until eggs are thickened but still moist. Garnish with sour cream and capers.

"I put a red dot on my calendar for each day I exercise. Then I can glance at my calendar and see if there are a lot of red dots. No dots means I need to get moving!" —Sheila B.

1 Serving: Calories 200 (Calories from Fat 130); Total Fat 14g (Saturated Fat 4.5g; Trans Fat 0g; Omega-3 0g); Cholesterol 435mg; Sodium 460mg; Total Carbohydrate 2g (Dietary Fiber 0g; Sugars 2g); Protein 17g **% Daily Value:** Potassium 5%; Vitamin A 15%; Vitamin C 0%; Calcium 6%; Iron 8%; Folic Acid 10% **Exchanges:** 2 1/2 Medium-Fat Meat
Carbohydrate Choices: 0

Apricot Breakfast Bread

PREP TIME: 25 Minutes   **START TO FINISH:** 2 Hours 25 Minutes   **1 LOAF** (16 slices)

1 cup all-purpose flour	1 cup buttermilk
3/4 cup whole wheat flour	2 tablespoons canola oil
3/4 cup packed brown sugar	1/2 cup chopped dried apricots
1 teaspoon baking soda	1/3 cup chopped walnuts
1 teaspoon ground cinnamon	1 tablespoon granulated sugar
1/4 teaspoon salt	1/2 teaspoon ground cinnamon
1 egg or 2 egg whites	

1. Heat oven to 350°F (or 325°F if using dark or nonstick pan). Grease bottom and sides of 8 × 4- or 9 × 5-inch loaf pan with shortening or cooking spray; coat with flour.

2. In medium bowl, mix flours, brown sugar, baking soda, 1 teaspoon cinnamon and the salt; set aside.

3. In another medium bowl, stir egg, buttermilk and oil with spoon until well blended. Add buttermilk mixture to flour mixture and stir just until moistened (some lumps will remain). Stir in apricots and walnuts. Spread in pan.

4. In small bowl, mix granulated sugar and 1/2 teaspoon cinnamon; sprinkle evenly over batter in pan.

5. Bake 50 to 60 minutes or until golden brown and toothpick inserted in center comes out clean. Cool 10 minutes; remove bread from pan to wire rack. Cool completely, about 1 hour. When completely cool, wrap in plastic wrap. Best served the next day.

BETTY'S TIP
You wouldn't know it by the flavor, but this moist bread is low in fat. Canola oil is a great choice to use in recipes because it's high in mono- and polyunsaturated fat which are beneficial for your heart.

1 Slice: Calories 150 (Calories from Fat 35); Total Fat 4g (Saturated Fat 0g; Trans Fat 0g; Omega-3 0g); Cholesterol 15mg; Sodium 140mg; Total Carbohydrate 25g (Dietary Fiber 2g; Sugars 14g); Protein 3g   **% Daily Value:** Potassium 4%; Vitamin A 4%; Vitamin C 0%; Calcium 4%; Iron 6%; Folic Acid 4%   **Exchanges:** 1 Starch, 1/2 Other Carbohydrate, 1/2 Fat **Carbohydrate Choices:** 1 1/2

Cranberry-Orange Bread

PREP TIME: 20 Minutes   **START TO FINISH:** 2 Hours 30 Minutes   **1 LOAF** (24 slices)

NOTE FROM DR. R

Besides eating
cereal for breakfast,
adding it to recipes
is an easy way to get
the extra vitamins,
minerals and whole
grains that the
cereal provides.

BREAD

2 cups Whole Grain Total® cereal

3/4 cup water

1 tablespoon grated orange or lemon peel

1/4 cup orange or lemon juice

1/2 teaspoon vanilla

2 cups all-purpose flour

1 cup granulated sugar

2 tablespoons canola oil

1 1/2 teaspoons baking powder

1/2 teaspoon baking soda

1/2 teaspoon salt

1 egg or 2 egg whites

1 cup fresh or frozen cranberries

ORANGE GLAZE

1/2 cup powdered sugar

1/4 teaspoon grated orange peel

2 to 3 teaspoons orange juice

1. Heat oven to 350°F. Grease bottom only of 9 × 5-inch loaf pan with shortening or cooking spray. Place cereal in food-storage plastic bag or between sheets of waxed paper; crush with rolling pin (or crush in blender or food processor).

2. In large bowl, mix crushed cereal, water, orange peel, orange juice and vanilla; let stand 10 minutes. Stir in remaining bread ingredients except cranberries. Gently stir in cranberries. Pour into pan.

3. Bake 50 to 60 minutes or until toothpick inserted in center comes out clean. Cool 10 minutes. Loosen sides of loaf; remove from pan to wire rack. Cool completely, about 1 hour.

4. In small bowl, mix all glaze ingredients until smooth and thin enough to drizzle; drizzle over loaf. Wrap tightly and store at room temperature up to 4 days or refrigerate up to 10 days.

1 Slice: Calories 110 (Calories from Fat 15); Total Fat 1.5g (Saturated Fat 0g; Trans Fat 0g; Omega-3 0g); Cholesterol 10mg; Sodium 135mg; Total Carbohydrate 23g (Dietary Fiber 0g; Sugars 12g); Protein 2g   **% Daily Value:** Potassium 1%; Vitamin A 0%; Vitamin C 8%; Calcium 15%; Iron 15%; Folic Acid 15%   **Exchanges:** 1/2 Starch, 1 Other Carbohydrate **Carbohydrate Choices:** 1 1/2

Oatmeal-Tropical Fruit Muffins

PREP TIME: 10 Minutes **START TO FINISH:** 30 Minutes **12 MUFFINS**

1 cup buttermilk or sour milk

1 cup old-fashioned or quick-cooking oats

1/2 cup packed brown sugar

1/4 cup canola oil

1 egg or 2 egg whites

1/2 cup all-purpose flour

1/2 cup whole wheat flour

2 teaspoons baking soda

1/2 teaspoon salt

1 teaspoon ground cinnamon

1/2 cup dried tropical fruit mix

1. Heat oven to 400°F. In small bowl; pour buttermilk over oats; let stand 5 minutes. Place paper baking cup in each of 12 regular-size muffin cups.

2. In large bowl, mix brown sugar, oil and egg with spoon. Stir in flours, baking soda, salt and cinnamon just until flour is moistened. Stir in oat mixture; fold in fruit mix. Divide batter among muffin cups (3/4 full).

3. Bake 15 to 20 minutes or until golden brown. Immediately remove from pan to wire rack.

NOTE FROM DR. R
Eating breakfast sets the stage for the rest of the day in terms of energy and nutrition. Breakfast eaters tend to have diets that contain more vitamins, minerals and fiber and less fat than those who don't.

"I practice yoga once a week. Sometimes I have to force myself to go, but afterward, I'm always glad I did." —Heidi L.

1 Muffin: Calories 170 (Calories from Fat 50); Total Fat 6g (Saturated Fat 1g; Trans Fat 0g; Omega-3 0g); Cholesterol 20mg; Sodium 340mg; Total Carbohydrate 26g (Dietary Fiber 2g; Sugars 13g); Protein 4g **% Daily Value:** Potassium 5%; Vitamin A 2%; Vitamin C 0%; Calcium 4%; Iron 6%; Folic Acid 4% **Exchanges:** 1 Starch, 1/2 Other Carbohydrate, 1 Fat **Carbohydrate Choices:** 2

Chocolate Chip–Cherry Scones

PREP TIME: 20 Minutes **START TO FINISH:** 45 Minutes **12 SCONES**

2 cups all-purpose flour

1/4 cup sugar

2 teaspoons baking powder

1/2 teaspoon baking soda

1/2 teaspoon salt

1/4 cup firm butter or margarine

1 container (6 oz) cherry orchard low-fat yogurt

1/2 cup dried cherries or cherry-flavored dried cranberries

1/4 cup semisweet chocolate chips

Unsweetened baking cocoa, if desired

1. Heat oven to 400°F. Spray cookie sheet with cooking spray.

2. In medium bowl, mix flour, sugar, baking powder, baking soda and salt. Cut in butter, using pastry blender (or pulling 2 table knives through ingredients in opposite directions), until mixture looks like fine crumbs. Stir in yogurt, cherries and chocolate chips (dough will seem dry and crumbly).

3. On lightly floured surface, shape dough into a ball. Knead dough lightly 10 times. Divide dough in half. On cookie sheet, pat each half of dough into 6-inch circle. Cut each circle into 6 wedges, using sharp knife, but do not separate wedges.

4. Bake 10 to 15 minutes or until golden brown. Immediately remove from cookie sheet to wire rack. Carefully separate wedges. Cool 10 minutes. Sprinkle lightly with cocoa. Serve warm.

1 Scone: Calories 180 (Calories from Fat 45); Total Fat 5g (Saturated Fat 3g; Trans Fat 0g; Omega-3 0g); Cholesterol 10mg; Sodium 270mg; Total Carbohydrate 29g (Dietary Fiber 1g; Sugars 11g); Protein 3g   **% Daily Value:** Potassium 3%; Vitamin A 6%; Vitamin C 0%; Calcium 8%; Iron 6%; Folic Acid 8%   **Exchanges:** 1 Starch, 1 Other Carbohydrate, 1 Fat **Carbohydrate Choices:** 2

Cranberry-Pecan Granola

PREP TIME: 35 Minutes   **START TO FINISH:** 35 Minutes   **8 SERVINGS** (3/4 cup each)

3 cups old-fashioned oats

1/4 cup chopped pecans

1/4 cup frozen (thawed) orange juice concentrate

1/4 cup real maple syrup or maple-flavored syrup

1/2 teaspoon ground cinnamon

2 teaspoons canola oil

2 cups Wheat Chex® cereal

1 1/3 cups sweetened dried cranberries (about 6 oz)

1. Heat oven to 325°F. In large bowl, mix oats and pecans.

2. In small bowl, mix juice concentrate, syrup, cinnamon and oil until well blended. Drizzle over oat mixture; toss well to coat evenly. Stir in cereal. Spread on 2 large cookie sheets or in 2 (15 × 10 × 1-inch) pans.

3. Bake 20 to 25 minutes, stirring granola frequently and changing positions of cookie sheets once halfway through baking, until light golden brown. Stir half of cranberries into each half of granola.

NOTE FROM DR. R
Many women don't get enough iron. This granola is high in iron and is a great breakfast or snack. And if you drink a glass of orange juice with it, the vitamin C may help your body absorb the iron more readily.

"I like being strong for my kids so I can run and play with them without wimping out."   —Stacy P.

1 Serving: Calories 310 (Calories from Fat 50); Total Fat 6g (Saturated Fat 0.5g; Trans Fat 0g; Omega-3 0g); Cholesterol 0mg; Sodium 110mg; Total Carbohydrate 58g (Dietary Fiber 6g; Sugars 26g); Protein 7g   **% Daily Value:** Potassium 7%; Vitamin A 4%; Vitamin C 10%; Calcium 6%; Iron 30%; Folic Acid 30%   **Exchanges:** 2 Starch, 2 Other Carbohydrate, 1 Fat **Carbohydrate Choices:** 4

Maintain a Healthy Weight

Maintaining a healthy weight can help you look better, feel better and have more energy. It can also help reduce the chance of developing cancer, diabetes and heart disease. The best diet is making wise food choices and being active every day. If you make changes gradually, you'll adopt new ways of thinking that result in new behaviors and improved habits. However you choose to lose, here are six stick-to-it strategies sure to help:

1. **Be committed.** Losing weight and keeping it off takes time, effort and dedication. Make sure you're ready to make the necessary changes and that you are starting when you are not distracted by other major life issues, such as buying a home or changing jobs. Motivate yourself by focusing on the benefits, such as having more energy and improving your health. Eating for wellness's sake is about balancing the food you eat with the energy you expend.

2. **Get support.** Though you are the only one in control of losing and keeping the weight off, support from your partner, family and friends can make a big difference. Select people who will listen, encourage you and perhaps even participate in exercise or healthy eating. Some people do better when they enlist professional help, like a dietitian or a personal exercise trainer; others benefit from group support they receive at specific weight loss programs.

3. **Be realistic.** Slow, steady weight loss—one to two pounds per week—is the safest, most effective way to lose weight and keep it off. To lose one to two pounds per week, you need to create a shortage of 500 to 1000 calories a day by increasing exercise and reducing calories. Losing weight more rapidly means losing water weight or muscle tissue, rather than fat. Changing your habits over time is the key to successful weight loss and maintenance. Make your goals eating healthy and exercising regularly.

4. **Be active.** The best exercises for burning calories are aerobic—involving continuous, rhythmic use of your muscles, such as walking briskly, swimming, jumping rope, dancing, jogging, running and cycling. If it's an activity you enjoy, you're bound to stay with it longer. Your workout should be intense enough to feel like you're working yet also able to have a conversation during the activity. Having an exercise buddy is a great way to stay motivated. Strength training, an important component, is also beneficial for weight loss because it builds muscle while boosting your metabolism.

5. **Follow the wellness mantra of balance, variety and moderation.** Balance the foods you eat with the amount of activity you get each day. Eat a variety of foods over the course of a week. Aim for moderation in portion sizes and quantity of food. Eating for wellness can be simple and tasty, as the recipes in this cookbook show, and you don't have to give up your favorite foods or feel deprived.

6. **Cue in to portion sizes.** A big piece of the puzzle in losing weight is eating the proper amounts of foods. Portion sizes in restaurants and marketplaces are larger than needed, so it's hard to know what a true serving size is. The chart can help you visualize the correct portion sizes of the foods you eat. To start, measure your portions until you can start to "eyeball" them accurately.

METABOLISM CHANGES AS A WOMAN ENTERS MENOPAUSE, A SLOWER METABOLISM MAY FOLLOW. (THE AVERAGE WEIGHT GAIN DURING MENOPAUSE IS 10 TO 20 POUNDS.) YOU MAY WANT TO MAKE CHANGES TO YOUR DIET AND LIFESTYLE TO PREVENT WEIGHT GAIN. TO HELP KEEP YOUR WEIGHT STEADY:

- KEEP PORTION SIZES REALISTIC (SEE #6 ABOVE).

- EXERCISE EVERY DAY.

- EAT THE FOODS THAT PACK THE MOST NUTRIENTS WITH THE LEAST AMOUNT OF CALORIES (SEE #5 LEFT).

- TREAT FOODS THAT ARE HIGH IN FAT, LIKE CANDY, CHIPS, BAKERY DESSERTS, ETC., AS SPECIAL OCCASION TREATS, NOT A REGULAR PART OF YOUR DIET.

SERVING SIZE CARD:

Cut out and fold on the dotted line. Laminate for longtime use.

1 Serving Looks Like . . .

GRAIN PRODUCTS

1 cup of cereal flakes = fist

1 pancake = compact disc

½ cup of cooked rice, pasta, or potato = ½ baseball

1 slice of bread = cassette tape

1 piece of cornbread = bar of soap

1 Serving Looks Like . . .

VEGETABLES AND FRUIT

1 cup of salad greens = baseball

1 baked potato = fist

1 med. fruit = baseball

½ cup of fresh fruit = ½ baseball

¼ cup of raisins = large egg

1 Serving Looks Like . . .

DAIRY AND CHEESE

1½ oz. cheese = 4 stacked dice or 2 cheese slices

½ cup of ice cream = ½ baseball

FATS

1 tsp. margarine or spreads = 1 dice

1 Serving Looks Like . . .

MEAT AND ALTERNATIVES

3 oz. meat, fish, and poultry = deck of cards

3 oz. grilled/baked fish = checkbook

2 Tbsp. peanut butter = ping pong ball

Triple-Berry Oatmeal Muesli

PREP TIME: 25 Minutes   **START TO FINISH:** 40 Minutes   **6 SERVINGS**

2 3/4 cups old-fashioned oats or barley flakes
1/2 cup sliced almonds
2 containers (6 oz each) banana crème low-fat yogurt
1 1/2 cups fat-free (skim) milk
1/4 cup ground flaxseed or flaxseed meal
1/2 cup fresh blueberries
1/2 cup fresh raspberries
1/2 cup sliced fresh strawberries

NOTE FROM DR. R
This muesli is a combination of great-tasting, good-for-you foods. Flaxseed, the highest plant source of omega-3 fatty acids, has been shown to reduce cholesterol and triglyceride levels.

1. Heat oven to 350°F. On cookie sheet, spread oats and almonds. Bake 18 to 20 minutes, stirring occasionally, until light golden brown; cool 15 minutes.

2. In large bowl, mix yogurt and milk until well blended. Stir in oats, almonds and flaxseed. Top each serving with berries.

"Every night my daughter and I list three things that we are grateful for. We range from the very specific, 'I am grateful I did OK on the math test,' to the general, 'I am grateful for flowers.' It helps to put things into perspective." —Anne F.

1 Serving: Calories 310 (Calories from Fat 80); Total Fat 9g (Saturated Fat 1.5g; Trans Fat 0g; Omega-3 1g); Cholesterol 0mg; Sodium 60mg; Total Carbohydrate 46g (Dietary Fiber 8g; Sugars 16g); Protein 13g   **% Daily Value:** Potassium 13%; Vitamin A 8%; Vitamin C 20%; Calcium 20%; Iron 15%; Folic Acid 10%   **Exchanges:** 2 Starch, 1/2 Fruit, 1/2 Skim Milk, 1/2 High-Fat Meat, 1/2 Fat   **Carbohydrate Choices:** 3

On-the-Go Apple Breakfast Bars

PREP TIME: 30 Minutes   **START TO FINISH:** 2 Hours 30 Minutes   **16 BARS**

1 1/2 cups dried apples, finely chopped

3/4 cup chopped pecans

2 1/2 cups Whole Grain Total® cereal

1/3 cup honey

1/4 cup golden raisins

1 tablespoon packed brown sugar

1/3 cup chunky or creamy peanut butter

1/4 cup apple butter

1/2 teaspoon ground cinnamon

1/2 cup old-fashioned or quick-cooking oats

1/4 cup roasted sunflower nuts

1. Line bottom and sides of 8-inch square pan with foil; spray with cooking spray. Sprinkle 1/2 cup of the apples and 1/4 cup of the pecans over bottom of pan. Place cereal in food-storage plastic bag or between sheets of waxed paper; coarsely crush with rolling pin (or coarsely crush in blender or food processor); set aside.

2. In 4-quart Dutch oven, heat 1/2 cup of the apples, the honey, raisins and brown sugar to boiling over medium-high heat, stirring occasionally. Reduce heat to medium. Cook uncovered about 1 minute, stirring constantly, until hot and bubbly; remove from heat.

3. Stir peanut butter into cooked mixture until melted. Stir in apple butter and cinnamon. Stir in oats, sunflower nuts and 1/4 cup of the pecans until well mixed. Stir in crushed cereal.

4. Press mixture very firmly (or bars will crumble) and evenly onto apples and pecans in pan. Sprinkle with remaining 1/2 cup apples and 1/4 cup pecans; press lightly into bars. Refrigerate about 2 hours or until set. For bars, cut into 8 rows by 2 rows. Store covered in refrigerator.

"I take yoga in the morning, when I'm at my best. It has improved my breathing and flexibility, and I just feel better."   —Lola W.

BETTY'S TIP
The beauty of this breakfast bar is that it can be made ahead and stored in the refrigerator. Its hearty flavor and texture make it ideal for days when "on the go" is a must.

1 Bar: Calories 180 (Calories from Fat 70); Total Fat 8g (Saturated Fat 1g; Trans Fat 0g; Omega-3 0g); Cholesterol 0mg; Sodium 85mg; Total Carbohydrate 25g (Dietary Fiber 3g; Sugars 16g); Protein 3g   **% Daily Value:** Potassium 4%; Vitamin A 2%; Vitamin C 10%; Calcium 20%; Iron 25%; Folic Acid 25%   **Exchanges:** 1 Starch, 1/2 Other Carbohydrate, 1 1/2 Fat
Carbohydrate Choices: 1 1/2

Apple-Mint Iced Green Tea

PREP TIME: 10 Minutes   **START TO FINISH:** 35 Minutes   **6 SERVINGS** (1 cup each)

6 tea bags green tea with mint
4 cups boiling water
2 cups apple juice
Fresh mint sprigs, if desired

NOTE FROM DR. R
Tea has long been linked to relaxation. And green tea contains antioxidants, which may provide preventive protection against certain diseases. Served hot or cold, this tea combines apple and mint and is a refreshing choice anytime.

1. In large heatproof bowl or pitcher, place tea bags. Pour boiling water over tea bags. Cover; let steep 10 minutes. Remove tea bags. Cool tea 15 minutes.

2. Stir apple juice into tea. Pour over ice. Garnish with mint.

"I walk with my dog most mornings. We both benefit from the exercise and the relaxing quiet of the morning." —Lola W.

1 Serving: Calories 40 (Calories from Fat 0); Total Fat 0g (Saturated Fat 0g; Trans Fat 0g; Omega-3 0g); Cholesterol 0mg; Sodium 10mg; Total Carbohydrate 10g (Dietary Fiber 0g; Sugars 8g); Protein 0g   **% Daily Value:** Potassium 5%; Vitamin A 0%; Vitamin C 0%; Calcium 0%; Iron 0%; Folic Acid 2%   **Exchanges:** 1/2 Other Carbohydrate   **Carbohydrate Choices:** 1/2

VITAMIN C   CALCIUM   IRON   FIBER   FOLIC ACID   POTASSIUM

Chocolate–Peanut Butter–Banana Smoothie

PREP TIME: 5 Minutes   **START TO FINISH:** 2 Hours 5 Minutes   **3 SERVINGS** (1 cup each)

2 ripe medium bananas, peeled, cut into 2-inch chunks
2 cups chocolate-flavored soymilk or chocolate-flavored fat-free (skim) milk
3 tablespoons chocolate topping
2 tablespoons creamy peanut butter

1. Freeze banana chunks 2 hours.

2. In blender, place frozen banana chunks and remaining ingredients. Cover; blend on high speed about 30 seconds or until smooth. Serve immediately.

BETTY'S TIP
To freeze bananas, peel and freeze at least 2 hours or overnight. Or whenever you have a banana that is too ripe to eat, just toss it in the freezer for making this popular shake.

1 Serving: Calories 350 (Calories from Fat 80); Total Fat 9g (Saturated Fat 2g; Trans Fat 0g; Omega-3 0g); Cholesterol 0mg; Sodium 170mg; Total Carbohydrate 57g (Dietary Fiber 5g; Sugars 31g); Protein 10g   **% Daily Value:** Potassium 18%; Vitamin A 8%; Vitamin C 10%; Calcium 20%; Iron 15%; Folic Acid 10%   **Exchanges:** 1 Starch, 1 Fruit, 1 Other Carbohydrate, 1 Skim Milk, 1 1/2 Fat   **Carbohydrate Choices:** 4

Creamy Mango Smoothies

PREP TIME: 10 Minutes   **START TO FINISH:** 10 Minutes   **6 SERVINGS** (1 cup each)

2 mangoes, seed removed, peeled and chopped (2 cups)
2 cups mango sorbet
2 containers (6 oz each) French vanilla low-fat yogurt
1 1/2 cups fat-free (skim) milk or soymilk

In blender, place all ingredients. Cover; blend on high speed until smooth.

BETTY'S TIP

For the best flavor and color, choose ripe mangoes; look for skins that are yellow with blushes of red. Mango adds vitamins A and C, and the yogurt and milk add calcium and vitamin D.

"I've learned that it takes healthy eating and exercise to keep my weight down. They go hand in hand."   —Cathy P.

1 Serving: Calories 200 (Calories from Fat 10); Total Fat 1g (Saturated Fat 0.5g; Trans Fat 0g; Omega-3 0g); Cholesterol 0mg; Sodium 75mg; Total Carbohydrate 43g (Dietary Fiber 1g; Sugars 36g); Protein 5g   **% Daily Value:** Potassium 9%; Vitamin A 15%; Vitamin C 30%; Calcium 20%; Iron 0%; Folic Acid 4%   **Exchanges:** 1 Fruit, 1 1/2 Other Carbohydrate, 1/2 Skim Milk   **Carbohydrate Choices:** 3

Creamy Mango Smoothies

2

Energy-Boosting
Snacks and Breads

Tame your hunger with bites of
inviting appetizers and snacks

Chilly Garden Pizza

PREP TIME: 15 Minutes **START TO FINISH:** 15 Minutes **16 SERVINGS**

1 container (6.5 oz) 50%-less-fat garlic-and-herb spreadable cheese
1 package (10 oz) prebaked thin Italian pizza crust (12 inch)
1 cup chopped fresh spinach
3/4 cup diced seeded cucumber
1 large tomato, chopped (1 cup)
1/2 cup sliced fresh mushrooms
1 tablespoon chopped fresh basil leaves
1/4 teaspoon salt
1/8 teaspoon pepper
1 cup shredded carrots

1. Spread cheese over pizza crust.

2. Top with spinach, cucumber, tomato, mushrooms and basil. Sprinkle with salt and pepper. Top with carrots.

NOTE FROM DR. R
Enjoy the bounty of your garden while you get your vitamins and minerals. Spinach and carrots are loaded with beta-carotene, a powerful antioxidant which converts to vitamin A and is important for good eye health.

"I try to be mindful of what I'm eating and how much." —Cathy P.

1 Serving: Calories 100 (Calories from Fat 45); Total Fat 5g (Saturated Fat 3g; Trans Fat 0g; Omega-3 0g); Cholesterol 15mg; Sodium 170mg; Total Carbohydrate 10g (Dietary Fiber 0g; Sugars 1g); Protein 3g **% Daily Value:** Potassium 3%; Vitamin A 25%; Vitamin C 4%; Calcium 0%; Iron 4%; Folic Acid 6% **Exchanges:** 1/2 Starch, 1/2 High-Fat Meat **Carbohydrate Choices:** 1/2

Grilled Margherita Pizza

PREP TIME: 25 Minutes **START TO FINISH:** 25 Minutes **9 SERVINGS** (4 pieces each)

2 cloves garlic, finely chopped

1 teaspoon olive oil

1 teaspoon dried oregano leaves

1 package (14 oz) prebaked original Italian pizza crust (12 inch)

2 plum (Roma) tomatoes, thinly sliced

2 tablespoons coarsely chopped fresh basil leaves

1 cup shredded reduced-fat Italian cheese blend (4 oz)

1. Heat gas or charcoal grill. In small bowl, mix garlic, oil and oregano; brush over pizza crust. Top with tomatoes, basil and cheese.

2. Place pizza on grill. Cover grill; cook over medium-low heat 7 to 9 minutes, moving pizza around grill every 2 minutes to prevent bottom from burning, until cheese is melted.

3. Cut pizza into 36 squares. Serve immediately.

BETTY'S TIP

Finely shredded mozzarella cheese can be used instead of the Italian blend. If you'd rather bake the pizza, heat the oven to 450°F and bake on an ungreased cookie sheet for 8 to 10 minutes.

"I protect my exercise time by scheduling it on my calendar. If I don't, work and family take over and I never make the time I need for myself." —Jean S.

1 Serving: Calories 170 (Calories from Fat 50); Total Fat 6g (Saturated Fat 3g; Trans Fat 0g; Omega-3 0g); Cholesterol 15mg; Sodium 330mg; Total Carbohydrate 20g (Dietary Fiber 1g; Sugars 0g); Protein 8g **% Daily Value:** Potassium 2%; Vitamin A 6%; Vitamin C 0%; Calcium 10%; Iron 8%; Folic Acid 10% **Exchanges:** 1 1/2 Starch, 1/2 High-Fat Meat **Carbohydrate Choices:** 1

Bruschetta Pita Wedges

PREP TIME: 10 Minutes   **START TO FINISH:** 20 Minutes   **6 SERVINGS** (2 wedges each)

2 whole wheat pita breads (7 inch)
1 tablespoon fat-free balsamic vinaigrette or fat-free Italian dressing
1 tablespoon chopped fresh or 1 teaspoon dried basil leaves
2 large plum (Roma) tomatoes, seeded, chopped (1 cup)
1 clove garlic, finely chopped
1/3 cup plain fat-free hummus
1/2 cup shredded part-skim mozzarella cheese
1 tablespoon shredded Parmesan cheese

NOTE FROM DR. R
These quick and classy appetizers can be served with a glass of crisp Chardonnay or Chianti. A daily drink can be beneficial for your heart by boosting good (HDL) cholesterol and may even protect against certain types of strokes. Because moderation is key when drinking, be sure to keep it to one drink per day.

1. Heat oven to 400°F. On large cookie sheet, place pita breads. Bake 6 to 8 minutes or until slightly crisp.

2. In medium bowl, mix vinaigrette, basil, tomatoes and garlic.

3. Spread half of the hummus over each pita bread. Spoon tomato mixture over hummus. Sprinkle with cheeses.

4. Bake 5 to 6 minutes or until tomato mixture is hot. Cut each pita bread into 6 wedges.

"I love using fresh herbs—both for the aroma and the flavor. Fresh basil, oregano, thyme and rosemary are great!"   —Cindy L.

1 Serving: Calories 140 (Calories from Fat 35); Total Fat 4g (Saturated Fat 1.5g; Trans Fat 0g; Omega-3 0g); Cholesterol 5mg; Sodium 290mg; Total Carbohydrate 19g (Dietary Fiber 3g; Sugars 3g); Protein 7g   **% Daily Value:** Potassium 5%; Vitamin A 6%; Vitamin C 4%; Calcium 10%; Iron 8%; Folic Acid 8%   **Exchanges:** 1 1/2 Starch, 1/2 Medium-Fat Meat   **Carbohydrate Choices:** 1

Bruschetta Pita Wedges

Roasted Carrot and Herb Spread

PREP TIME: 20 Minutes **START TO FINISH:** 1 Hour 20 Minutes **16 SERVINGS** (2 tablespoons spread and 2 crackers each)

1 lb ready-to-eat baby-cut carrots

1 dark-orange sweet potato, peeled, cut into 1-inch pieces (2 1/2 cups)

1 small onion, cut into 8 wedges, separated

2 tablespoons olive oil

1 clove garlic, finely chopped

1 tablespoon chopped fresh or 1 teaspoon dried thyme leaves

1/4 teaspoon salt

1/8 teaspoon freshly ground pepper

Assorted whole-grain crackers or vegetable chips

BETTY'S TIP
Red garnet sweet potatoes—or any of the deep-orange variety—help give this dip its intense color, flavor and nutrition, but you can use any kind of sweet potato that you like.

1. Heat oven to 350°F. Spray 15 × 10 × 1-inch pan with cooking spray.

2. Place carrots, sweet potato and onion in pan; drizzle with oil. Sprinkle with garlic, thyme, salt and pepper; stir to coat. Bake uncovered about 1 hour, stirring occasionally, until vegetables are tender.

3. In food processor, place vegetable mixture. Cover; process until blended. Spoon into serving bowl. Serve warm, or cover and refrigerate until serving. Serve with crackers.

"My husband and I ride to work together—we de-stress on the way home and by the time we reach our house, we are ready to enjoy our evening." —Suzanne S.

1 Serving: Calories 80 (Calories from Fat 25); Total Fat 3g (Saturated Fat 0.5g; Trans Fat 0g; Omega-3 0g); Cholesterol 0mg; Sodium 120mg; Total Carbohydrate 12g (Dietary Fiber 2g; Sugars 3g); Protein 1g **% Daily Value:** Potassium 5%; Vitamin A 130%; Vitamin C 4%; Calcium 0%; Iron 4%; Folic Acid 4% **Exchanges:** 1/2 Starch, 1/2 Other Carbohydrate, 1/2 Fat **Carbohydrate Choices:** 1

Shrimp and Red Potato Snacks

PREP TIME: 15 Minutes **START TO FINISH:** 30 Minutes **20 SNACKS**

5 small red potatoes, about 1 1/2 inches in diameter

2 teaspoons olive oil

1/4 teaspoon salt

10 cooked deveined peeled medium shrimp, thawed if frozen, tail shells removed

1/4 cup reduced-fat garlic-and-herb spreadable cheese (from 4-oz container)

Dill weed sprigs

1. Heat oven to 400°F. Line cookie sheet with foil or cooking parchment paper; lightly spray with cooking spray. Cut each potato into four 1/4-inch slices, trimming off round ends. Coat with oil and salt. Place on cookie sheet.

2. Bake 15 to 18 minutes or until tender and edges begin to turn light golden brown. Cool about 10 minutes.

3. Meanwhile, cut each shrimp lengthwise in half. To serve, spread about 1/2 teaspoon cheese on each potato slice; top with shrimp half and small dill weed sprig.

> **BETTY'S TIP**
> Sometimes it helps relieve stress if you can do part of a recipe ahead. For this one, you can slice and bake the potatoes the day before, then cover and refrigerate until serving time.

"Whenever I am feeling stressed, I realize I have gone to an extreme—too much food and not enough exercise."   —Lisa B.

1 Snack: Calories 45 (Calories from Fat 10); Total Fat 1g (Saturated Fat 0g; Trans Fat 0g; Omega-3 0g); Cholesterol 5mg; Sodium 50mg; Total Carbohydrate 7g (Dietary Fiber 0g; Sugars 0g); Protein 1g   **% Daily Value:** Potassium 7%; Vitamin A 0%; Vitamin C 4%; Calcium 2%; Iron 4%; Folic Acid 0%   **Exchanges:** 1/2 Starch   **Carbohydrate Choices:** 1/2

Mozzarella-Pepperoncini Platter

PREP TIME: 15 Minutes   **START TO FINISH:** 15 Minutes   **16 SERVINGS**

1 lb fresh reduced-fat mozzarella cheese,
cut into 1/4-inch slices

2/3 cup coarsely chopped drained garlic-dill
Italian pepperoncini peppers (from 16-oz jar)

1/3 cup chopped drained roasted red bell peppers
(from 7-oz jar)

16 thin slices French bread, lightly toasted,
or whole-grain crackers

1. On serving platter, arrange mozzarella slices in a single layer.

2. Sprinkle pepperoncini peppers and bell peppers over cheese. Serve with bread.

NOTE FROM DR. R
Just one serving of this appetizer gives you a boost of calcium. Besides its well-known role in bone health, research shows that getting adequate calcium may help reduce the risk of certain cancers and plays a role in maintaining blood pressure.

"I go up and down the stairs for a fast exercise break a couple of times during the day. That really gets my heart rate up." —Sherri F.

1 Serving: Calories 110 (Calories from Fat 50); Total Fat 6g (Saturated Fat 3.5g; Trans Fat 0g; Omega-3 0g); Cholesterol 15mg; Sodium 200mg; Total Carbohydrate 6g (Dietary Fiber 0g; Sugars 0g); Protein 8g   **% Daily Value:** Potassium 1%; Vitamin A 8%; Vitamin C 20%; Calcium 20%; Iron 0%; Folic Acid 4%   **Exchanges:** 1/2 Starch, 1 Medium-Fat Meat   **Carbohydrate Choices:** 1/2

Mozzarella-Pepperoncini Platter

Potato Bites

PREP TIME: 40 Minutes   START TO FINISH: 55 Minutes   22 SERVINGS (2 bites each)

1 package (24 oz) refrigerated mashed potatoes (about 2 cups)
1 1/2 cups frozen sweet peas (from 1-lb bag)
1/3 cup chopped red onion
1 teaspoon ground coriander
1/2 teaspoon ground cumin
1/4 teaspoon salt
1/8 teaspoon ground red pepper (cayenne)
1 cup plain dry bread crumbs
2 eggs
2 tablespoons fat-free (skim) milk
Cooking spray
Tomato chutney or chunky-style salsa, if desired

BETTY'S TIP
The easy way to make potato balls that are the same size? Use a small ice-cream scoop. To serve, skewer each bite with a colorful fringed toothpick.

1. Heat oven to 400°F. Line cookie sheet with foil or cooking parchment paper; spray foil or paper with cooking spray. In medium bowl, mix potatoes, peas, onion, coriander, cumin, salt and red pepper.

2. In shallow bowl, place bread crumbs. In another shallow bowl, beat eggs and milk with fork or wire whisk. Shape potato mixture by tablespoonfuls into about 1-inch balls. Roll balls in bread crumbs to coat, then dip into egg mixture and coat again with bread crumbs. Place on cookie sheet. Spray tops of balls with cooking spray.

3. Bake 10 to 14 minutes or until light golden brown and hot. Serve warm with chutney.

1 Serving: Calories 30 (Calories from Fat 5); Total Fat 1g (Saturated Fat 0g; Trans Fat 0g; Omega-3 0g); Cholesterol 10mg; Sodium 50mg; Total Carbohydrate 4g (Dietary Fiber 0g; Sugars 0g); Protein 1g   **% Daily Value:** Potassium 1%; Vitamin A 2%; Vitamin C 0%; Calcium 0%; Iron 0%; Folic Acid 0%   **Exchanges:** 1/2 Other Carbohydrate   **Carbohydrate Choices:** 0

Grilled Vegetable Salsa

PREP TIME: 1 Hour 10 Minutes   **START TO FINISH:** 1 Hour 25 Minutes   **18 SERVINGS** (1/3 cup salsa and 6 chips each)

2 ears corn, husked, cleaned and broken crosswise in half

2 medium zucchini, cut lengthwise in half, then cut crosswise into 1 1/2-inch pieces

1 medium red bell pepper, cut into 8 pieces

1 medium red onion, cut into wedges, separated

2 jalapeño chiles, cut in half, seeded

1 tablespoon olive oil

6 plum (Roma) tomatoes, cut lengthwise in half, seeded

2 teaspoons grated lime peel

2 tablespoons chopped fresh cilantro

1 teaspoon salt

Tortilla chips

1. Heat gas or charcoal grill. In large bowl, toss corn, zucchini, bell pepper, onion and chiles with oil. Place in grill basket (grill "wok").

2. Place basket on grill. Cover grill; cook over medium heat 25 to 30 minutes, shaking basket or stirring occasionally, until vegetables are tender. Add tomatoes to basket. Cover grill; cook 1 to 2 minutes longer or until tomatoes are hot. Remove basket from grill; cool vegetables 15 minutes.

3. Cut corn off cobs (about 1 cup kernels); chop all remaining vegetables into small pieces. In large bowl, mix vegetables, lime peel, cilantro and salt. Serve immediately, or cover and refrigerate up to 24 hours. Serve with tortilla chips. Store covered in refrigerator.

NOTE FROM DR. R

Vegetables are a good source of soluble and insoluble fiber, making them a great weapon against heart disease. Since much of the fiber is contained in the skins, avoid peeling the skins whenever you can.

1 Serving: Calories 90 (Calories from Fat 35); Total Fat 3.5g (Saturated Fat 0g; Trans Fat 0g; Omega-3 0g); Cholesterol 0mg; Sodium 200mg; Total Carbohydrate 12g (Dietary Fiber 2g; Sugars 2g); Protein 2g   **% Daily Value:** Potassium 5%; Vitamin A 10%; Vitamin C 15%; Calcium 0%; Iron 4%; Folic Acid 8%   **Exchanges:** 1/2 Starch, 1/2 Vegetable, 1/2 Fat
Carbohydrate Choices: 1

Zesty Corn Dip with Veggies

PREP TIME: 10 Minutes   **START TO FINISH:** 1 Hour 10 Minutes   **24 SERVINGS** (about 3 tablespoons dip and 1/4 cup veggies each)

2 packages (8 oz each) reduced-fat cream cheese (Neufchâtel), softened
1/4 cup lime juice
1 tablespoon ground red chiles or chili powder
1 tablespoon ground cumin
1/2 teaspoon salt
Dash pepper
1 can (7 oz) whole kernel corn, drained
1/4 cup chopped walnuts
1 small onion, chopped (1/4 cup)
6 cups assorted vegetables (jicama strips, grape tomatoes, bell pepper strips, carrot and celery sticks)

BETTY'S TIP
This is a yummy combination of flavors and colors. For a fun presentation fill hollowed-out large bell peppers with the dip and arrange on a tray lined with corn husks.

1. In large bowl, beat cream cheese, lime juice, chiles, cumin, salt and pepper with electric mixer on medium speed until smooth. Stir in corn, walnuts and onion.

2. Refrigerate at least 1 hour. Serve with vegetables.

1 Serving: Calories 70 (Calories from Fat 40); Total Fat 4.5g (Saturated Fat 2g; Trans Fat 0g; Omega-3 0g); Cholesterol 10mg; Sodium 135mg; Total Carbohydrate 5g (Dietary Fiber 1g; Sugars 3g); Protein 3g   **% Daily Value:** Potassium 4%; Vitamin A 25%; Vitamin C 10%; Calcium 4%; Iron 4%; Folic Acid 4%   **Exchanges:** 1/2 Vegetable, 1/2 High-Fat Meat   **Carbohydrate Choices:** 1/2

Zesty Corn Dip with Veggies

Quick Guacamole

PREP TIME: 10 Minutes **START TO FINISH:** 10 Minutes **16 SERVINGS** (2 tablespoons dip and 6 chips each)

2 large ripe avocados, pitted, peeled and chopped
1 tablespoon lime juice
1 plum (Roma) tomato, chopped (1/3 cup)
1 tablespoon chopped fresh cilantro
1/4 teaspoon salt
Dash ground red pepper (cayenne)
Blue corn tortilla chips

1. In medium bowl, mix all ingredients except tortilla chips.

2. Serve guacamole with tortilla chips.

NOTE FROM DR. R
Guacamole is always a hit. Besides having fiber, potassium and B vitamins, avocados contain disease-fighting antioxidants and the good fats needed for a healthy heart. Moderation is the key to reaping the benefits from this delicious tropical fruit.

"I try to do something fun every day. On a busy workday, it might just be calling a friend or spending 10 minutes on a crossword puzzle." —Jeanne A.

1 Serving: Calories 70 (Calories from Fat 40); Total Fat 4.5g (Saturated Fat 0.5g; Trans Fat 0g; Omega-3 0g); Cholesterol 0mg; Sodium 70mg; Total Carbohydrate 5g (Dietary Fiber 2g; Sugars 0g); Protein 0g   **% Daily Value:** Potassium 4%; Vitamin A 0%; Vitamin C 4%; Calcium 0%; Iron 0%; Folic Acid 6%   **Exchanges:** 1/2 Starch, 1 Fat   **Carbohydrate Choices:** 1/2

Quick Guacamole

Raspberry-Mint
Marshmallow Creme Dip

PREP TIME: 25 Minutes   **START TO FINISH:** 2 Hours 25 Minutes   **15 SERVINGS** (2 tablespoons dip and 6 fruit pieces each)

4 oz (from 8-oz package) reduced-fat cream cheese (Neufchâtel), softened
1 cup marshmallow creme
1 container (6 oz) lemon low-fat yogurt
1/2 cup fresh raspberries
2 teaspoons chopped fresh mint leaves
15 fresh strawberries, stems removed, cut lengthwise in half
3 kiwifruit, each cut into 10 chunks
30 pieces (2-inch) fresh pineapple

1. In medium bowl, beat cream cheese, marshmallow creme, yogurt and raspberries with electric mixer on high speed until smooth. Stir in mint.

2. Cover dip; refrigerate at least 2 hours but no longer than 12 hours. Serve dip with strawberries, kiwifruit and pineapple.

BETTY'S TIP
Add to the fun of this delightful dip by serving it in a unique way. Cut 1 medium cantaloupe in half and scoop out the fruit almost down to the peel. Fill with dip, then garnish with mint sprigs.

"Kicking the soccer ball, shooting a few hoops or hitting the tennis ball with my kids is a good way to exercise and add a little fun to my day." —Cheri O.

1 Serving: Calories 80 (Calories from Fat 15); Total Fat 1.5g (Saturated Fat 1g; Trans Fat 0g; Omega-3 0g); Cholesterol 0mg; Sodium 35mg; Total Carbohydrate 14g (Dietary Fiber 1g; Sugars 11g); Protein 2g   **% Daily Value:** Potassium 4%; Vitamin A 4%; Vitamin C 50%; Calcium 4%; Iron 0%; Folic Acid 4%   **Exchanges:** 1 Other Carbohydrate, 1/2 Fat   **Carbohydrate Choices:** 1

Raspberry-Mint Marshmallow Creme Dip

Caribbean Dip with Lime Chips

PREP TIME: 20 Minutes   **START TO FINISH:** 20 Minutes   **24 SERVINGS** (2 tablespoons dip and 2 chips each)

BETTY'S TIP
This is such a
to-die-for dip
that people are
bound to ask for the
recipe! Make this
beautiful, layered
dip up to 4 hours
ahead; cover tightly
and refrigerate.
Make the chips
ahead of time, too,
and wrap tightly.

LIME CHIPS
1/2 teaspoon grated lime peel
2 tablespoons lime juice
2 teaspoons olive oil
2 teaspoons honey
Dash salt
4 fat-free flour tortillas (8 inch)

DIP
1 package (8 oz) reduced-fat cream cheese (Neufchâtel), softened
1/2 cup fat-free sour cream
1 tablespoon taco seasoning mix (from 1.25-oz package)
1 can (15 oz) black beans, drained, well rinsed
1/2 cup chopped red bell pepper
1/2 cup chopped mango
2 tablespoons chopped fresh cilantro
1 to 2 teaspoons finely chopped jalapeño chiles

1. Heat oven to 350°F. Spray large cookie sheet with cooking spray. In small bowl, mix lime peel, lime juice, oil, honey and salt. Brush on both sides of each tortilla; place tortillas on cookie sheet. Cut each tortilla into 12 wedges; arrange in single layer on cookie sheet. Bake 8 to 10 minutes or until crisp and light golden brown; cool.

2. In small bowl, mix cream cheese, sour cream and taco seasoning mix with spoon or electric mixer on medium speed until well mixed. Spread on 10-inch round serving plate.

3. Top cream cheese mixture with remaining ingredients. Serve immediately, or refrigerate until serving. Serve with chips. Store leftover chips in airtight container at room temperature.

"I take the time to go for a walk with my husband, even in the cold winter. It gives us time together away from everything else. Having a walking partner helps keep me motivated." —Glenna F.

1 Serving: Calories 80 (Calories from Fat 20); Total Fat 2g (Saturated Fat 1g; Trans Fat 0g; Omega-3 0g); Cholesterol 5mg; Sodium 150mg; Total Carbohydrate 13g (Dietary Fiber 2g; Sugars 2g); Protein 4g   **% Daily Value:** Potassium 3%; Vitamin A 6%; Vitamin C 15%; Calcium 4%; Iron 6%; Folic Acid 6%   **Exchanges:** 1 Starch   **Carbohydrate Choices:** 1

Baked Coconut Shrimp

PREP TIME: 40 Minutes **START TO FINISH:** 40 Minutes **ABOUT 31 SERVINGS** (1 shrimp and 1 teaspoon sauce each)

3/4 cup apricot preserves
2 tablespoons lime juice
1/2 teaspoon ground mustard
1/4 cup all-purpose flour
2 tablespoons packed brown sugar
1/4 teaspoon salt
Dash ground red pepper (cayenne)
1 egg or 2 egg whites
1 cup shredded coconut
1 lb uncooked deveined peeled medium shrimp (31 to 35), thawed if frozen
2 tablespoons butter or margarine, melted

1. In 1-quart saucepan, mix apricot preserves, 1 tablespoon of the lime juice and the mustard. Cook over low heat, stirring occasionally, just until preserves are melted. Refrigerate while making shrimp.

2. Move oven rack to lowest position. Heat oven to 425°F. Spray rack in broiler pan with cooking spray.

3. In shallow bowl, mix flour, brown sugar, salt and red pepper. In another shallow bowl, beat egg and remaining 1 tablespoon lime juice. In third shallow bowl, place coconut.

4. Coat each shrimp with flour mixture, then dip each side into egg mixture and coat well with coconut. Place on rack in broiler pan. Drizzle with butter.

5. Bake 7 to 8 minutes or until shrimp are pink and coating is beginning to brown. Serve with preserves mixture.

BETTY'S TIP

If you have time, you can prepare the shrimp up to 2 hours ahead. Refrigerate covered, and bake just before serving. Then save a bit of time by serving these terrific low-fat appetizers with purchased cocktail sauce.

1 Serving: Calories 60 (Calories from Fat 20); Total Fat 2g (Saturated Fat 1.5g; Trans Fat 0g; Omega-3 0g); Cholesterol 30mg; Sodium 60mg; Total Carbohydrate 8g (Dietary Fiber 0g; Sugars 6g); Protein 3g **% Daily Value:** Potassium 1%; Vitamin A 0%; Vitamin C 0%; Calcium 0%; Iron 2%; Folic Acid 0% **Exchanges:** 1/2 Other Carbohydrate, 1/2 Very Lean Meat, 1/2 Fat **Carbohydrate Choices:** 1/2

Keep Your Bones Strong

Keeping your bones strong is important to prevent osteoporosis, a bone-thinning disease that primarily affects women after menopause. The bones get progressively weaker, and women may not suspect a problem until they actually fracture a hip or wrist or notice a decrease in their height. The risk of developing osteoporosis increases with age. The good news is that you may be able to prevent it or slow the process, even if you have the risk factors for osteoporosis:

➤ A history of the disease

➤ A thin or small-framed woman

➤ History of irregular or skipped periods

➤ Smoking or drinking more than 7 drinks/week

➤ Not getting enough calcium

➤ Not doing weight-bearing exercises (see list of examples below)

➤ Having taken steroids or other bone-thinning medications

During the prime bone-building years of childhood and early adulthood, bone is added to your skeleton faster than old bone is destroyed. By age 30, your bones are as dense and strong as they'll ever be. After that, bone loss gradually begins to outpace bone building. While you can't control heredity, you can modify your lifestyle to keep your bones in tip-top shape:

Get enough calcium and vitamin D. Calcium is important for many functions in your body throughout life. Your needs for this important mineral change over time. If you are age 50 or younger, 1000 milligrams of calcium daily is needed. Once you hit 50, the amount jumps to 1500 milligrams of calcium daily. It's wise to consume enough calcium every day since your body takes calcium out of your bones if it doesn't get enough from your diet.

The Calcium Cupboard	Milligrams
1 cup low-fat or fat-free yogurt	400
1 cup skim or low-fat milk	350
1 cup calcium-fortified orange juice	350
1 ounce cheese	200
1 cup soymilk (calcium fortified)	80 to 200
1/2 cup almonds	180
1/2 cup low-fat cottage cheese	150
1/2 cup frozen yogurt	100
3/4 cup ready-to-eat cereal	100 to 1000
1/2 cup baked beans	60

Good Sources of Vitamin D Exposure to sunlight*	(IU)
3 1/2 ounces cooked salmon	360
3 ounces canned tuna	200
1 cup low-fat/skim milk	100
1 cup fortified yogurt	80 to 100
3/4 cup ready-to-eat cereal	40 to 50
1 egg	25

*The body makes vitamin D when exposed to sunlight. About 10 to 15 minutes of sun exposure two or three times a week may be enough to provide adequate vitamin D. (Avoid peak sun exposure times of 11:00 a.m. to 3:00 p.m. every day.)

1. **Get vitamin D regularly.** Vitamin D helps calcium be absorbed in the body. Too little can mean not enough calcium is deposited inside bones. 200 International Units (IUs) are recommended daily.

2. **Consider calcium supplements.** Though food is the best source of calcium, even women who eat healthy foods may not always get enough calcium, especially if they don't eat dairy foods. Talk to your doctor about making up the difference with supplements. Your body never fully absorbs all of the calcium you take in, but eating it or taking it in several servings or doses throughout the day will help it be absorbed more easily.

3. **Look out for calcium robbers (sodium, caffeine and protein).** To safeguard your calcium stores, eat less processed, canned and fast foods (they're high in sodium), as well as chips, pickles and other salty foods. Also, drink no more than 2 cups of coffee a day. Women between 30 and 50 are advised to get only about 10% to 35% of their total calories from protein each day.

4. **Exercise.** Like muscle, bone is living tissue that becomes stronger with activity. Young women who exercise achieve greater bone mass than those who do not. Women over 30 can help prevent bone loss with regular weight-bearing exercise. Besides making bones more dense, exercise helps maintain muscle strength, coordination and balance, which help prevent falls and fractures.

The Best Calcium Supplement for You

Calcium exists in nature only in combination with other compounds. For that reason, several different calcium compounds are used in supplements, including:

- ➤ Calcium Carbonate (Tums, Os-Cal)

- ➤ Calcium Citrate (Citracal)

- ➤ Calcium Phosphate (Posture)

The compounds contain different amounts of *elemental calcium*, the actual amount of calcium in the supplement. Read the label to carefully determine how much elemental calcium is in the supplement and how many pills to take. The "best" one to take is the one that meets your needs in terms of amount, how your body tolerates it, how convenient it is, how much it costs and how widely available it is. Calcium carbonate (Tums) is recommended to quiet an upset stomach. Do not take more than the recommended amount of calcium without your doctor's advice, and make sure your doctor knows what other supplements, like iron, you may be taking, as calcium interferes with iron absorption.

BEST BONE-BUILDING EXERCISES

THE BEST BONE-BUILDING EXERCISES ARE THE WEIGHT-BEARING KIND, WHICH FORCE YOU TO WORK AGAINST GRAVITY. THEY ARE:

- WALKING OR HIKING

- JOGGING

- CLIMBING STAIRS

- DANCING

- PLAYING TENNIS

- WEIGHT LIFTING

AT LEAST 30 TO 60 MINUTES OF PHYSICAL ACTIVITY ON MOST DAYS IS RECOMMENDED. SWIMMING AND BICYCLING, THOUGH THEY HELP BUILD AND MAINTAIN STRONG MUSCLES AND HAVE EXCELLENT CARDIOVASCULAR BENEFITS, MAY NOT BE THE BEST WAY TO EXERCISE YOUR BONES.

Girlfriends' Gorp

PREP TIME: 10 Minutes **START TO FINISH:** 10 Minutes **14 SERVINGS** (1/2 cup each)

3 cups Wheat Chex® or Multi-Bran Chex® cereal
1 1/2 cups butter-flavored pretzel sticks
1 cup fat-free caramel corn
2/3 cup roasted soybeans
1/2 cup dried cranberries
1/3 cup dark or semisweet chocolate chips

NOTE FROM DR. R
Roasted soybeans, or soy nuts, contain all the benefits of soy in a fun snack. Research suggests that when women replace some of the animal-protein foods they eat with soy foods, their blood cholesterol levels tended to drop.

1. In gallon-size food-storage plastic bag or 3-quart container, mix all ingredients.

2. Seal bag and shake ingredients to mix, or stir ingredients in container. Store tightly covered.

"Sometimes I stay up ridiculously late reading a really good book because I love to read and I think it is fun for my soul." —Jeanne A.

1 Serving: Calories 130 (Calories from Fat 25); Total Fat 2.5g (Saturated Fat 1g; Trans Fat 0g; Omega-3 0g); Cholesterol 0mg; Sodium 200mg; Total Carbohydrate 22g (Dietary Fiber 2g; Sugars 8g); Protein 4g **% Daily Value:** Potassium 4%; Vitamin A 2%; Vitamin C 2%; Calcium 4%; Iron 20%; Folic Acid 25% **Exchanges:** 1 Starch, 1/2 Other Carbohydrate, 1/2 Fat **Carbohydrate Choices:** 1 1/2

Raspberry-Chocolate Muffins

PREP TIME: 10 Minutes **START TO FINISH:** 35 Minutes **12 MUFFINS**

1 1/3 cups Fiber One® cereal
1 1/3 cups buttermilk
1/4 cup canola oil
1 egg or 2 egg whites
1 cup all-purpose flour
3/4 cup sugar
1/4 cup unsweetened baking cocoa
2 teaspoons baking soda
1/4 teaspoon salt
2/3 cup fresh or frozen (thawed and drained) raspberries

1. Heat oven to 375°F. Place paper baking cup in each of 12 regular-size muffin cups, or grease bottoms only of muffin cups with shortening or cooking spray. Place cereal in food-storage plastic bag or between sheets of waxed paper; crush with rolling pin (or crush in blender or food processor).

2. In medium bowl, stir crushed cereal and buttermilk; let stand 5 minutes. Stir in oil and egg. Stir in flour, sugar, cocoa, baking soda and salt until moistened. Gently stir in raspberries. Divide batter evenly among muffin cups.

3. Bake 20 to 25 minutes or until toothpick inserted in center comes out clean. Immediately remove from pan.

"I love classical chamber music and listen to it on my way to work. It's a quieter, gentler way to make commuting more pleasant." —Andi B.

BETTY'S TIP
Combining the popular tastes of chocolate and raspberry, these fantastic muffins are packed with fiber. Fiber is the part of plant foods your body cannot digest—it helps keep you regular—getting fiber from a variety of food sources every day is beneficial.

1 Muffin: Calories 190 (Calories from Fat 60); Total Fat 6g (Saturated Fat 1g; Trans Fat 0g; Omega-3 0g); Cholesterol 20mg; Sodium 320mg; Total Carbohydrate 29g (Dietary Fiber 4g; Sugars 14g); Protein 4g **% Daily Value:** Potassium 4%; Vitamin A 0%; Vitamin C 2%; Calcium 6%; Iron 10%; Folic Acid 10% **Exchanges:** 1 Starch, 1 Other Carbohydrate, 1 Fat **Carbohydrate Choices:** 2

Best-Ever Brown Bread

PREP TIME: 10 Minutes   **START TO FINISH:** 3 Hours 10 Minutes   **1 LOAF** (16 slices)

1 1/2 cups whole wheat flour
1 cup all-purpose flour
2/3 cup packed dark brown sugar
1/2 cup old-fashioned oats
1/3 cup ground flaxseed or flaxseed meal
1 teaspoon baking soda
1 teaspoon salt
1 2/3 cups buttermilk
1 tablespoon old-fashioned oats

1. Heat oven to 350°F. Spray 8 × 4-inch loaf pan with cooking spray.

2. In large bowl, mix flours, brown sugar, 1/2 cup oats, the flaxseed, baking soda and salt. Stir in buttermilk just until mixed. Pour batter into pan. Sprinkle with 1 tablespoon oats.

3. Bake 45 to 55 minutes or until toothpick inserted in center comes out clean. Cool in pan on wire rack 5 minutes. Remove from pan to wire rack. Cool completely, about 2 hours, before slicing.

"I keep healthy snacks handy at work."   —Rita R.

1 Slice: Calories 140 (Calories from Fat 15); Total Fat 2g (Saturated Fat 0g; Trans Fat 0g; Omega-3 0g); Cholesterol 0mg; Sodium 250mg; Total Carbohydrate 27g (Dietary Fiber 3g; Sugars 10g); Protein 4g   **% Daily Value:** Potassium 5%; Vitamin A 0%; Vitamin C 0%; Calcium 6%; Iron 8%; Folic Acid 6%   **Exchanges:** 1 Starch, 1 Other Carbohydrate   **Carbohydrate Choices:** 2

Mini Rosemary Scones

PREP TIME: 25 Minutes   **START TO FINISH:** 55 Minutes   **18 MINI SCONES**

1 cup all-purpose flour

1 cup whole wheat flour

2 tablespoons sugar

2 teaspoons baking powder

1/2 teaspoon baking soda

1/2 teaspoon salt

2 teaspoons grated lemon peel

1 tablespoon finely chopped fresh
or 1 teaspoon dried rosemary leaves,
crushed

3 tablespoons firm butter or margarine

1/2 cup fat-free sour cream

1/4 cup canola oil

1 tablespoon fresh lemon juice

1. Heat oven to 400°F. Spray cookie sheet with cooking spray.

2. In medium bowl, mix flours, sugar, baking powder, baking soda, salt, lemon peel and rosemary. Cut in butter, using pastry blender (or pulling 2 table knives through ingredients in opposite directions), until mixture looks like fine crumbs. Stir in sour cream, oil and lemon juice.

3. On lightly floured surface, knead dough lightly 10 times. Divide dough into thirds. On cookie sheet, pat each third of dough into 5-inch circle. Cut each circle into 6 wedges, using sharp knife, but do not separate wedges.

4. Bake 12 to 17 minutes or until edges are golden brown. Immediately remove from cookie sheet to wire rack. Carefully separate wedges. Cool 5 to 10 minutes. Serve warm.

"If I've skipped a few workouts, I don't beat myself up. I just get back on the treadmill and start over." —Lisa B.

NOTE FROM DR. R
If you haven't already, consider an activity that has an impact on your body to help strengthen your bones, such as walking, jogging or dancing, anything where you're on your feet, working against gravity.

1 Mini Scone: Calories 110 (Calories from Fat 45); Total Fat 5g (Saturated Fat 1.5g; Trans Fat 0g; Omega-3 0g); Cholesterol 5mg; Sodium 180mg; Total Carbohydrate 13g (Dietary Fiber 1g; Sugars 2g); Protein 2g   **% Daily Value:** Potassium 1%; Vitamin A 0%; Vitamin C 0%; Calcium 4%; Iron 4%; Folic Acid 4%   **Exchanges:** 1 Starch, 1 Fat   **Carbohydrate Choices:** 1

Three-Seed Flatbread

PREP TIME: 10 Minutes **START TO FINISH:** 1 Hour 15 Minutes **12 SERVINGS**

6 frozen unbaked large whole wheat rolls (from 48-oz package)

2 teaspoons olive oil

3 cloves garlic, finely chopped

1 teaspoon ground flaxseed or flaxseed meal

1/2 teaspoon black sesame seed or poppy seed

1/2 teaspoon white sesame seed

1/2 teaspoon salt

1/4 teaspoon dried basil leaves

2 tablespoons shredded Parmesan cheese

NOTE FROM DR. R

Olive oil is a great choice for this three-seed bread. It contains monounsaturated fat and antioxidants. A simple change, like replacing butter with olive oil, has been shown to help lower cholesterol.

1. On microwavable plate, place frozen rolls. Cover with microwavable plastic wrap; microwave on High 25 seconds. Turn rolls over; rotate plate 1/2 turn. Microwave on High 25 seconds longer to thaw.

2. Spray 13 × 9-inch pan with cooking spray. On lightly floured surface, knead roll dough together. Pat dough in bottom of pan; brush with oil. Sprinkle with remaining ingredients.

3. Cover; let rise in warm place about 40 minutes or until slightly puffy.

4. Heat oven to 350°F. Bake 20 to 22 minutes or until golden brown. Cut into 12 squares.

"Instead of going to a spa, I try to create that special ambience in my home. I play soft music, light a candle and give my feet a good soaking."   —Cheri O.

1 Serving: Calories 70 (Calories from Fat 20); Total Fat 2g (Saturated Fat 0.5g; Trans Fat 0g; Omega-3 0g); Cholesterol 0mg; Sodium 230mg; Total Carbohydrate 10g (Dietary Fiber 2g; Sugars 2g); Protein 3g   **% Daily Value:** Potassium 2%; Vitamin A 0%; Vitamin C 0%; Calcium 4%; Iron 4%; Folic Acid 2%   **Exchanges:** 1/2 Starch, 1/2 Fat   **Carbohydrate Choices:** 1/2

Three-Seed Flatbread

3

Satisfying Soups and Stews

Nourish your body and soul with a

soothing cup of soup or stew

Slow Cooker Southwest Chicken Soup

PREP TIME: 15 Minutes   **START TO FINISH:** 7 Hours 45 Minutes   **6 SERVINGS** (about 1 1/2 cups each)

1 lb boneless skinless chicken thighs, cut into 1-inch pieces

2 medium dark-orange sweet potatoes, peeled, cut into 1-inch pieces (2 cups)

1 large onion, chopped (1 cup)

2 cans (14.5 oz each) diced tomatoes with green chiles, undrained

1 can (14 oz) reduced-sodium chicken broth

1 teaspoon dried oregano leaves

1/2 teaspoon ground cumin

1 cup frozen whole kernel corn (from 1-lb bag)

1/2 cup chopped green bell pepper

8 yellow or blue corn tortillas (5 or 6 inch)

2 tablespoons chopped fresh cilantro

NOTE FROM DR. R

Sweet potatoes contain beta-carotene, which your body converts to vitamin A and keeps your eyesight sharp. They also contain phytonutrients, which are thought to improve the body's ability to fight off disease and infection.

1. In 3 1/2- to 4-quart slow cooker, mix chicken, sweet potatoes, onion, tomatoes, broth, oregano and cumin.

2. Cover; cook on Low heat setting 7 to 8 hours.

3. Stir corn and bell pepper into soup. Increase heat setting to High. Cover; cook about 30 minutes or until chicken is no longer pink in center and vegetables are tender.

4. Meanwhile, heat oven to 450°F. Spray 2 cookie sheets with cooking spray. Cut each tortilla into strips; place in single layer on cookie sheets. Bake about 6 minutes or until crisp but not brown; cool. Spoon soup into bowls. Top with tortilla strips. Sprinkle with cilantro.

"First thing every morning, I go for a walk, even in the winter. It refreshes me and gets me ready for the day." —Carol G.

1 Serving: Calories 300 (Calories from Fat 60); Total Fat 7g (Saturated Fat 2g; Trans Fat 0g; Omega-3 0g); Cholesterol 45mg; Sodium 660mg; Total Carbohydrate 37g (Dietary Fiber 7g; Sugars 11g); Protein 23g   **% Daily Value:** Potassium 26%; Vitamin A 150%; Vitamin C 25%; Calcium 15%; Iron 15%; Folic Acid 15%   **Exchanges:** 2 Starch, 1 Vegetable, 2 Lean Meat **Carbohydrate Choices:** 2 1/2

Slow Cooker
Chicken-Barley Stew

PREP TIME: 15 Minutes   **START TO FINISH:** 8 Hours 30 Minutes   **6 SERVINGS** (1 1/2 cups each)

3 large carrots, sliced (2 cups)

2 medium stalks celery, sliced (1 cup)

1 large onion, chopped (1 cup)

2 bone-in chicken breasts (about 1 1/4 lb), skin removed

5 cups water

3/4 cup uncooked medium pearled barley

2 teaspoons chicken bouillon granules

1/2 teaspoon salt

1/4 teaspoon pepper

1 can (14.5 oz) diced tomatoes, undrained

2 tablespoons chopped fresh parsley

1 teaspoon dried thyme leaves

1. In 4- to 5-quart slow cooker, place carrots, celery and onion. Place chicken breasts on vegetables. Add remaining ingredients except parsley and thyme.

2. Cover; cook on Low heat setting 8 to 9 hours.

3. Remove chicken from cooker; place on cutting board. Remove meat from bones and chop into 1/2- to 1-inch pieces; discard bones.

4. Stir chicken, parsley and thyme into stew. Increase heat setting to High. Cover; cook 10 to 15 minutes longer or until chicken is thoroughly heated.

BETTY'S TIP
The Dietary Guidelines for Americans recommends 3 servings of whole grains daily. One serving is 1 slice of whole wheat bread, 1/2 cup of cooked barley or 3/4 cup of a whole-grain cereal. This stew gives you 1 serving—team it with a slice of whole-grain bread, and you have 2 servings—easy.

1 Serving: Calories 220 (Calories from Fat 25); Total Fat 3g (Saturated Fat 0.5g; Trans Fat 0g; Omega-3 0g); Cholesterol 40mg; Sodium 650mg; Total Carbohydrate 30g (Dietary Fiber 7g; Sugars 6g); Protein 19g   **% Daily Value:** Potassium 16%; Vitamin A 100%; Vitamin C 10%; Calcium 8%; Iron 15%; Folic Acid 8%   **Exchanges:** 1 1/2 Starch, 1 Vegetable, 2 Very Lean Meat   **Carbohydrate Choices:** 2

Turkey–Wild Rice Soup

PREP TIME: 10 Minutes   **START TO FINISH:** 35 Minutes   **6 SERVINGS** (1 1/2 cups each)

2 tablespoons butter or margarine
1/2 cup all-purpose flour
2 cans (14 oz each) reduced-sodium chicken broth
1 package (8 oz) 98% fat-free oven-roasted turkey breast, cubed (about 2 cups)
2 cups water
2 tablespoons instant chopped onion
1 package (6 oz) original-flavor long-grain and wild rice mix
2 cups soymilk or fat-free (skim) milk

BETTY'S TIP
Wild rice is really the seed of an aquatic grass. Whatever you want to call it, the wild rice adds a delicious nutty flavor and slightly chewy texture to this quick and tasty soup.

1. In 5-quart Dutch oven, melt butter over medium heat. Stir in flour with wire whisk until well blended. Slowly stir in broth with wire whisk. Stir in turkey, water, onion, rice and contents of seasoning packet.

2. Heat to boiling over high heat, stirring occasionally. Reduce heat to medium-low. Cover; simmer about 25 minutes or until rice is tender.

3. Stir in soymilk; heat just to boiling.

"I love taking a bubble bath so much that I get up a half-hour early every day just to make time for one. The bubbly water wakes me up and gets me off to a good start!"   —Andi B.

1 Serving: Calories 200 (Calories from Fat 50); Total Fat 5g (Saturated Fat 3g; Trans Fat 0g; Omega-3 0g); Cholesterol 45mg; Sodium 530mg; Total Carbohydrate 20g (Dietary Fiber 0g; Sugars 3g); Protein 18g   **% Daily Value:** Potassium 8%; Vitamin A 6%; Vitamin C 0%; Calcium 15%; Iron 10%; Folic Acid 10%   **Exchanges:** 1 1/2 Starch, 2 Very Lean Meat, 1/2 Fat
Carbohydrate Choices: 1

Caribbean Turkey Stew

PREP TIME: 20 Minutes   **START TO FINISH:** 1 Hour   **5 SERVINGS** (1 1/2 cups each)

1 tablespoon canola oil

1 medium onion, coarsely chopped (1/2 cup)

4 cloves garlic, finely chopped

1 1/2 lb turkey breast tenderloins, cut into 1-inch pieces

1/2 teaspoon ground nutmeg

1/4 teaspoon salt

1/4 teaspoon pepper

1 dark-orange sweet potato, peeled, cut into 1-inch pieces (1 1/2 cups)

2 dried bay leaves

4 small red potatoes, cut into eighths (1 1/2 cups)

2 cups chicken broth

2 cups frozen sweet peas (from 1-lb bag)

1. In 4 1/2-quart Dutch oven, heat oil over medium-high heat. Cook onion and garlic in oil 4 to 5 minutes, stirring frequently, until onion is softened.

2. Sprinkle turkey pieces with nutmeg, salt and pepper. Stir into onion mixture. Cook 5 to 6 minutes, stirring occasionally, until turkey is no longer pink.

3. Stir in remaining ingredients except peas. Heat to boiling; reduce heat to medium-low. Cover; cook 18 to 20 minutes or until potatoes are tender.

4. Stir in frozen peas. Cover; cook 4 to 5 minutes, stirring occasionally, until peas are hot. Remove bay leaves.

NOTE FROM DR. R
Eating soup or stew if you are trying to lose weight is a good idea because the sheer volume of soup in the stomach gives a sense of fullness and may help you eat less overall. Just make certain it's packed with nutrients, like this terrific stew is.

"I don't waste time driving around looking for the closest parking spot. I park at the back of the lot for extra steps, and I don't have to worry that I can't find my car because it's always in the same spot." —Sherri F.

1 Serving: Calories 300 (Calories from Fat 45); Total Fat 5g (Saturated Fat 1g; Trans Fat 0g; Omega-3 0g); Cholesterol 90mg; Sodium 640mg; Total Carbohydrate 26g (Dietary Fiber 5g; Sugars 7g); Protein 38g   **% Daily Value:** Potassium 26%; Vitamin A 180%; Vitamin C 15%; Calcium 6%; Iron 20%; Folic Acid 10%   **Exchanges:** 1 Starch, 1/2 Other Carbohydrate, 1 Vegetable, 4 1/2 Very Lean Meat, 1/2 Fat   **Carbohydrate Choices:** 2

Italian Beef and Vegetable Soup

PREP TIME: 20 Minutes **START TO FINISH:** 40 Minutes **5 SERVINGS** (about 1 1/2 cups each)

NOTE FROM DR. R
Eating soups is a
great way to work in
vegetables without
even noticing it.
Vegetables add
fiber, vitamins A
and C, folic acid,
and color and
crunch!

2 teaspoons all-purpose flour
1/4 teaspoon salt
1/4 teaspoon pepper
1/2 lb boneless beef round steak, cut into 1/2-inch cubes
1 tablespoon olive oil
1 can (15 oz) cannellini beans, drained, rinsed
1 can (14.5 oz) diced tomatoes with basil, garlic and oregano, undrained
2 cups frozen Italian-blend vegetables (from 1-lb bag)
3 cups water
Grated Parmesan cheese, if desired

1. In 1-quart resealable food-storage plastic bag, place flour, salt and pepper. Seal bag; shake until blended. Add beef. Seal bag; shake until beef is evenly coated with flour mixture.

2. In 3-quart heavy saucepan or Dutch oven, heat oil over medium-high heat. Cook beef in oil 4 to 5 minutes, stirring occasionally, until brown on all sides.

3. Stir in remaining ingredients except cheese. Heat to boiling; reduce heat. Simmer uncovered 15 to 20 minutes or until vegetables are tender. Serve with cheese.

*"Yoga is a great stress reducer. I used to get terrible back
pain, related to stress. Since I've been practicing yoga, it has completely
gone away."* —Stacy P.

1 Serving: Calories 220 (Calories from Fat 40); Total Fat 4.5g (Saturated Fat 1g; Trans Fat 0g; Omega-3 0g); Cholesterol 25mg; Sodium 250mg; Total Carbohydrate 25g (Dietary Fiber 7g; Sugars 4g); Protein 19g **% Daily Value:** Potassium 21%; Vitamin A 6%; Vitamin C 8%; Calcium 10%; Iron 30%; Folic Acid 20% **Exchanges:** 1 Starch, 1/2 Other Carbohydrate, 2 Lean Meat **Carbohydrate Choices:** 1 1/2

Italian Beef and Vegetable Soup

Slow Cooker Beef-Barley Soup

PREP TIME: 10 Minutes   **START TO FINISH:** 8 Hours 20 Minutes   **6 SERVINGS** (1 1/3 cups each)

1 1/2 lb beef stew meat
2 medium carrots, sliced (1 cup)
1 medium onion, chopped (1/2 cup)
1 cup sliced fresh mushrooms
2 cans (10.5 oz each) condensed beef consommé
3 cups water
1/2 cup uncooked medium pearled barley
2 dried bay leaves
1 cup frozen baby sweet peas (from 1-lb bag)

BETTY'S TIP
Simmering slowly all day adds fantastic flavor to this homey soup. Adding the peas at the end preserves their fresh flavor and bright green color—and also saves nutrients!

1. In 4- to 5-quart slow cooker, mix all ingredients except peas.

2. Cover; cook on Low heat setting 8 to 9 hours.

3. About 10 minutes before serving, stir in peas. Increase heat setting to High. Cover; cook about 10 minutes or until peas are cooked through. Remove bay leaves.

"I feel more energized and able to meet the needs of family and work if I have 'renewal' time for myself. Going for a walk, knitting or working in my garden renew my spirit and give me energy." —Alison E.

1 Serving: Calories 320 (Calories from Fat 120); Total Fat 14g (Saturated Fat 5g; Trans Fat 0.5g; Omega-3 0g); Cholesterol 65mg; Sodium 610mg; Total Carbohydrate 21g (Dietary Fiber 4g; Sugars 3g); Protein 29g   **% Daily Value:** Potassium 17%; Vitamin A 60%; Vitamin C 4%; Calcium 4%; Iron 20%; Folic Acid 8%   **Exchanges:** 1 Starch, 1 Vegetable, 3 1/2 Lean Meat, 1/2 Fat   **Carbohydrate Choices:** 1 1/2

Sirloin Three-Bean Chili

PREP TIME: 35 Minutes   **START TO FINISH:** 55 Minutes   **8 SERVINGS** (about 1 1/4 cups each)

1 tablespoon canola oil
2 lb boneless beef sirloin, cut into 1-inch cubes
1 large onion, coarsely chopped (1 cup)
1 medium green bell pepper, coarsely chopped (1 cup)
2 cans (28 oz each) diced tomatoes, undrained
1 can (15 to 16 oz) pinto beans, drained, rinsed
1 can (15 to 16 oz) kidney beans, drained, rinsed
1 can (15 oz) black beans, drained, rinsed
1 cup beef broth
1 1/2 tablespoons ground cumin
1 tablespoon chili powder

1. In 4-quart Dutch oven, heat oil over medium-high heat. Cook 1 pound of beef at a time in oil, stirring occasionally, until brown; remove from Dutch oven.

2. Add onion and bell pepper to Dutch oven. Cook 2 to 3 minutes, stirring occasionally, until crisp-tender. Stir in remaining ingredients except beef.

3. Cover; cook over medium heat 10 minutes. Stir in beef. Cook uncovered 3 to 8 minutes or until beef is tender.

NOTE FROM DR. R
Doing your part for a healthy heart can make a big difference in your life. Eating foods high in fiber and low in fat and sodium, combined with daily exercise and finding ways to relax, are things you can do.

"I used to think I could do everything; now I know I can't. It's made me prioritize and realize what's really important, and I focus on that."   —Billie F.

1 Serving: Calories 410 (Calories from Fat 60); Total Fat 7g (Saturated Fat 1.5g; Trans Fat 0g; Omega-3 0g); Cholesterol 65mg; Sodium 430mg; Total Carbohydrate 46g (Dietary Fiber 13g; Sugars 8g); Protein 41g   **% Daily Value:** Potassium 35%; Vitamin A 10%; Vitamin C 30%; Calcium 15%; Iron 45%; Folic Acid 60%   **Exchanges:** 3 Starch, 4 1/2 Very Lean Meat, 1/2 Fat **Carbohydrate Choices:** 3

Slow Cooker Hearty Pork Stew

PREP TIME: 25 Minutes   **START TO FINISH:** 7 Hours 10 Minutes   **6 SERVINGS** (1 1/2 cups each)

1 1/2 lb boneless pork loin roast, trimmed of fat, cut into 1-inch cubes

3 medium carrots, cut into 1/4-inch slices (1 1/2 cups)

1 medium onion, chopped (1/2 cup)

2 cups 1/2-inch cubes peeled parsnips

1 1/2 cups 1-inch cubes peeled butternut squash

4 cups chicken broth

1 tablespoon chopped fresh or 1 teaspoon dried sage leaves

2 teaspoons chopped fresh or 3/4 teaspoon dried thyme leaves

1/2 teaspoon pepper

2 tablespoons all-purpose flour

2 tablespoons butter or margarine, softened

BETTY'S TIP

This recipe also works well with other root vegetables, like sliced parsnips, rutabagas or beets. It's important to eat a variety of foods to give your body all the nutrients it needs.

1. In 4- to 5-quart slow cooker, mix all ingredients except flour and butter.

2. Cover; cook on Low heat setting 6 to 7 hours.

3. In small bowl, mix flour and butter; gradually stir into stew until blended. Increase heat setting to High. Cover; cook 30 to 45 minutes, stirring occasionally, until thickened.

1 Serving: Calories 320 (Calories from Fat 130); Total Fat 14g (Saturated Fat 6g; Trans Fat 0g; Omega-3 0g); Cholesterol 85mg; Sodium 780mg; Total Carbohydrate 18g (Dietary Fiber 3g; Sugars 6g); Protein 30g   **% Daily Value:** Potassium 24%; Vitamin A 140%; Vitamin C 10%; Calcium 6%; Iron 10%; Folic Acid 15%   **Exchanges:** 1 Starch, 4 Lean Meat, 1/2 Fat
Carbohydrate Choices: 1

Slow Cooker Hearty Pork Stew

Old-Fashioned Oven Beef Stew

PREP TIME: 15 Minutes   **START TO FINISH:** 4 Hours 15 Minutes   **6 SERVINGS** (1 1/2 cups each)

1 1/2 lb beef stew meat
3 tablespoons all-purpose flour
2 bags (1 lb each) frozen vegetables for stew
1 can (14.5 oz) diced tomatoes, undrained
2 cans (10 oz each) condensed beef consommé
1 tablespoon sugar
1/8 teaspoon pepper
2 dried bay leaves

NOTE FROM DR. R
Many marketplace and restaurant portions are much bigger than normal portion sizes. Use the chart on page 239 to help you visualize the correct portion sizes of the foods you eat most often. If you'd like to reduce the fat in this recipe, use sirloin steak cubes instead of stew meat.

1. Heat oven to 325°F. In 4-quart Dutch oven or 13 × 9-inch (3-quart) glass baking dish, toss beef with flour. Add frozen vegetables.

2. In large bowl, stir tomatoes, beef consommé, sugar, pepper and bay leaves. Pour over beef and vegetables; gently stir until mixed.

3. Cover; bake 3 hours 30 minutes to 4 hours or until beef is tender. Remove bay leaves.

"Sometimes when I'm having a hard time quieting my thoughts, I knit. It forces me to concentrate on the here and now, especially since I am new to knitting." —Heidi L.

1 Serving: Calories 350 (Calories from Fat 120); Total Fat 14g (Saturated Fat 5g; Trans Fat 0.5g; Omega-3 0g); Cholesterol 65mg; Sodium 710mg; Total Carbohydrate 27g (Dietary Fiber 4g; Sugars 8g); Protein 28g   **% Daily Value:** Potassium 27%; Vitamin A 130%; Vitamin C 15%; Calcium 6%; Iron 25%; Folic Acid 10%   **Exchanges:** 1 1/2 Starch, 1 Vegetable, 3 Medium-Fat Meat   **Carbohydrate Choices:** 2

Savory Millet and Potato Stew

PREP TIME: 35 Minutes   **START TO FINISH:** 35 Minutes   **6 SERVINGS** (about 1 1/3 cups each)

5 cups reduced-sodium chicken broth

2 tablespoons reduced-sodium soy sauce

1 bag (1 lb) frozen broccoli, carrots and cauliflower (or other combination)

1 cup diced red potatoes

1 cup uncooked millet

1 teaspoon dried thyme leaves

1/4 to 1/2 teaspoon pepper

1 large onion, chopped (1 cup)

4 cloves garlic, finely chopped

1. In 4-quart saucepan or Dutch oven, heat broth and soy sauce to boiling. Stir in remaining ingredients. Heat to boiling; reduce heat to medium.

2. Cover; cook 12 to 16 minutes, stirring occasionally, until millet and potatoes are tender.

"First thing in the morning, I drink a glass of water to rehydrate. It gets me going."   —Val B.

NOTE FROM DR. R
Thick and rich tasting, millet is a tiny, high-protein, low-fat whole grain that cooks in just a few minutes. Whole grains are concentrated sources of nutrients and phytochemicals, thought to have heart and health protective benefits.

1 Serving: Calories 200 (Calories from Fat 15); Total Fat 1.5g (Saturated Fat 0g; Trans Fat 0g; Omega-3 0g); Cholesterol 0mg; Sodium 660mg; Total Carbohydrate 37g (Dietary Fiber 6g; Sugars 3g); Protein 9g   **% Daily Value:** Potassium 16%; Vitamin A 35%; Vitamin C 25%; Calcium 6%; Iron 15%; Folic Acid 20%   **Exchanges:** 2 Starch, 1 Vegetable **Carbohydrate Choices:** 2 1/2

Slow Cooker Lentil Stew with Cornbread Dumplings

PREP TIME: 15 Minutes   **START TO FINISH:** 7 Hours 50 Minutes   8 servings (about 1 cup stew and 1 dumpling each)

STEW

1 lb dried lentils (2 cups), sorted, rinsed

3 cups water

1 teaspoon ground cumin

1 teaspoon salt-free seasoning blend

3 medium carrots, thinly sliced (1 1/2 cups)

1 medium yellow or red bell pepper, cut into 1-inch pieces

1 medium onion, chopped (1/2 cup)

1 can (14.5 oz) diced tomatoes with green chiles, undrained

1 can (14 oz) vegetable broth

DUMPLINGS

1/2 cup all-purpose flour

1/2 cup yellow cornmeal

1 teaspoon baking powder

1/4 teaspoon salt

1/4 cup fat-free (skim) milk

2 tablespoons canola oil

1 egg or 2 egg whites, slightly beaten

BETTY'S TIP

Either chicken or beef broth can be substituted for the vegetable broth. If you'd like to reduce the sodium even more, try using less broth and more water, or use reduced-sodium broth.

1. In 3 1/2- to 4-quart slow cooker, mix all stew ingredients.

2. Cover; cook on Low heat setting 7 to 8 hours.

3. In medium bowl, mix flour, cornmeal, baking powder and 1/4 teaspoon salt. Stir in milk, oil and egg just until moistened. Drop dough by spoonfuls onto hot lentil mixture. Increase heat setting to High. Cover; cook 25 to 35 minutes or until toothpick inserted in center of dumplings comes out clean.

"Early on, *become part of a group or club of great girlfriends.*
These friends are with you (and you with them) through all of life's stresses."
—Vicki A.

1 Serving: Calories 330 (Calories from Fat 45); Total Fat 5g (Saturated Fat 0.5g; Trans Fat 0g; Omega-3 0g); Cholesterol 25mg; Sodium 650mg; Total Carbohydrate 52g (Dietary Fiber 12g; Sugars 6g); Protein 18g   **% Daily Value:** Potassium 25%; Vitamin A 70%; Vitamin C 30%; Calcium 20%; Iron 35%; Folic Acid 80%   **Exchanges:** 3 Starch, 1 Vegetable, 1 Very Lean Meat, 1/2 Fat   **Carbohydrate Choices:** 3 1/2

Slow Cooker Lentil Stew with Cornbread Dumplings

Minestrone Soup

PREP TIME: 40 Minutes   **START TO FINISH:** 40 Minutes   **6 SERVINGS** (1 2/3 cups each)

1 can (28 oz) whole tomatoes, undrained
1 can (15 to 16 oz) great northern beans, undrained
1 can (15 to 16 oz) kidney beans, undrained
1 can (15.25 oz) whole kernel corn, undrained
2 medium stalks celery, thinly sliced (1 cup)
1 small zucchini, sliced (1 cup)
1 medium onion, chopped (1/2 cup)
1 cup shredded cabbage
1/2 cup uncooked elbow macaroni or broken spaghetti
2 cups water
1 teaspoon Italian seasoning
1 extra-large vegetarian vegetable bouillon cube
1 clove garlic, finely chopped
Grated Parmesan cheese, if desired

NOTE FROM DR. R
Eat beans and other fiber foods often to get enough fiber every day. Fiber provides a sense of fullness and satisfies your appetite. It's also important for good digestive health.

1. In 4-quart Dutch oven, heat all ingredients except cheese to boiling, breaking up tomatoes; reduce heat to low.

2. Cover; simmer 15 to 20 minutes, stirring occasionally, until macaroni and vegetables are tender. Serve with cheese.

"I schedule time to exercise, just like I schedule a doctor's appointment. That way I don't have any excuses, like 'I don't have time.'"

—Sheila B.

1 Serving: Calories 320 (Calories from Fat 15); Total Fat 1.5g (Saturated Fat 0g; Trans Fat 0g; Omega-3 0g); Cholesterol 0mg; Sodium 860mg; Total Carbohydrate 59g (Dietary Fiber 12g; Sugars 8g); Protein 16g   **% Daily Value:** Potassium 32%; Vitamin A 8%; Vitamin C 25%; Calcium 15%; Iron 35%; Folic Acid 50%   **Exchanges:** 3 1/2 Starch, 1 Vegetable, 1/2 Very Lean Meat   **Carbohydrate Choices:** 4

Minestrone Soup

Keep Your Heart Healthy

Cancer may seem like more of a health threat, nearly twice as many women in the United States die of heart disease and stroke as die from all forms of cancer, including breast cancer. Heart disease is the leading cause of death in women age 65 and older in the United States. Key factors increase the risk of heart disease and stroke, and the more risk factors you have, the greater your chance of a heart attack or stroke.

Risk factors you *can* control:

Don't smoke: Women who smoke cigarettes or cigars have a much higher risk of death from heart disease or stroke. Secondhand smoke also increases the risk. And women smokers who use birth control pills have a higher risk of heart attack and stroke than do the nonsmokers who use them.

Keep your cholesterol down: High levels of LDL (bad) cholesterol raise the risk of heart disease and heart attack. High levels of HDL (good) cholesterol lower the risk of heart disease. Research shows that low levels of HDL cholesterol are a higher risk factor for women than for men.

Control your blood pressure: Women have an increased risk of developing high blood pressure if they are 20 pounds or more over a healthy weight for their height and build, have a family history of high blood pressure, are pregnant, take birth control pills or have reached menopause. On average, African-American women have higher blood pressure levels than Caucasian women.

Be physically active: Inactive women are almost twice as likely to develop heart disease as those who are active. The American Heart Association (AHA) recommends at least 30 to 60 minutes of physical activity on most or all days of the week.

Control your weight: If your body carries too much fat, particularly near your waist, you're at higher risk for high blood pressure, high cholesterol, high triglycerides, diabetes, heart disease and stroke.

Know the symptoms of a woman's heart attack. As with men, women's most common heart attack symptom is chest pain or discomfort. But women are somewhat more likely than men to experience some of the other common symptoms, particularly shortness of breath, nausea/vomiting and back or jaw pain.

Chest pain is the most common symptom of a heart attack for women and men. A woman's symptoms for a heart attack can be different from a man's. By not recognizing trouble, you may put off seeking help. Some heart attacks are sudden and intense—the "movie heart attack," where no one doubts what's happening. But most heart attacks start slowly, with mild pain or discomfort. Often people affected aren't sure what's wrong and wait too long before getting help. Here are signs that can mean a heart attack is happening:

- Chest discomfort. Most heart attacks involve discomfort in the center of the chest that lasts more than a few minutes, or that goes away and comes back. It can feel like uncomfortable pressure, squeezing, fullness or pain.

- Discomfort in other areas of the upper body. Symptoms can include pain or discomfort in one or both arms, the back, neck, jaw or stomach.

- Shortness of breath. May occur with or without chest discomfort.

- Other signs: These may include breaking out in a cold sweat, nausea or lightheadedness.

Control your diabetes: Women with diabetes have a much higher risk of heart attack and stroke. Women with diabetes may be overweight, have high blood pressure and high cholesterol, increasing their risk even more.

Other risk factors:

Birth control pills: Today's low-dose oral contraceptives carry a much lower risk of heart disease and stroke than did earlier versions. The exception is in women who smoke or already have high blood pressure.

High triglycerides (total fats in the blood): A high triglyceride level often goes with high levels of total cholesterol and LDL, lower levels of HDL and an increased risk of diabetes. Research suggests high triglyceride levels may increase the risk for heart disease and stroke for women.

Take Wellness to Heart. Women are the greatest caregivers in the world, taking care of husbands, children and parents. Direct some of that caring toward yourself, and take these small, heart-saving steps:

1. **Eat well.** Include whole grains, fruits, veggies, fish and fiber to make sure you are getting the most nutrients from the calories you take in.

2. **Take your medicine.** If you take medicine to reduce your cholesterol or blood pressure, take it without fail.

3. **Be active.** Try to work in some kind of exercise every day, even if it's only for a short time. Take the time to go for a walk before work or during lunch.

4. **Take time for yourself.** Spend a few minutes each day doing something you enjoy—whether it's reading, meditating, doing yoga, gardening—anything that helps you relax and just makes you feel good.

5. **Get plenty of rest.** Sleep is your body's way of recharging itself and regaining energy. Encourage your body to fall asleep by slowing down at least 30 minutes before bedtime and by limiting caffeine late in the day.

6. **Express yourself.** If things are bothering you, talk to family, good friends or others who care. Express your feelings, thoughts and hopes in a journal. Being able to share your feelings will help you release tension.

Alcohol abuse: Excess drinking and binge drinking can contribute to obesity, high triglycerides, cancer and other diseases, and can raise blood pressure, cause heart failure and lead to stroke.

Your response to stress: Research is being done to understand the role stress plays in the development of heart disease.

Risk factors you *cannot* control:

Age: Risk of heart disease and stroke rises with age.

Gender: More than half of total stroke deaths occur in women.

Family history: Women are more likely to develop heart disease or stroke if close blood relatives had them (siblings, parents).

Race: African-American women have a greater risk of heart disease and stroke and are more likely than Caucasian women to die of strokes.

Previous heart attack or stroke: Women who've had a heart attack or stroke are at higher risk of having a second heart attack or stroke. Women who've had a stroke are at much higher risk of having another one or of having a heart attack.

Vegetable Stew with Polenta

PREP TIME: 20 Minutes   **START TO FINISH:** 1 Hour 15 Minutes   **4 SERVINGS** (1 1/2 cups each)

1 tablespoon olive oil

1 medium onion, coarsely chopped (1/2 cup)

1 medium yellow or green bell pepper, coarsely chopped (1 cup)

4 cloves garlic, finely chopped

2 medium carrots, cut into 1/4-inch slices (1 cup)

2 cans (14.5 oz each) diced tomatoes with basil, garlic and oregano, undrained

1 can (15 to 16 oz) black-eyed peas, drained, rinsed

1 can (19 oz) cannellini beans, drained, rinsed

1 cup water

1 teaspoon Italian seasoning

1/4 teaspoon pepper

1 roll (1 lb) refrigerated polenta

1 cup frozen cut green beans (from 1-lb bag)

NOTE FROM DR. R
This is a very nutrient-dense recipe, meaning that for the calories, this stew is loaded with fiber, vitamins A and C, calcium, folic acid and potassium. Eating a variety of foods enhances good health.

1. In 4 1/2- to 5-quart Dutch oven, heat oil over medium heat. Cook onion, bell pepper and garlic in oil 5 to 6 minutes, stirring frequently, until onion is softened.

2. Stir in remaining ingredients except polenta and green beans. Heat to boiling; reduce heat to medium-low. Cover; cook 35 to 40 minutes, stirring occasionally, until carrots are tender and stew is hot. Meanwhile, cook polenta as directed on roll; keep warm.

3. Stir frozen green beans into stew. Cover; cook 5 to 6 minutes, stirring occasionally, until beans are hot. To serve, spoon stew over polenta.

1 Serving: Calories 460 (Calories from Fat 45); Total Fat 5g (Saturated Fat 1g; Trans Fat 0g; Omega-3 0g); Cholesterol 0mg; Sodium 790mg; Total Carbohydrate 81g (Dietary Fiber 16g; Sugars 12g); Protein 23g   **% Daily Value:** Potassium 45%; Vitamin A 80%; Vitamin C 80%; Calcium 25%; Iron 60%; Folic Acid 90%   **Exchanges:** 4 Starch, 1 Other Carbohydrate, 1 Vegetable, 1 Very Lean Meat, 1/2 Fat   **Carbohydrate Choices:** 5 1/2

Sweet Potato–Pear Soup

PREP TIME: 25 Minutes **START TO FINISH:** 45 Minutes **5 SERVINGS** (about 1 1/2 cups each)

2 teaspoons canola oil

1 small onion, chopped (1/4 cup)

1 medium stalk celery, chopped (1/2 cup)

1/2 cup apple juice

1/2 teaspoon dried thyme leaves

1/2 teaspoon paprika

3 medium dark-orange sweet potatoes (about 1 1/2 lb), peeled, diced (4 1/2 cups)

1 medium pear, peeled, diced (1 cup)

2 cans (14 oz each) reduced-sodium chicken broth

Chopped fresh thyme, if desired

1. In 3-quart saucepan, heat oil over medium heat. Cook onion and celery in oil 4 to 5 minutes, stirring occasionally, until tender.

2. Stir in remaining ingredients except fresh thyme. Heat to boiling; reduce heat. Cover; simmer 15 to 20 minutes or until sweet potato is tender.

3. Into blender or food processor, add half of the soup. Cover; blend on medium speed 1 to 2 minutes or until smooth; return to saucepan. Blend remaining soup. Heat blended soup 1 to 2 minutes or until hot. Garnish with fresh thyme.

BETTY'S TIP

For a crunchy texture with this smooth soup, add bagel chips, pita chips or oyster crackers. Adding a green salad that includes beans, tomatoes and a sprinkling of cheese, along with a whole-grain breadstick or roll, makes a satisfying meal.

"I do a little bit of housecleaning every day so my weekends are free for fun things." —Brenda S.

1 Serving: Calories 180 (Calories from Fat 20); Total Fat 2g (Saturated Fat 0g; Trans Fat 0g; Omega-3 0g); Cholesterol 0mg; Sodium 420mg; Total Carbohydrate 35g (Dietary Fiber 6g; Sugars 17g); Protein 5g **% Daily Value:** Potassium 24%; Vitamin A 470%; Vitamin C 25%; Calcium 8%; Iron 8%; Folic Acid 6% **Exchanges:** 1 1/2 Starch, 1 Other Carbohydrate **Carbohydrate Choices:** 2

Fabulous Fish

Nurture yourself with sensational

seafood or flavorful fish

Broiled Salmon with Orange-Mustard Glaze

PREP TIME: 20 Minutes **START TO FINISH:** 20 Minutes **4 SERVINGS**

1 lb salmon fillets, cut into 4 pieces
2 tablespoons orange marmalade
2 teaspoons mustard seed
1/4 teaspoon salt
1/8 teaspoon red pepper sauce

NOTE FROM DR. R
Salmon contains omega-3 fatty acids, a fat that has heart-protective benefits. Though it's important to keep the overall fat in your diet low, omega-3 is one you want to eat more of, as it contributes to good heart health.

1. Set oven control to broil. Spray broiler pan rack with cooking spray. Place salmon, skin side down, on rack in broiler pan. Broil with tops 4 inches from heat 10 to 15 minutes or until fish flakes easily with fork.

2. Meanwhile, in small bowl, mix remaining ingredients. Spread on salmon during last 5 minutes of broiling.

"I do isometric exercises when I'm waiting in line, in the car or on hold on the phone. That way, I feel like at least I'm getting something done." —Kelly T.

1 Serving: Calories 190 (Calories from Fat 60); Total Fat 7g (Saturated Fat 2g; Trans Fat 0g; Omega-3 1.5g); Cholesterol 75mg; Sodium 220mg; Total Carbohydrate 7g (Dietary Fiber 0g; Sugars 5g); Protein 25g **% Daily Value:** Potassium 17%; Vitamin A 2%; Vitamin C 2%; Calcium 2%; Iron 6%; Folic Acid 0% **Exchanges:** 1/2 Other Carbohydrate, 3 1/2 Very Lean Meat, 1 Fat **Carbohydrate Choices:** 1/2

Salmon with Ginger-Citrus Salsa

PREP TIME: 30 Minutes   **START TO FINISH:** 2 Hours 40 Minutes   **4 SERVINGS**

SALMON

1 lemon

4 cups water

6 thin slices gingerroot

1/2 teaspoon salt

1/4 teaspoon coarsely ground pepper

1 lb salmon fillets, cut into 4 pieces

SALSA

2 navel oranges, peeled, finely chopped

1 lime, peeled, finely chopped

1/2 cup chopped red bell pepper

2 tablespoons chopped fresh chives

1 tablespoon honey

1 teaspoon grated gingerroot

1 teaspoon olive oil

1. Grate enough peel from lemon to make 2 teaspoons; set aside for salsa. Cut lemon into slices. In 10- or 12-inch skillet, heat lemon slices, water, sliced gingerroot, salt and pepper to boiling. Boil 3 minutes; reduce heat to medium-low.

2. Add salmon, skin side down, to skillet. Cover and cook 7 to 10 minutes or until salmon flakes easily with fork. Carefully remove salmon with slotted spoon; place in baking dish. Cover; refrigerate at least 2 hours but no longer than 24 hours. Discard liquid mixture in skillet.

3. In medium glass or plastic bowl, mix oranges, lime, bell pepper, chives, honey, grated gingerroot, oil and reserved 2 teaspoons lemon peel.

4. To serve, carefully remove skin from salmon; place salmon on serving plate. Spoon salsa over salmon, using slotted spoon.

NOTE FROM DR. R
Salmon is a good choice for many reasons. One is that it is high in polyunsaturated fats, which can reduce the risk of heart disease by not elevating cholesterol levels as saturated fats do.

1 Serving: Calories 240 (Calories from Fat 70); Total Fat 8g (Saturated Fat 2g; Trans Fat 0g; Omega-3 1.5g); Cholesterol 75mg; Sodium 370mg; Total Carbohydrate 17g (Dietary Fiber 3g; Sugars 12g); Protein 25g   **% Daily Value:** Potassium 23%; Vitamin A 20%; Vitamin C 70%; Calcium 6%; Iron 6%; Folic Acid 8%   **Exchanges:** 1 Other Carbohydrate, 3 1/2 Very Lean Meat, 1 Fat **Carbohydrate Choices:** 1

Salmon-Pasta Toss

PREP TIME: 25 Minutes   **START TO FINISH:** 25 Minutes   **4 SERVINGS**

8 oz uncooked linguine

1 tablespoon olive oil

12 oz skinless salmon fillets,
cut into 1-inch pieces

1 cup sliced fresh mushrooms

12 asparagus spears,
cut into 1-inch pieces

2 cloves garlic, finely chopped

1/4 cup chopped fresh or
2 teaspoons dried basil leaves

12 grape tomatoes

2 medium green onions,
sliced (2 tablespoons)

4 teaspoons cornstarch

1 cup chicken broth

1/4 cup shredded Parmesan cheese

1. Cook and drain linguine as directed on package, omitting salt.

2. Meanwhile, in 12-inch nonstick skillet, heat oil over medium heat. Cook salmon in oil 4 to 5 minutes, stirring gently and frequently, until salmon flakes easily with fork (salmon may break apart). Remove from skillet.

3. Increase heat to medium-high. Add mushrooms, asparagus and garlic to skillet; cook and stir 2 minutes. Stir in basil, tomatoes and onions; cook and stir 1 minute longer.

4. In 2-cup glass measuring cup, stir cornstarch into broth. Add to vegetable mixture. Cook and stir 1 to 2 minutes or until sauce is thickened and bubbly. Stir in salmon. Serve over linguine. Sprinkle with cheese.

"I don't deny myself my favorite foods—I just find ways to eat more healthy versions of them, like oven French fries, hamburgers made with 93% lean meat and light mayonnaise in potato salad."   —Lori F.

BETTY'S TIP

If the salmon you purchased has skin, remove the skin before cutting the salmon into pieces. Place the fillet, skin side down, on a cutting board. Using a sharp knife, cut between the flesh and skin, angling knife down toward the skin and using a sawing motion. Grip the skin tightly with the other hand after a small portion has been removed.

1 Serving: Calories 440 (Calories from Fat 110); Total Fat 12g (Saturated Fat 3g; Trans Fat 0g; Omega-3 1g); Cholesterol 60mg; Sodium 410mg; Total Carbohydrate 52g (Dietary Fiber 5g; Sugars 3g); Protein 32g   **% Daily Value:** Potassium 22%; Vitamin A 15%; Vitamin C 15%; Calcium 10%; Iron 20%; Folic Acid 50%   **Exchanges:** 3 Starch, 1 Vegetable, 3 Lean Meat **Carbohydrate Choices:** 3 1/2

Salmon-Pasta Toss

Corn 'n Crab Cakes

PREP TIME: 20 Minutes   **START TO FINISH:** 1 Hour   **4 SERVINGS**

1/2 cup frozen whole kernel corn (from 1-lb bag), thawed

4 medium green onions, chopped (1/4 cup)

1/3 cup fat-free mayonnaise or salad dressing

1 tablespoon 40%-less-sodium taco seasoning mix (from 1.25-oz package)

2 cans (6 oz each) white crabmeat, drained, cartilage removed

1 egg or 2 egg whites

2 tablespoons water

1/2 cup plain dry bread crumbs

3 tablespoons chunky-style salsa

BETTY'S TIP
The fat-free mayonnaise provides moisture and tenderness without the extra fat of regular mayonnaise and you won't miss the extra salt in the taco seasoning. These crab cakes contain a good amount of potassium, an extra bonus to help balance the sodium.

1. Line cookie sheet with waxed paper. In medium bowl, mix corn, onions, mayonnaise, taco seasoning mix and crabmeat. Shape into 8 patties, using slightly less than 1/4 cup for each patty. Place on cookie sheet; freeze 15 minutes.

2. Heat oven to 450°F. Spray another cookie sheet with cooking spray. In shallow bowl, mix beat egg and water until blended. In another shallow bowl or pie plate, place bread crumbs.

3. Dip each patty into egg mixture, coating both sides, then coat with bread crumbs. Place on sprayed cookie sheet. Bake 15 minutes; turn patties. Bake about 10 minutes longer or until golden brown. Serve with salsa.

"I try to balance work with relaxation. Spending time with my family, curling up with a good book or watching my favorite TV show help me relieve tension and ease my mind."   —Danya H.

1 Serving: Calories 180 (Calories from Fat 35); Total Fat 3.5g (Saturated Fat 1g; Trans Fat 0g; Omega-3 0g); Cholesterol 120mg; Sodium 690mg; Total Carbohydrate 19g (Dietary Fiber 2g; Sugars 4g); Protein 19g   **% Daily Value:** Potassium 12%; Vitamin A 6%; Vitamin C 4%; Calcium 10%; Iron 10%; Folic Acid 15%   **Exchanges:** 1 Starch, 2 1/2 Very Lean Meat, 1/2 Fat **Carbohydrate Choices:** 1

Cajun Catfish Sandwiches

PREP TIME: 15 Minutes   **START TO FINISH:** 40 Minutes   **4 SERVINGS**

1 cup corn flake crumbs

1 tablespoon Cajun seasoning

1/4 cup fat-free (skim) milk

4 catfish fillets (4 oz each)

1 1/2 cups coleslaw mix (shredded cabbage and carrots)

3 tablespoons fat-free coleslaw dressing

4 whole-grain hamburger buns

1 lemon, cut into 4 wedges

1. Heat oven to 425°F. Line cookie sheet with foil; spray with cooking spray.

2. In shallow dish, mix corn flake crumbs and Cajun seasoning. Into another shallow dish, pour milk.

3. Dip each catfish fillet into milk, then coat with corn flake mixture. Place on foil.

4. Bake 10 minutes; turn. Bake 10 to 15 minutes longer or until fish flakes easily with fork.

5. Meanwhile, in small bowl, mix coleslaw mix and dressing. Place catfish in buns; squeeze lemon juice over catfish. Top each fillet with about 1/4 cup coleslaw.

NOTE FROM DR. R
One easy way to get three servings of whole grains a day is to make sure that the bread or buns you eat are whole grain.

"One thing I do is walk up and down escalators. It's an easy way to work in exercise on my way somewhere." —Karen C.

1 Serving: Calories 340 (Calories from Fat 80); Total Fat 9g (Saturated Fat 2g; Trans Fat 0g; Omega-3 1g); Cholesterol 90mg; Sodium 870mg; Total Carbohydrate 35g (Dietary Fiber 4g; Sugars 11g); Protein 29g   **% Daily Value:** Potassium 19%; Vitamin A 40%; Vitamin C 25%; Calcium 10%; Iron 30%; Folic Acid 20%   **Exchanges:** 1 1/2 Starch, 1/2 Other Carbohydrate, 1 Vegetable, 3 Lean Meat   **Carbohydrate Choices:** 2

Calypso Shrimp with Black Bean–Citrus Salsa

PREP TIME: 20 Minutes **START TO FINISH:** 2 Hours 30 Minutes **4 SERVINGS**

BETTY'S TIP

You can make this salad ahead of time; cover and refrigerate the cooked shrimp separately from the salsa. Just before serving, arrange on plates. You can use red beans instead of black beans if you like.

SHRIMP AND MARINADE

2 teaspoons grated orange peel

1/4 cup orange juice

1/2 teaspoon seasoned salt

4 cloves garlic, finely chopped

1 lb uncooked large shrimp (21 to 30), peeled, deveined

1 tablespoon canola oil

SALSA

1 can (15 oz) black beans, drained, rinsed

1 medium orange, peeled, divided into segments, membrane removed and cut in half

1/4 cup chunky-style salsa

2 tablespoons chopped fresh cilantro

1 teaspoon grated lime peel

2 cloves garlic, finely chopped

1. In 8-inch square (2-quart) glass baking dish, mix orange peel, orange juice, seasoned salt and 4 cloves chopped garlic. Add shrimp; turn to coat. Cover with plastic wrap; refrigerate up to 2 hours to marinate.

2. In medium bowl, mix all salsa ingredients. Cover; let stand until ready to serve (or refrigerate if longer than 30 minutes).

3. In 10-inch nonstick skillet, heat oil over medium-high heat. Drain shrimp; discard marinade. Cook shrimp in oil 2 to 3 minutes, stirring frequently, until shrimp are pink.

4. Among 4 dinner plates, divide salsa. Arrange shrimp around salsa.

1 Serving: Calories 280 (Calories from Fat 45); Total Fat 5g (Saturated Fat 0.5g; Trans Fat 0g; Omega-3 0.5g); Cholesterol 160mg; Sodium 470mg; Total Carbohydrate 33g (Dietary Fiber 7g; Sugars 7g); Protein 26g **% Daily Value:** Potassium 17%; Vitamin A 8%; Vitamin C 50%; Calcium 10%; Iron 30%; Folic Acid 35% **Exchanges:** 1 Starch, 1 Other Carbohydrate, 3 1/2 Very Lean Meat, 1/2 Fat **Carbohydrate Choices:** 2

Calypso Shrimp with Black Bean–Citrus Salsa

Shrimp Kabobs and Warm Spinach Salad

PREP TIME: 20 Minutes   **START TO FINISH:** 50 Minutes   **4 SERVINGS**

KABOBS

8 wooden skewers (8 to 10 inch)

1/4 cup dry white wine or chicken broth

2 teaspoons olive oil

1 teaspoon grated lemon peel

2 tablespoons lemon juice

3 cloves garlic, finely chopped

1 tablespoon chopped fresh or
1 teaspoon dried basil leaves

1 lb uncooked deveined peeled
large shrimp (21 to 30), thawed if frozen,
tail shells removed

SALAD

6 cups spinach leaves

2 plum (Roma) tomatoes, chopped (2/3 cup)

2 tablespoons chopped onion

3 tablespoons fat-free balsamic vinaigrette

1. Soak wooden skewers in water at least 30 minutes to prevent burning.

2. Meanwhile, in shallow glass or plastic dish or heavy-duty resealable food-storage plastic bag, mix wine, oil, lemon peel, lemon juice, garlic and basil. Add shrimp, turning to coat with marinade. Cover dish or seal bag; refrigerate at least 30 minutes but no longer than 2 hours to marinate.

3. Heat gas or charcoal grill. Remove shrimp from marinade; reserve marinade. Thread shrimp on skewers, leaving space between each.

4. Place kabobs on grill. Cover grill; cook over medium heat 3 to 5 minutes, turning and brushing 2 or 3 times with marinade, until shrimp are pink.

5. Meanwhile, in large bowl, toss spinach, tomatoes, onion and vinaigrette. On serving plate, place spinach salad; top with shrimp kabobs.

1 Serving: Calories 130 (Calories from Fat 30); Total Fat 3.5g (Saturated Fat 0.5g; Trans Fat 0g; Omega-3 0g); Cholesterol 160mg; Sodium 400mg; Total Carbohydrate 6g (Dietary Fiber 2g; Sugars 3g); Protein 19g   **% Daily Value:** Potassium 15%; Vitamin A 90%; Vitamin C 35%; Calcium 8%; Iron 20%; Folic Acid 25%   **Exchanges:** 1 Vegetable, 2 1/2 Very Lean Meat, 1/2 Fat   **Carbohydrate Choices:** 1/2

Grilled Seafood Salad with Shallot-Thyme Vinaigrette

PREP TIME: 30 Minutes   **START TO FINISH:** 1 Hour   **6 SERVINGS**

VINAIGRETTE

1/4 cup balsamic vinegar

3 tablespoons olive oil

2 tablespoons white wine vinegar

1 tablespoon finely chopped shallot

1 tablespoon chopped fresh or
1 teaspoon dried thyme leaves

1 tablespoon Dijon mustard

1 tablespoon water

1/4 teaspoon salt

SALAD

12 uncooked large shrimp, thawed if frozen, peeled, deveined

1 lb swordfish, marlin or tuna steaks,
3/4 to 1 inch thick

1 medium fennel bulb, cut into wedges

10 cups bite-size pieces mixed salad greens

1/2 small red onion, thinly sliced

12 cherry tomatoes, cut in half

12 pitted Kalamata or ripe olives

1. In tightly covered container, shake all vinaigrette ingredients. In shallow glass or plastic dish or heavy-duty resealable food-storage plastic bag, place shrimp and fish. Add 1/4 cup of the vinaigrette; turn shrimp and fish to coat. Cover dish or seal bag; refrigerate 30 minutes to marinate. Reserve remaining vinaigrette.

2. Heat gas or charcoal grill. Remove shrimp and fish from marinade; reserve marinade. Place fish and fennel on grill. Cover grill; cook over medium heat 5 minutes; brush with marinade. Add shrimp. Cover grill; cook about 5 minutes, turning and brushing fish, fennel and shrimp with marinade 2 or 3 times, until shrimp are pink, fish flakes easily with fork and fennel is tender. Discard any remaining marinade.

3. On serving platter, arrange salad greens. Cut fish into bite-size pieces. Arrange fish, fennel, shrimp and remaining salad ingredients on greens. Serve with reserved vinaigrette.

"I read labels for all the foods I eat. I limit the amount of fat I eat, especially saturated and trans fats." —Nanci D.

NOTE FROM DR. R
Although the total amount of fat in this salad is a bit higher than in others, it's mostly from polyunsaturated (good) fats. Grilling not only adds extra flavor to your food, it's a healthy way to cook because it doesn't add extra fat. Broiling, simmering, roasting and braising are all healthy ways to cook because they don't add fat.

1 Serving: Calories 210 (Calories from Fat 110); Total Fat 12g (Saturated Fat 2g; Trans Fat 0g; Omega-3 1g); Cholesterol 65mg; Sodium 350mg; Total Carbohydrate 9g (Dietary Fiber 4g; Sugars 3g); Protein 18g   **% Daily Value:** Potassium 25%; Vitamin A 100%; Vitamin C 45%; Calcium 10%; Iron 15%; Folic Acid 30%   **Exchanges:** 2 Vegetable, 2 Very Lean Meat, 2 Fat
Carbohydrate Choices: 1/2

Cuban-Style Tilapia Salad

PREP TIME: 30 Minutes   **START TO FINISH:** 30 Minutes   **4 SERVINGS**

DRESSING
1/2 cup pineapple juice
1 teaspoon grated lime peel
2 tablespoons lime juice
1 tablespoon canola oil
1/4 teaspoon seasoned salt

TILAPIA AND SALAD
4 tilapia or other mild-flavored fish fillets (about 5 oz each)
Cooking spray
2 tablespoons lime juice
1/2 teaspoon seasoned salt
4 cups mixed salad greens
2 cups fresh or canned (drained) pineapple chunks
1/4 cup fresh mint leaves

BETTY'S TIP
For a heartier salad, add 1 cup canned black beans, drained and rinsed. Divide the beans among the plates with the greens. Serve with whole-grain bread and skim milk.

1. In 1-cup glass measuring cup, beat all dressing ingredients with wire whisk.

2. Set oven control to broil. On rack in broiler pan, place fish; spray tops of fish with cooking spray. Sprinkle tops of fish with 2 tablespoons lime juice and the seasoned salt. Broil with tops 4 to 6 inches from heat 6 to 8 minutes or until fish flakes easily with fork.

3. Meanwhile, on each of 4 plates, arrange 1 cup salad greens. Divide pineapple among plates. Place fish on or next to greens. Sprinkle greens and fish with mint. Serve with dressing.

"I try to keep work at work and home at home, which allows me to focus on each as I need to and not be distracted with either one." —Lynn V.

1 Serving: Calories 230 (Calories from Fat 50); Total Fat 5g (Saturated Fat 0.5g; Trans Fat 0g; Omega-3 1g); Cholesterol 75mg; Sodium 390mg; Total Carbohydrate 17g (Dietary Fiber 2g; Sugars 12g); Protein 28g   **% Daily Value:** Potassium 20%; Vitamin A 60%; Vitamin C 80%; Calcium 6%; Iron 8%; Folic Acid 25%   **Exchanges:** 1 Fruit, 1 Vegetable, 3 1/2 Very Lean Meat, 1/2 Fat   **Carbohydrate Choices:** 1

Cuban-Style Tilapia Salad

Keep Your Skin and Hair Healthy

Healthy Skin

Who says beauty is only skin deep? There is much more to your skin than what others see on the surface. Your skin is your body's largest organ, and it plays a very important role in regulating your body's fluids and temperature. Your skin contains the nerve endings that let you know if something is hard or soft, hot or cold, dull or sharp. Healthy skin is the sign of a healthy body. Keep your skin healthy by:

- ➤ Getting adequate amounts of rest (easier said than done, at times). Strive for at least six to eight hours a night.

- ➤ Drinking lots of water to help regulate the body's fluids.

- ➤ Not smoking. The nicotine in cigarettes causes blood vessels to constrict and prevents blood, oxygen and nutrients from flowing to body tissues.

- ➤ Eating lots of fruits and vegetables—they're the best source of the vitamins C and A that the skin needs—whole grains and vitamin E–rich nuts like almonds.

- ➤ Avoiding the sun, especially during peak hours for sunburn, 11:00 a.m. to 3:00 p.m.

Moisturizing Facial Mask

TRY THIS REFRESHING, MOISTURIZING FACIAL MASK TO KEEP YOUR SKIN GLOWING. (AN ADDED BONUS: IT WILL ALSO RELAX YOU, IT SMELLS WONDERFUL!)

1 1/2 tablespoons dried rosemary leaves
Glass or plastic bottle with stopper or secure cap
1/2 cup old-fashioned or quick-cooking oats
3 tablespoons finely chopped or ground almonds
Plastic container or jar with lid

1. Crumble rosemary leaves with your fingers into 1-quart bowl. Pour 2 cups boiling water over leaves. Let stand 15 minutes or until cool. Strain leaves from water; discard leaves.

2. Pour rosemary-infused water into bottle; seal.

3. Mix oats and almonds in container; seal.

4. To use mask, place about 2 tablespoons oats mixture in small bowl. Add about 2 tablespoons rosemary-infused water, 1 teaspoon at a time, until a thick paste forms. Set aside.

5. Wash your face, and apply a warm, wet washcloth for a few minutes.

6. Remove washcloth. Gently spread oatmeal mixture on face, avoiding eyes and lips. Leave on 15 minutes.

7. Wash off mask with warm, wet washcloth.

Soothe Your Feet with This Relaxing, Yet Invigorating Foot Soak

2 cups Epsom salts
Glass or plastic jar or container with lid
Essential oil of your choice, if desired*
Small bottle of body lotion, if desired

*Do not apply essential oils directly to skin; always dilute with another oil or water. Consult your physician before using essential oils if you are pregnant or your skin is sensitive to light.

1. Pour Epsom salts into jar; seal.

2. Mix 1/2 cup Epsom salts and 1 gallon warm water in dishpan; add 8 drops essential oil. Soak feet in water at least 15 minutes. Towel dry.

3. Rub feet with lotion. Wear slippers or socks until lotion is absorbed to protect carpets.

Healthy Hair Begins on the Inside

Like your skin, your hair needs nutrition from the inside out. The critical principle in hair health is that the hair base, the follicle, is fed with nutrients from the blood supply to the scalp. Shining, lustrous hair is a reflection of your inner health. The reverse is also true—specific nutritional deficiencies can affect your hair. Make certain you eat:

➤ Fatty fish like salmon, tuna and mackerel, along with walnuts, almonds, canola oil and flaxseed. All are high in omega-3 fatty acids that are essential for overall health.

➤ Plenty of fruits and vegetables to get folic acid, vitamins A and C and antioxidants. Eat a variety of fruits, like different types of berries, citrus fruits, melons and grapes. For vegetables, include dark leafy greens, beets, broccoli, carrots and fresh herbs.

➤ Milk and dairy products, which give you protein and calcium.

➤ Whole grains and legumes for B vitamins and antioxidants.

➤ Fish, chicken, eggs and soy products for lean protein, iron and trace minerals.

➤ Also, drink lots of water to keep your hair and scalp hydrated.

EATING GOOD FOOD IS THE SINGLE BEST THING YOU CAN DO TO MAINTAIN THE NATURAL HEALTH AND BEAUTY OF YOUR HAIR. BECAUSE TRACE MINERALS LIKE ZINC AND MAGNESIUM ALSO AFFECT HAIR, BE CERTAIN TO EAT FOODS LIKE BEEF AND POTATOES, THAT ARE HIGH IN ZINC AND POTASSIUM. ALSO, GIVE YOUR SCALP A NICE MASSAGE A FEW TIMES A WEEK TO KEEP OXYGENATED BLOOD MOVING TO YOUR ROOTS. NOT ONLY IS IT GOOD FOR YOUR HAIR AND SCALP, IT ALSO FEELS GOOD AND WILL RELAX YOU!

Tilapia Florentine

PREP TIME: 30 Minutes   **START TO FINISH:** 30 Minutes   **4 SERVINGS**

4 tilapia or other mild-flavor fish fillets (5 oz each)
1/3 cup reduced-fat mayonnaise or salad dressing
2 teaspoons fresh lemon juice
1 teaspoon Dijon mustard
1/2 teaspoon dried tarragon leaves
1/4 teaspoon lemon-pepper seasoning
4 teaspoons garlic-herb dry bread crumbs
2 teaspoons olive oil
1 1/2 cups sliced fresh mushrooms (4 oz)
1 tablespoon fresh lemon juice
6 cups lightly packed fresh spinach leaves (9 oz)
1/2 teaspoon salt

BETTY'S TIP
Tilapia is a very popular fish with a mild flavor that pairs well with tarragon. If you like tarragon, you're in for a treat. Not a tarragon lover? You may want to cut back a bit on the amount.

1. Heat oven to 450°F. Spray 11 × 7-inch pan with cooking spray.

2. Place fish fillets in pan. In small bowl, mix mayonnaise, 2 teaspoons lemon juice, the mustard, tarragon and lemon-pepper seasoning until blended. Spread mayonnaise mixture evenly over fish fillets. Sprinkle with bread crumbs.

3. Bake 10 to 12 minutes or until fish flakes easily with fork.

4. Meanwhile, in 12-inch skillet, heat oil over medium heat. Cook mushrooms in oil about 5 minutes, stirring occasionally, until softened. Stir in 1 tablespoon lemon juice. Gradually stir in spinach. Cook about 3 minutes, stirring occasionally, just until spinach is wilted. Sprinkle with salt.

5. To serve, place spinach on each fish fillet.

1 Serving: Calories 240 (Calories from Fat 100); Total Fat 11g (Saturated Fat 2g; Trans Fat 0g; Omega-3 1g); Cholesterol 80mg; Sodium 680mg; Total Carbohydrate 7g (Dietary Fiber 2g; Sugars 2g); Protein 29g   **% Daily Value:** Potassium 21%; Vitamin A 120%; Vitamin C 6%; Calcium 10%; Iron 15%; Folic Acid 25%   **Exchanges:** 1 Vegetable, 4 Very Lean Meat, 2 Fat **Carbohydrate Choices:** 1/2

Grilled Lemon-Garlic Halibut Steaks with Pea Pods

PREP TIME: 20 Minutes   **START TO FINISH:** 30 Minutes   **4 SERVINGS**

1/4 cup lemon juice

1 tablespoon olive oil

1/4 teaspoon salt

1/4 teaspoon pepper

2 cloves garlic, finely chopped

4 halibut or tuna steaks, about 1 inch thick (about 2 lb)

1/4 cup chopped fresh parsley

1 tablespoon grated lemon peel

2 cups snow pea pods, strings removed

1. Brush grill rack with canola oil. Heat gas or charcoal grill. In shallow glass or plastic dish or resealable plastic food-storage bag, mix lemon juice, oil, salt, pepper and garlic. Add fish; turn several times to coat. Cover dish or seal bag; refrigerate 10 minutes to marinate.

2. Remove fish from marinade; reserve marinade. Place fish on grill. Cover grill; cook over medium heat 9 to 13 minutes, turning once and brushing with marinade, until fish flakes easily with fork (tuna will be slightly pink in center). Discard any remaining marinade. Sprinkle fish with parsley and lemon peel; cover with foil to keep warm.

3. In 1-quart saucepan, heat 1 inch water to boiling over high heat. Add pea pods. Cook 2 to 3 minutes or until crisp-tender; drain. Serve fish with pea pods.

BETTY'S TIP

You will need 1 large lemon for 1 tablespoon grated lemon peel and 1/4 cup of juice; room-temperature lemons will yield more juice than those that are cold.

1 Serving: Calories 210 (Calories from Fat 50); Total Fat 6g (Saturated Fat 1g; Trans Fat 0g; Omega-3 1g); Cholesterol 100mg; Sodium 310mg; Total Carbohydrate 4g (Dietary Fiber 1g; Sugars 1g); Protein 36g   **% Daily Value:** Potassium 18%; Vitamin A 15%; Vitamin C 20%; Calcium 6%; Iron 8%; Folic Acid 8%   **Exchanges:** 1 Vegetable, 5 Very Lean Meat, 1/2 Fat **Carbohydrate Choices:** 0

Tuna with Avocado-Kiwi Salsa

PREP TIME: 40 Minutes   **START TO FINISH:** 1 Hour 10 Minutes   **6 SERVINGS**

TUNA

1 1/2 lb tuna steaks, 3/4 to
1 inch thick

1/4 cup lime juice

2 teaspoons chili oil

2 tablespoons finely chopped
fresh cilantro

1 clove garlic, finely chopped

1/2 teaspoon salt

SALSA

1 small avocado, pitted, peeled and coarsely
chopped (1 cup)

1 kiwifruit, peeled, chopped (1/2 cup)

3 medium green onions, chopped (3 tablespoons)

1 small jalapeño chile, seeded, finely chopped
(1 tablespoon)

2 tablespoons lime juice

2 tablespoons chopped fresh cilantro

1/4 teaspoon salt

1. If tuna steaks are large, cut into 6 serving pieces. In shallow glass or plastic dish, mix remaining tuna ingredients. Add tuna; turn to coat with marinade. Cover; refrigerate, turning once, at least 30 minutes but no longer than 2 hours to marinate.

2. Meanwhile, in medium bowl, mix all salsa ingredients; refrigerate.

3. Spray grill rack with cooking spray. Heat gas or charcoal grill. Remove tuna from marinade; reserve marinade. Place tuna on grill. Cover grill; cook over medium heat 11 to 16 minutes, brushing 2 or 3 times with marinade and turning once, until tuna flakes easily with fork and is slightly pink in center. Discard any remaining marinade. Top tuna with salsa.

"I like watching TV shows that make me feel like a part of the discussion group—one of the girls. I tape my favorite show while I'm at work so I can enjoy it later." —Nancy L.

1 Serving: Calories 210 (Calories from Fat 100); Total Fat 11g (Saturated Fat 2.5g; Trans Fat 0g; Omega-3 1.5g); Cholesterol 65mg; Sodium 360mg; Total Carbohydrate 6g (Dietary Fiber 2g; Sugars 2g); Protein 23g   **% Daily Value:** Potassium 20%; Vitamin A 4%; Vitamin C 20%; Calcium 2%; Iron 6%; Folic Acid 6%   **Exchanges:** 1/2 Other Carbohydrate, 3 1/2 Lean Meat **Carbohydrate Choices:** 1/2

Tuna with Avocado-Kiwi Salsa

Grilled Swordfish with Black Bean and Corn Salsa

PREP TIME: 45 Minutes **START TO FINISH:** 1 Hour 15 Minutes **6 SERVINGS**

NOTE FROM DR. R
Swordfish is a fine choice because it contains omega-3 fatty acids. Combined with black beans and corn, this dish is a good source of many vitamins and minerals.

SWORDFISH

1 teaspoon finely grated lime peel

3 tablespoons lime juice

1/2 teaspoon ground cumin

1/4 teaspoon salt

1/8 teaspoon pepper

2 cloves garlic, finely chopped

Liquid from canned tomatoes used in salsa (about 1/2 cup)

3 swordfish steaks (10 to 12 oz each), cut in half

SALSA

1 can (15 oz) Southwestern black beans, drained, rinsed

1 can (11 oz) whole kernel corn, drained

1 can (10 oz) original or mild diced tomatoes with green chiles, drained, liquid reserved

4 medium green onions, chopped (1/4 cup)

1 tablespoon olive oil

2 teaspoons dry sherry or red wine vinegar

1/4 teaspoon salt

1/8 teaspoon pepper

1. In shallow glass or plastic dish, mix all swordfish ingredients except the swordfish. Add swordfish; turn to coat with marinade. Cover; refrigerate at least 30 minutes but no longer than 2 hours to marinate.

2. Meanwhile, in medium bowl, mix all salsa ingredients. Let stand at room temperature.

3. Spray grill rack with cooking spray. Heat gas or charcoal grill. Remove fish from marinade; reserve marinade. Place fish on grill. Cover grill; cook over medium heat 15 to 20 minutes, brushing 2 or 3 times with marinade and turning once, until fish flakes easily with fork. Discard any remaining marinade. Serve fish with room-temperature salsa.

"I build my meals around getting five or more servings of fruits and veggies a day, so that by the end of the day, I've had all I need." —Kelly T.

1 Serving: Calories 310 (Calories from Fat 90); Total Fat 10g (Saturated Fat 2g; Trans Fat 0g; Omega-3 1.5g); Cholesterol 75mg; Sodium 680mg; Total Carbohydrate 25g (Dietary Fiber 7g; Sugars 5g); Protein 31g **% Daily Value:** Potassium 23%; Vitamin A 15%; Vitamin C 10%; Calcium 8%; Iron 15%; Folic Acid 6% **Exchanges:** 1 Starch, 1/2 Other Carbohydrate, 4 Very Lean Meat, 1 1/2 Fat **Carbohydrate Choices:** 1 1/2

Grilled Fish Tacos

PREP TIME: 20 Minutes   **START TO FINISH:** 35 Minutes   **4 SERVINGS**

2 tablespoons lime juice

2 teaspoons chili powder

1 teaspoon ground cumin

2 tilapia or cod fillets (5 oz each)

4 whole wheat tortillas (6 inch)

1 cup shredded lettuce

1/2 cup black beans (from 15-oz can), drained, rinsed

1/4 cup chopped seeded tomato

1/4 cup shredded reduced-fat Cheddar cheese (1 oz)

1/4 cup fat-free sour cream, if desired

2 tablespoons chopped fresh cilantro

1. In heavy-duty resealable food-storage plastic bag, mix lime juice, chili powder and cumin. Add fish; seal bag. Turn bag several times to coat fish with marinade. Refrigerate 15 to 30 minutes to marinate.

2. Brush grill rack with canola oil. Heat gas or charcoal grill. Place fish on grill. Cover grill; cook over medium heat 4 to 6 minutes, turning after 2 minutes, until fish flakes easily with fork.

3. Cut fish into bite-size pieces; divide fish among tortillas. Fill with lettuce, beans, tomato, cheese, sour cream and cilantro.

BETTY'S TIP
This is a lighter version of the popular fast-food item, and the beans add more fiber. If you have leftover black beans, just place in a food-storage container and refrigerate. Toss into soups, salads or casseroles.

1 Serving: Calories 170 (Calories from Fat 20); Total Fat 2.5g (Saturated Fat 0.5g; Trans Fat 0g; Omega-3 0g); Cholesterol 40mg; Sodium 240mg; Total Carbohydrate 17g (Dietary Fiber 4g; Sugars 2g); Protein 19g   **% Daily Value:** Potassium 12%; Vitamin A 10%; Vitamin C 4%; Calcium 10%; Iron 10%; Folic Acid 15%   **Exchanges:** 1 Starch, 2 1/2 Very Lean Meat   **Carbohydrate Choices:** 1

Marvelous Meat and Poultry

5

Savor the tantalizing flavor and tenderness of a meaty main dish

Grilled Jerk Flank Steak

PREP TIME: 25 Minutes **START TO FINISH:** 4 Hours 30 Minutes **6 SERVINGS**

3 tablespoons teriyaki marinade and sauce (from 15-oz bottle)
1 tablespoon canola oil
2 teaspoons pumpkin pie spice
1/2 teaspoon dried thyme leaves
1/2 teaspoon salt
1/4 teaspoon pepper
2 cloves garlic, finely chopped
1 jalapeño chile with seeds, finely chopped
1 1/2 lb beef flank steak

NOTE FROM DR. R
If you've given up red meat because you think it's high in fat, try using leaner choices such as flank steak. This recipe has an unusual and fun combination of flavors.

1. In heavy-duty resealable food-storage plastic bag, place all ingredients except beef. Add beef; seal bag and turn to coat beef. Refrigerate at least 4 hours but no longer than 24 hours to marinate.

2. Heat gas or charcoal grill. Remove beef from marinade; discard marinade.

3. Place beef on grill. Cover grill; cook over hot heat about 10 minutes, turning once, until slightly pink when cut in center. Let stand 5 minutes. To serve, cut across grain into thin slices.

To Broil: Place marinated steak on rack in broiler pan. Broil with top 4 to 5 inches from heat about 10 minutes, turning once, until slightly pink when cut in center.

"Cooking or baking something delicious and yet still healthy makes me feel good. It satisfies my cravings, and I feel like I've indulged." —Brenda S.

1 Serving: Calories 180 (Calories from Fat 70); Total Fat 8g (Saturated Fat 3g; Trans Fat 0g; Omega-3 0g); Cholesterol 50mg; Sodium 170mg; Total Carbohydrate 0g (Dietary Fiber 0g; Sugars 0g); Protein 26g **% Daily Value:** Potassium 6%; Vitamin A 0%; Vitamin C 0%; Calcium 0%; Iron 15%; Folic Acid 2% **Exchanges:** 3 1/2 Lean Meat **Carbohydrate Choices:** 0

Sirloin Steak with Caramelized Onions

PREP TIME: 40 Minutes   **START TO FINISH:** 40 Minutes   **4 SERVINGS**

1 tablespoon olive oil

2 large sweet onions, sliced (4 cups)

1 tablespoon Dijon mustard

1 teaspoon soy sauce

1 lb boneless beef sirloin steak, about 1 inch thick

1/8 teaspoon salt

1/4 teaspoon pepper

1. Heat gas or charcoal grill.

2. In 12-inch nonstick skillet, heat oil over medium heat. Cook onions in oil 15 to 20 minutes, stirring occasionally, until onions are very soft and caramelized. Stir in mustard and soy sauce.

3. Meanwhile, sprinkle both sides of beef steak with salt and pepper; place on grill. Cover grill; cook over medium heat 10 to 12 minutes for medium doneness, turning once.

4. Slice steak thinly across grain. Serve with onions.

BETTY'S TIP

Let food safety rule! Use a different plate and tongs to take raw food to the grill and to take cooked food off the grill.

"No matter how much work piles up, eating lunch away from my desk allows me to focus on refreshing for the second half of the day." —Suzanne S.

1 Serving: Calories 220 (Calories from Fat 70); Total Fat 7g (Saturated Fat 1.5g; Trans Fat 0g; Omega-3 0g); Cholesterol 65mg; Sodium 280mg; Total Carbohydrate 12g (Dietary Fiber 2g; Sugars 5g); Protein 27g   **% Daily Value:** Potassium 12%; Vitamin A 0%; Vitamin C 6%; Calcium 4%; Iron 15%; Folic Acid 8%   **Exchanges:** 1/2 Other Carbohydrate, 1 Vegetable, 3 1/2 Very Lean Meat, 1 Fat   **Carbohydrate Choices:** 1

Grilled Italian Steak and Vegetables

PREP TIME: 25 Minutes   **START TO FINISH:** 40 Minutes   **4 SERVINGS**

1/2 cup fat-free balsamic vinaigrette dressing

1/4 cup chopped fresh basil leaves

1 1/2 teaspoons peppered seasoned salt

2 beef boneless New York strip steaks, about 1 inch thick (8 to 10 oz each)

1 lb asparagus spears, cut into 2-inch pieces

1 medium red onion, cut into thin wedges

1 yellow bell pepper, cut into 8 pieces

NOTE FROM DR. R
Beef contains high-quality protein, iron, folic acid, zinc and many other nutrients that are important for overall good health. The vegetables add a big hit of vitamins and minerals in this great-tasting recipe.

1. In large bowl, mix 2 tablespoons of the dressing, 2 tablespoons of the basil and 3/4 teaspoon of the peppered seasoned salt; set aside for vegetables. In shallow glass or plastic dish or resealable food-storage plastic bag, mix remaining dressing, basil and peppered seasoned salt; add beef. Cover dish or seal bag; refrigerate 15 minutes to marinate.

2. Heat gas or charcoal grill. Add asparagus, onion and bell pepper to reserved dressing mixture; toss to coat. Place in disposable 8-inch square foil pan or grill basket (grill "wok"). Reserve dressing in bowl.

3. Remove beef from marinade; reserve marinade. Place pan of vegetables on grill. Cover grill; cook 5 minutes. Add beef to grill next to pan. Cover grill; cook beef and vegetables 10 to 12 minutes, turning beef once and stirring vegetables occasionally, until beef is desired doneness and vegetables are tender. Brush beef with reserved marinade during last 5 minutes of cooking.

4. Add vegetables to bowl with reserved dressing; toss to coat. Cut beef into thin slices. Discard any remaining marinade. Serve vegetables with beef. Drizzle with additional dressing if desired.

To Broil: Place pan of vegetables on rack in broiler pan; broil with top 4 to 6 inches from heat 5 minutes. Add beef to rack. Broil beef and vegetables 10 to 12 minutes, turning beef once and stirring vegetables occasionally, until beef is desired doneness and vegetables are tender. Brush beef with reserved marinade during last 5 minutes of cooking.

1 Serving: Calories 220 (Calories from Fat 70); Total Fat 8g (Saturated Fat 3g; Trans Fat 0g; Omega-3 0g); Cholesterol 50mg; Sodium 1010mg; Total Carbohydrate 9g (Dietary Fiber 2g; Sugars 6g); Protein 29g   **% Daily Value:** Potassium 13%; Vitamin A 15%; Vitamin C 60%; Calcium 4%; Iron 15%; Folic Acid 25%   **Exchanges:** 1 Vegetable, 4 Lean Meat **Carbohydrate Choices:** 1/2

Grilled Italian Steak and Vegetables

Beef Kabobs with
Edamame Succotash

PREP TIME: 40 Minutes   **START TO FINISH:** 2 Hours 40 Minutes   **6 SERVINGS**

NOTE FROM DR. R
Edamame, fresh
soybeans available
shelled or in their
pods, are the latest
rage. Not only are
they colorful and
hearty, they are also
a complete protein
(containing all the
essential amino
acids needed in the
diet), a rare quality
for a plant protein!

SUCCOTASH

1 can (11 oz) whole kernel corn with red and green peppers, drained

1 1/2 cups frozen shelled edamame (soybeans), thawed

1 cup small cherry tomatoes, cut in half

1/2 cup chicken broth

1 tablespoon finely chopped canned chipotle chiles in adobo sauce

1/2 teaspoon salt

LIME-CHILE MARINADE

1 teaspoon grated lime peel

1/3 cup fresh lime juice

1 tablespoon finely chopped canned chipotle chiles in adobo sauce

1 teaspoon ground cumin

1/2 teaspoon salt

3 cloves garlic, finely chopped

KABOBS

1 1/2 lb boneless beef sirloin steak, 3/4 to 1 inch thick, cut into 1-inch pieces

1 medium red onion, cut into 24 wedges and separated

1. In 10-inch skillet, heat all succotash ingredients over medium heat 4 to 6 minutes, stirring occasionally, until edamame are crisp-tender; refrigerate.

2. In shallow glass or plastic dish or resealable food-storage plastic bag, mix all marinade ingredients. Add beef; stir to coat with marinade. Cover dish or seal bag; refrigerate at least 2 hours but no longer than 24 hours, stirring once, to marinate.

3. Heat gas or charcoal grill. Drain beef, reserving marinade. On each of twelve 10-inch metal skewers, thread beef and onion alternately, leaving 1/4-inch space between each piece. Brush onion with reserved marinade.

4. Place kabobs on grill. Cover grill; cook over medium heat 6 to 8 minutes for medium beef doneness, turning and brushing with reserved marinade occasionally. Discard any remaining marinade. Serve kabobs with succotash.

1 Serving: Calories 270 (Calories from Fat 70); Total Fat 7g (Saturated Fat 1.5g; Trans Fat 0g; Omega-3 0g); Cholesterol 65mg; Sodium 400mg; Total Carbohydrate 17g (Dietary Fiber 4g; Sugars 4g); Protein 33g   **% Daily Value:** Potassium 20%; Vitamin A 10%; Vitamin C 15%; Calcium 8%; Iron 20%; Folic Acid 20%   **Exchanges:** 1 Starch, 4 Very Lean Meat, 1 Fat **Carbohydrate Choices:** 1

Mini Greek Meat Loaves with Tzatziki Sauce

PREP TIME: 20 Minutes   **START TO FINISH:** 1 Hour   **4 SERVINGS** (2 mini meat loaves and 1/4 of sauce each)

MEAT LOAVES

1 lb extra-lean (at least 90%) ground beef

1/2 box (9-oz size) frozen spinach, cooked, well drained (about 1/2 cup)

1 small onion, finely chopped (1/4 cup)

1/3 cup old-fashioned or quick-cooking oats

2 oz crumbled feta cheese

1 egg plus 1 egg white

1 teaspoon dried oregano leaves, crushed

1/2 teaspoon garlic salt

1/4 teaspoon pepper

SAUCE

3/4 cup plain low-fat yogurt

1/2 medium cucumber, peeled, seeded and finely chopped (1/2 cup)

1 tablespoon olive oil

1/4 teaspoon salt

1 clove garlic, finely chopped

1. Heat oven to 350°F. Spray 8 regular-size muffin cups with cooking spray.

2. In medium bowl, mix all meat loaves ingredients. Scoop generous 1/3 cup meat mixture into each muffin cup, pressing down slightly.

3. Bake 30 to 35 minutes or until no longer pink in centers of loaves. (If using meat thermometer, insert so tip is in center of one loaf; thermometer should read at least 160°F.) Let stand in pan 5 minutes.

4. Meanwhile, in small bowl, mix all sauce ingredients; refrigerate until serving. Serve sauce with meat loaves.

"I sneak veggies into foods so that no one knows they're there—like shredded carrots in meatballs or meat loaf, corn and beans into the taco meat mix and pureed veggies into soups."   —Kelly T.

NOTE FROM DR. R
Tzatziki is a typical Greek sauce and is a nice complement to the meat loaves. Green leafy vegetables, like spinach, are high in antioxidants, which can help protect cells from damage, and are thought to protect against heart disease and certain types of cancer.

1 Serving: Calories 330 (Calories from Fat 160); Total Fat 18g (Saturated Fat 7g; Trans Fat 0.5g; Omega-3 0.5g); Cholesterol 140mg; Sodium 560mg; Total Carbohydrate 12g (Dietary Fiber 2g; Sugars 4g); Protein 31g   **% Daily Value:** Potassium 15%; Vitamin A 60%; Vitamin C 2%; Calcium 20%; Iron 20%; Folic Acid 15%   **Exchanges:** 1/2 Starch, 1/2 Other Carbohydrate, 4 Lean Meat, 1 Fat   **Carbohydrate Choices:** 1

Pork Lo Mein

PREP TIME: 25 Minutes   **START TO FINISH:** 25 Minutes   **4 SERVINGS**

1/2 lb boneless pork loin

2 1/2 cups sugar snap pea pods

1 1/2 cups ready-to-eat baby-cut carrots, cut lengthwise into 1/4-inch sticks

1/2 package (9-oz size) refrigerated linguine, cut into 2-inch pieces

1/3 cup chicken broth

1 tablespoon soy sauce

2 teaspoons cornstarch

1 teaspoon sugar

2 teaspoons finely chopped gingerroot

2 to 4 cloves garlic, finely chopped

2 teaspoons canola oil

1/2 cup thinly sliced red onion

Toasted sesame seed, if desired*

*To toast sesame seed, sprinkle in an ungreased heavy skillet and cook over medium-low heat 5 to 7 minutes, stirring frequently until browning begins, then stirring constantly until golden brown.

1. Trim fat from pork. Cut pork with grain into 2 × 1-inch strips; cut strips across grain into 1/8-inch slices (pork is easier to cut if partially frozen, about 1 1/2 hours). Remove strings from pea pods.

2. In 3-quart saucepan, heat 2 quarts water to boiling. Add pea pods, carrots and linguine; heat to boiling. Boil 2 to 3 minutes or just until linguine is tender; drain.

3. In small bowl, mix broth, soy sauce, cornstarch, sugar, gingerroot and garlic.

4. In 12-inch nonstick skillet or wok, heat oil over medium-high heat. Add pork and onion; stir-fry about 2 minutes or until pork is no longer pink. Stir broth mixture; stir into pork mixture. Stir in pea pods, carrots and linguine. Cook 2 minutes, stirring occasionally. Sprinkle with sesame seed.

NOTE FROM DR. R
If your goal is to lose weight, it's important to pick the way that seems best for you, not what is most popular or what works well for someone else. I often tell women to try to fit in more workout time every day.

1 Serving: Calories 200 (Calories from Fat 45); Total Fat 5g (Saturated Fat 1g; Trans Fat 0g; Omega-3 0g); Cholesterol 35mg; Sodium 370mg; Total Carbohydrate 21g (Dietary Fiber 4g; Sugars 6g); Protein 17g   **% Daily Value:** Potassium 15%; Vitamin A 120%; Vitamin C 20%; Calcium 4%; Iron 10%; Folic Acid 15%   **Exchanges:** 1 Starch, 1 Vegetable, 1 1/2 Lean Meat **Carbohydrate Choices:** 1 1/2

Pork Lo Mein

Pork Tenderloin with Apples and Sweet Potatoes

PREP TIME: 15 Minutes   **START TO FINISH:** 1 Hour 15 Minutes   **6 SERVINGS**

1/4 cup packed brown sugar

1/4 cup butter or margarine, melted

1 tablespoon cider vinegar

1 teaspoon salt

1/2 teaspoon garlic powder

1/2 teaspoon pepper

2 medium red cooking apples, sliced (about 2 cups)

2 medium dark-orange sweet potatoes, peeled, thinly sliced (about 2 1/2 cups)

1 medium onion, chopped (1/2 cup)

2 pork tenderloins (1 lb each)

BETTY'S TIP

Be sure to use pork tenderloins—not pork loins—in this recipe. Pork loins are much larger and less tender, and would take longer to cook. The tenderloin is the leanest cut of pork there is, a great choice for preparing low-fat meals.

1. Heat oven to 425°F. In medium bowl, mix brown sugar, butter, vinegar, salt, garlic powder and pepper. Reserve 2 tablespoons of the butter mixture. Add apples, sweet potatoes and onion to remaining butter mixture; toss to coat. In roasting pan or 13 × 9-inch (3-quart) glass baking dish, spread apple mixture. Cover tightly with foil; bake 20 minutes.

2. Meanwhile, brush pork with reserved butter mixture. Heat 10-inch nonstick skillet over medium-high heat until hot. Cook pork in skillet about 3 minutes, turning to brown all sides evenly.

3. Place pork on apple mixture. Bake uncovered 30 to 40 minutes or until pork has slight blush of pink in center and meat thermometer inserted in center reads 160°F.

1 Serving: Calories 360 (Calories from Fat 120); Total Fat 14g (Saturated Fat 7g; Trans Fat 0g; Omega-3 0g); Cholesterol 115mg; Sodium 540mg; Total Carbohydrate 25g (Dietary Fiber 3g; Sugars 17g); Protein 35g   **% Daily Value:** Potassium 24%; Vitamin A 170%; Vitamin C 10%; Calcium 4%; Iron 15%; Folic Acid 4%   **Exchanges:** 1/2 Starch, 1 Other Carbohydrate, 4 1/2 Lean Meat   **Carbohydrate Choices:** 1 1/2

Stir-Fried Pork with Mushrooms and Broccoli

PREP TIME: 25 Minutes   **START TO FINISH:** 25 Minutes   **4 SERVINGS**

2 cups uncooked instant brown rice

2 1/4 cups water

1 tablespoon cornstarch

1/4 cup teriyaki marinade (from 12-oz bottle)

1/2 cup water

1/2 teaspoon ground ginger

3 teaspoons canola oil

3/4 lb boneless pork loin, trimmed of fat, cut into thin 2-inch strips

2 cups broccoli florets

1 small onion, cut into thin wedges

1 package (8 oz) sliced mushrooms (3 cups)

1 medium red, yellow or orange bell pepper, cut into 1-inch pieces

2 cloves garlic, finely chopped

1. Cook rice in 2 1/4 cups water as directed on package, omitting butter and salt. Meanwhile, place cornstarch in small bowl or cup. Gradually stir in teriyaki marinade, 1/2 cup water and the ginger.

2. In 12-inch nonstick skillet or wok, heat 2 teaspoons of the oil over medium-high heat. Add pork; stir-fry 4 to 5 minutes or until no longer pink in center. Remove pork from skillet; keep warm.

3. Add remaining 1 teaspoon oil to skillet. Add broccoli, onion, mushrooms, bell pepper and garlic; stir-fry 4 to 5 minutes or until vegetable are crisp-tender.

4. Stir cornstarch mixture into broccoli mixture. Add pork; cook and stir until sauce is thickened. Serve over rice.

BETTY'S TIP
A flavorful stir-fry usually requires a bit of chopping. Get all the ingredients chopped before starting to stir-fry, then it comes together very quickly. Customize this recipe by using any vegetables you like, even ones that are already cut up.

1 Serving: Calories 410 (Calories from Fat 80); Total Fat 9g (Saturated Fat 1.5g; Trans Fat 0g; Omega-3 0g); Cholesterol 55mg; Sodium 770mg; Total Carbohydrate 56g (Dietary Fiber 5g; Sugars 6g); Protein 28g   **% Daily Value:** Potassium 21%; Vitamin A 25%; Vitamin C 80%; Calcium 4%; Iron 15%; Folic Acid 15%   **Exchanges:** 2 1/2 Starch, 1 Other Carbohydrate, 1 Vegetable, 2 1/2 Lean Meat   **Carbohydrate Choices:** 4

Rosemary Pork Roast
with Carrots

PREP TIME: 15 Minutes   **START TO FINISH:** 1 Hour 45 Minutes   **8 SERVINGS**

1 boneless pork center loin roast (about 2 1/2 lb)
1 teaspoon canola oil
2 teaspoons dried rosemary leaves, crushed
1/2 teaspoon salt
1/4 teaspoon pepper
2 lb ready-to-eat baby-cut carrots
1 large sweet onion, cut into 16 wedges
2 teaspoons canola oil
1/2 teaspoon salt
1/2 teaspoon garlic powder

NOTE FROM DR. R

An important part of wellness is the opportunity to prepare and eat the best possible foods to maintain your body. To keep the overall fat as low as possible, trim all visible fat on cuts of meat before cooking. This colorful dinner is a company-worthy meal just bursting with good-for-you meat and vegetables.

1. Heat oven to 400°F. Spray 15 × 10 × 1-inch pan with cooking spray. Remove fat from pork. Rub pork with 1 teaspoon oil; sprinkle with 1 teaspoon of the rosemary, 1/2 teaspoon salt and the pepper. Place in center of pan. Insert ovenproof meat thermometer so tip is in center of thickest part of pork.

2. In large bowl, mix carrots, onion, 2 teaspoons oil, remaining 1 teaspoon rosemary, 1/2 teaspoon salt and the garlic powder. Arrange carrot mixture around pork.

3. Roast uncovered 1 hour to 1 hour 30 minutes or until meat thermometer reads 160°F and vegetables are tender. Cover with tent of foil; let stand about 10 minutes before carving.

1 Serving: Calories 300 (Calories from Fat 120); Total Fat 13g (Saturated Fat 4g; Trans Fat 0g; Omega-3 0g); Cholesterol 90mg; Sodium 430mg; Total Carbohydrate 13g (Dietary Fiber 4g; Sugars 6g); Protein 33g   **% Daily Value:** Potassium 23%; Vitamin A 270%; Vitamin C 8%; Calcium 6%; Iron 8%; Folic Acid 8%   **Exchanges:** 1/2 Other Carbohydrate, 1 Vegetable, 4 1/2 Lean Meat   **Carbohydrate Choices:** 1

Rosemary Pork Roast with Carrots

Plum-Mustard Pork Chops

PREP TIME: 15 Minutes   **START TO FINISH:** 15 Minutes   **4 SERVINGS**

4 boneless pork loin chops, 1/2 inch thick (5 oz each)
1/4 teaspoon salt
1/4 teaspoon pepper
1/4 cup Asian plum sauce or apricot jam
4 teaspoons yellow mustard

1. Heat 10-inch nonstick skillet over medium-high heat. Sprinkle pork chops with salt and pepper. Cook pork in skillet 5 to 6 minutes, turning after 3 minutes, until no longer pink in center.

2. Meanwhile, in small bowl, mix plum sauce and mustard. Serve with pork.

NOTE FROM DR. R
There are more benefits from exercise than just feeling better and maintaining weight. Research shows that it can improve sleep, reduce the risk of stroke and certain cancers and help control blood sugar levels for people who have diabetes. So keep moving!

"I look for the low-fat, low-calorie dishes on restaurant menus."   —Nanci D.

1 Serving: Calories 210 (Calories from Fat 70); Total Fat 8g (Saturated Fat 3g; Trans Fat 0g; Omega-3 0g); Cholesterol 65mg; Sodium 400mg; Total Carbohydrate 11g (Dietary Fiber 0g; Sugars 7g); Protein 23g   **% Daily Value:** Potassium 9%; Vitamin A 0%; Vitamin C 2%; Calcium 0%; Iron 6%; Folic Acid 2%   **Exchanges:** 1/2 Other Carbohydrate, 3 1/2 Lean Meat   **Carbohydrate Choices:** 1

Chicken Linguine Alfredo

PREP TIME: 25 Minutes   **START TO FINISH:** 25 Minutes   **6 SERVINGS** (about 1 cup each)

LIGHT ALFREDO SAUCE

2 teaspoons butter or margarine

2 tablespoons finely chopped shallot

1 clove garlic, crushed

3 tablespoons all-purpose flour

1/2 cup reduced-fat sour cream

1/2 cup grated Parmesan cheese

1/2 teaspoon salt

1/8 teaspoon white pepper

LINGUINE MIXTURE

8 oz uncooked linguine

1 1/4 lb chicken breast strips for stir-fry

1 pint (2 cups) fat-free half-and-half

1 jar (7 oz) roasted red bell peppers, drained, thinly sliced

1/3 cup shredded Parmesan cheese

2 tablespoons chopped fresh parsley

1. In 2-quart saucepan, melt butter over medium heat. Add shallot and garlic; cook and stir 1 minute. Remove crushed garlic from saucepan. In medium bowl, beat half-and-half and flour with wire whisk; add to saucepan. Heat to boiling, stirring frequently. Beat in sour cream with wire whisk. Reduce heat to low; cook 1 to 2 minutes or until heated. Remove from heat; stir in grated cheese, salt and white pepper.

2. In 4-quart Dutch oven, cook linguine as directed on package. Drain; rinse with hot water. Return to Dutch oven to keep warm.

3. Meanwhile, heat 12-inch nonstick skillet over medium-high heat. Add chicken; cook about 5 minutes, stirring frequently, until no longer pink in center.

4. Add chicken, bell peppers and Alfredo sauce to linguine; stir to mix. Cook over low heat until thoroughly heated. Garnish each serving with shredded cheese and parsley.

NOTE FROM DR. R
Whether it's deciding to eat healthier, adding more activity or making other changes, realize that going slow is okay. Success is greatest for those who set realistic goals and break their goals into small, doable steps. Small changes add up over time, so treat yourself well.

1 Serving: Calories 430 (Calories from Fat 110); Total Fat 13g (Saturated Fat 6g; Trans Fat 0g; Omega-3 0g); Cholesterol 80mg; Sodium 760mg; Total Carbohydrate 44g (Dietary Fiber 3g; Sugars 8g); Protein 35g   **% Daily Value:** Potassium 14%; Vitamin A 40%; Vitamin C 45%; Calcium 30%; Iron 15%; Folic Acid 25%   **Exchanges:** 2 Starch, 1 Other Carbohydrate, 4 Lean Meat   **Carbohydrate Choices:** 3

Stuffed Pasta Shells

PREP TIME: 30 Minutes   **START TO FINISH:** 55 Minutes   **5 SERVINGS**

15 uncooked jumbo pasta shells
1/2 lb lean ground turkey
1 teaspoon Italian seasoning
1/2 teaspoon fennel seed
1/4 teaspoon pepper
2 cups sliced fresh mushrooms

1 medium onion, chopped (1/2 cup)
4 cloves garlic, finely chopped
1 cup fat-free cottage cheese
1 egg or 2 egg whites
2 cups tomato pasta sauce
1/4 cup shredded Parmesan cheese (1 oz)

BETTY'S TIP
To keep sodium under control, look for a pasta sauce with a sodium content of 400 milligrams or less per serving and try to balance the sodium with foods that contain potassium.

1. Heat oven to 350°F. Cook and drain pasta as directed on package, omitting salt.

2. Meanwhile, in 10-inch nonstick skillet, cook turkey, Italian seasoning, fennel seed and pepper over medium heat 8 to 10 minutes, stirring occasionally, until turkey is no longer pink; remove turkey mixture from skillet.

3. In same skillet, cook mushrooms, onion and garlic over medium heat 6 to 8 minutes, stirring occasionally, until vegetables are tender. Stir in turkey mixture, cottage cheese and egg.

4. Spray 13 × 9-inch (3-quart) glass baking dish with cooking spray. Spoon about 1 tablespoon turkey mixture into each pasta shell. Place in baking dish. Spoon pasta sauce over shells.

5. Cover with foil. Bake 20 to 25 minutes or until hot. Sprinkle with Parmesan cheese.

"A break for physical activity, whether it's a workout at the gym or a walk around the block, clears my mind and helps me face the challenges of the day." —Mindy H.

1 Serving: Calories 370 (Calories from Fat 90); Total Fat 10g (Saturated Fat 3g; Trans Fat 0g; Omega-3 0g); Cholesterol 80mg; Sodium 810mg; Total Carbohydrate 44g (Dietary Fiber 4g; Sugars 13g); Protein 26g   **% Daily Value:** Potassium 18%; Vitamin A 10%; Vitamin C 10%; Calcium 15%; Iron 15%; Folic Acid 20%   **Exchanges:** 2 Starch, 1 Other Carbohydrate, 3 Lean Meat   **Carbohydrate Choices:** 3

Stuffed Pasta Shells

Spinach and Chicken Skillet

PREP TIME: 30 Minutes   **START TO FINISH:** 30 Minutes   **6 SERVINGS**

6 boneless skinless chicken breasts (about 1 3/4 lb)
1 cup fat-free (skim) milk
1/2 cup fat-free chicken broth
1 medium onion, chopped (1/2 cup)
1 bag (10 oz) washed fresh spinach, chopped
1/4 teaspoon salt
1/4 teaspoon pepper
1/4 teaspoon ground nutmeg

BETTY'S TIP
Milk is an excellent source of calcium and vitamin D, nutrients you need for healthy bones and teeth, and to help prevent osteoporosis. In addition, research shows including low-fat dairy products as part of a reduced-calorie diet may aid in successful weight management.

1. Heat 12-inch nonstick skillet over medium heat. Cook chicken in skillet 2 minutes on each side; reduce heat to medium-low. Stir in milk, broth and onion. Cook about 5 minutes, turning chicken occasionally, until onion is tender.

2. Stir in spinach. Cook 3 to 4 minutes, stirring occasionally, until spinach is completely wilted and juice of chicken is clear when center of thickest part is cut (170°F). Remove chicken from skillet; keep warm.

3. Increase heat to medium. Cook spinach mixture about 3 minutes or until liquid has almost evaporated. Stir in salt, pepper and nutmeg. Serve chicken on spinach. Sprinkle with additional pepper if desired.

"I reduce my stress when traveling by taking lots of reading material so that if the flight is delayed or other things come up, I have something pleasant to do, and my stress level stays low."   —Rita R.

1 Serving: Calories 190 (Calories from Fat 40); Total Fat 4.5g (Saturated Fat 1.5g; Trans Fat 0g; Omega-3 0g); Cholesterol 80mg; Sodium 260mg; Total Carbohydrate 5g (Dietary Fiber 1g; Sugars 3g); Protein 32g   **% Daily Value:** Potassium 17%; Vitamin A 90%; Vitamin C 10%; Calcium 10%; Iron 15%; Folic Acid 25%   **Exchanges:** 1 Vegetable, 4 1/2 Very Lean Meat, 1/2 Fat   **Carbohydrate Choices:** 1/2

Feta-Topped Chicken with Bulgur

PREP TIME: 25 Minutes **START TO FINISH:** 25 Minutes **4 SERVINGS**

4 boneless skinless chicken breasts (about 1 1/4 lb)
2 tablespoons balsamic vinaigrette dressing
1 teaspoon Italian seasoning
1/4 teaspoon seasoned pepper
2/3 cup uncooked bulgur wheat
2 cups water
1 large plum (Roma) tomato, cut into 8 slices
1/4 cup crumbled feta cheese (1 oz)

1. Set oven control to broil. Brush both sides of chicken breasts with dressing. Sprinkle both sides with Italian seasoning and seasoned pepper. Place on rack in broiler pan.

2. Broil with tops 4 inches from heat about 10 minutes, turning once, until juice of chicken is clear when center of thickest part is cut (170°F).

3. Meanwhile, cook bulgur in water as directed on package, omitting salt.

4. Top chicken with tomato and cheese. Broil 2 to 3 minutes longer or until cheese is lightly browned. Serve with bulgur.

BETTY'S TIP
Bulgur wheat is a quick-cooking whole grain that's becoming more popular. Rather than just cooking it in water, you can cook it in chicken or vegetable broth for extra flavor.

1 Serving: Calories 250 (Calories from Fat 90); Total Fat 10g (Saturated Fat 3g; Trans Fat 0g; Omega-3 0g); Cholesterol 90mg; Sodium 360mg; Total Carbohydrate 7g (Dietary Fiber 2g; Sugars 2g); Protein 33g **% Daily Value:** Potassium 11%; Vitamin A 10%; Vitamin C 4%; Calcium 6%; Iron 8%; Folic Acid 4% **Exchanges:** 1/2 Starch, 4 1/2 Very Lean Meat, 1 1/2 Fat **Carbohydrate Choices:** 1/2

Tropical Chicken Salad

PREP TIME: 25 Minutes   **START TO FINISH:** 25 Minutes   **4 SERVINGS**

1 1/4 lb boneless skinless chicken breasts, cut into 1/2-inch strips
1 tablespoon blackened seasoning blend
1 tablespoon canola oil
1 bag (5 oz) mixed baby salad greens (4 cups)
2 medium mangoes, seeds removed, peeled and diced (2 cups)
1/2 medium red onion, sliced (3/4 cup)
1 small red bell pepper, chopped (1/2 cup)
2/3 cup fat-free raspberry vinaigrette

NOTE FROM DR. R
Loaded with mango and bell pepper, this salad is a tasty source of vitamins A and C. Vitamin A helps maintain healthy eyesight, hair and skin; vitamin C helps promote healthy gums, blood vessels, bones and teeth.

1. In heavy-duty resealable food-storage plastic bag, place chicken. Sprinkle seasoning blend over chicken; seal bag and shake until chicken is evenly coated.

2. In 10-inch nonstick skillet, heat oil over medium-high heat. Cook chicken in oil 7 to 10 minutes, stirring frequently, until no longer pink in center. Remove chicken from skillet; drain on paper towels.

3. In large bowl, toss salad greens, mangoes, onion and bell pepper; divide among 4 plates. Top with chicken. Drizzle with vinaigrette.

"I park as far away from my office as possible so I get the extra exercise from walking, and I take the stairs instead of riding the elevator or escalator." —Lori F.

1 Serving: Calories 340 (Calories from Fat 80); Total Fat 8g (Saturated Fat 1.5g; Trans Fat 0g; Omega-3 0.5g); Cholesterol 85mg; Sodium 590mg; Total Carbohydrate 34g (Dietary Fiber 4g; Sugars 20g); Protein 33g   **% Daily Value:** Potassium 19%; Vitamin A 80%; Vitamin C 120%; Calcium 6%; Iron 10%; Folic Acid 25%   **Exchanges:** 1 Fruit, 1 Other Carbohydrate, 1 Vegetable, 4 1/2 Very Lean Meat, 1 Fat   **Carbohydrate Choices:** 2

Asian Chicken Roll-Ups

PREP TIME: 15 Minutes   **START TO FINISH:** 15 Minutes   **4 SERVINGS**

2 tablespoons crunchy peanut butter

2 tablespoons teriyaki baste and glaze (from 12-oz bottle)

1 tablespoon packed brown sugar

1 tablespoon hot water

1 teaspoon sesame or canola oil

4 flour tortillas (8 inch)

8 slices (1 oz each) cooked deli chicken breast

1 1/2 cups shredded iceberg lettuce

1 1/2 cups shredded carrots (about 3 medium)

1/2 cup chopped fresh cilantro

1. In small bowl, beat peanut butter, teriyaki baste and glaze, brown sugar, water and oil with wire whisk until smooth.

2. Spread about 1 1/2 tablespoons peanut butter mixture over each tortilla. Top each with 2 slices chicken, about 1/3 cup lettuce, about 1/3 cup carrots and 2 tablespoons cilantro. Roll up tortillas.

BETTY'S TIP

For an extra boost of vitamin C and other vitamins and minerals, try chopped fresh spinach instead of the iceberg lettuce. If you haven't tried them yet, whole wheat tortillas give a whole-grain texture and flavor to this fun roll-up.

1 Serving: Calories 350 (Calories from Fat 110); Total Fat 13g (Saturated Fat 3g; Trans Fat 0.5g; Omega-3 0g); Cholesterol 45mg; Sodium 520mg; Total Carbohydrate 36g (Dietary Fiber 3g; Sugars 9g); Protein 22g   **% Daily Value:** Potassium 11%; Vitamin A 100%; Vitamin C 6%; Calcium 10%; Iron 15%; Folic Acid 20%   **Exchanges:** 2 Starch, 1 Vegetable, 2 Very Lean Meat, 2 Fat   **Carbohydrate Choices:** 2 1/2

Reduce Your Stress

A normal part of life, the reason for stress can be positive, like taking a vacation, or it can be negative, such as losing out on a promotion. Too much ongoing stress may make it harder to feel in control of things and may take its toll on your health.

Challenge Versus Stress?

Challenges in daily life are beneficial; they can give us the drive to learn, increase productivity and achieve new levels of success. When there are too many challenges at one time, you may feel overwhelmed and experience symptoms of negative stress. Stress is the body's response to the perception that you are somehow "under attack." That feeling may arise if you sense a threat to your physical or emotional well-being. When the brain senses a threat, it signals the release of stress hormones that prepare the body for "fight or flight." These stress hormones release a burst of glucose that gives the body energy to deal with the threat at hand. Stress can cause physical reactions that make it harder to fight infection and for cells to use their nutrients wisely.

Ways to Balance Stress

Fortunately, there are ways to manage stress that can help you feel more in control. When you become overstressed, you tax your immune system and you can get sick. Try these tips to keep your stress level in balance:

➤ Exercise regularly so you can better manage everyday physical or emotional stress, but not in the hour before bedtime.

➤ Get a good night's sleep, aiming for at least six to eight hours each night. Begin winding down at least 30 minutes before going to bed.

➤ Plan your day and week so you can control your schedule.

➤ Think positively to prevent the body's hormonal response to stress. Say to yourself, "I can handle this problem. It's not as bad as it seemed at first glance."

➤ Talk things out with someone when you need extra support. Find a good friend, a family member, a support group or a counselor to talk to.

➤ Try yoga, the practice of balancing mind, body and spirit by deep breathing, stretching, strengthening and meditating. Or try progressive muscle relaxation, by tensing and relaxing muscle groups in a sequenced pattern. Both practices can help you relax.

- ➤ Enjoy a quiet moment of contemplation, mindfulness or meditation by closing your eyes, focusing on one thought, word, image or sound, and allowing other thoughts to float away. Meditation can provide a sense of peacefulness and inner calm.

- ➤ Laugh out loud (at yourself, if necessary) to keep your spirits up. Studies show that laughter has a calming effect—having a smile on your face makes it easier to cope with stress. An ancient Chinese proverb says that a laugh is a smile that bursts.

- ➤ Try aromatherapy. Comforting aromas, like lavender, cinnamon, cloves, ginger, orange, peppermint, lemon and lime, have been found to help people relax.

- ➤ Listen to music. A great way to unwind, listening to music helps you focus on something besides the issue at hand.

DE-STRESSING RECIPES: TRY ONE OF THESE EASY, HOMEMADE REMEDIES TO HELP YOU WIND DOWN AFTER A STRESSFUL DAY OR EVENT.

Lemon Massage Oil

1/3 cup almond, canola or grapeseed oil
1/8 teaspoon vitamin E oil
5 drops lemon essential oil*
Glass bottle with stopper or secure cap

Never apply essential oils directly to skin; always dilute with another oil or water. Consult your physician before using essential oils if you are pregnant or your skin is sensitive to light.

1. Place almond oil, vitamin E oil and lemon essential oil in bottle. Seal and shake well.

2. Pour 1 tablespoon of oil into hand to warm it, then apply to body using a circular motion.

3. Store remaining oil in cool, dark place or in refrigerator. Let refrigerated oil return to room temperature before using.

Warming Neck Sock

3 packages (18 oz each) buckwheat kernels or groats (kasha)
1 cup or more dried lavender blossoms, hibiscus or clover flowers (or a combination of your choice)
Knee-high sock
Ribbon, if desired

1. Mix buckwheat groats and dried flowers in large paper grocery bag.

2. Pour buckwheat mixture from a corner of the bag into sock. It may be easier if you use a funnel or have someone hold the sock for you.

3. Tie knot in top of sock; tie ribbon around sock and over the knot.

4. Warm sock in microwave on High 2 minutes. (Be sure it is not hot before you touch it.) Place sock across the back of neck and shoulders and relax!

Grilled Chicken Skewers with Peanut Sauce

PREP TIME: 30 Minutes   **START TO FINISH:** 1 Hour 20 Minutes   **4 SERVINGS**

BETTY'S TIP
Rich in protein and heart-healthy fat, a little bit of peanut butter goes a long way. Just a tablespoon of this nutty spread can help you feel full, which can keep you from overindulging on other foods.

CHICKEN

8 bamboo skewers (8 inches long)

1 lb boneless skinless chicken breasts, cut into 1-inch pieces

1/4 cup teriyaki marinade and sauce (from 15-oz bottle)

RICE

1 cup uncooked instant brown rice

1 1/4 cups water

SAUCE

1/4 cup creamy peanut butter

1 tablespoon chopped fresh cilantro

3 tablespoons teriyaki marinade and sauce (from 15-oz bottle)

1 tablespoon lime juice

1/4 teaspoon red pepper sauce

4 medium green onions, chopped (1/4 cup)

2 cloves garlic, finely chopped

1. Soak bamboo skewers in water at least 30 minutes before using to prevent burning. In medium bowl, mix chicken and 1/4 cup teriyaki marinade. Cover; refrigerate 30 to 60 minutes to marinate.

2. Meanwhile, heat coals or gas grill for direct heat. In small bowl, stir all sauce ingredients until blended; set aside.

3. Remove chicken from marinade; discard marinade. Thread chicken on skewers. Place skewers on grill. Cover grill; cook over medium heat 8 to 10 minutes, turning once, until chicken is no longer pink in center.

4. Meanwhile, cook rice in water as directed on package, omitting butter and salt. Sprinkle chicken with additional chopped fresh cilantro if desired. Serve with sauce and rice.

To Broil: Place skewered chicken on rack in broiler pan. Broil with tops 4 to 5 inches from heat 8 to 10 minutes, turning once, until chicken is no longer pink in center.

"I never watch TV after 9:00 p.m. I reserve that time for reconnecting with my husband (maybe with a glass of wine) and for putting on my pj's and reading myself to sleep." —Andi B.

1 Serving: Calories 430 (Calories from Fat 120); Total Fat 13g (Saturated Fat 3g; Trans Fat 0g; Omega-3 0g); Cholesterol 70mg; Sodium 840mg; Total Carbohydrate 43g (Dietary Fiber 6g; Sugars 4g); Protein 34g   **% Daily Value:** Potassium 12%; Vitamin A 2%; Vitamin C 2%; Calcium 4%; Iron 10%; Folic Acid 8%   **Exchanges:** 2 Starch, 1 Other Carbohydrate, 4 Very Lean Meat, 2 Fat   **Carbohydrate Choices:** 3

Polynesian Chicken Salad

PREP TIME: 20 Minutes **START TO FINISH:** 20 Minutes **4 SERVINGS** (1 1/2 cups each)

2 teaspoons sesame seed

2 cups water

1 package (3 oz) chicken-flavor ramen noodle soup mix

1 can (8 oz) pineapple tidbits, drained, 2 tablespoons juice reserved

2 tablespoons white vinegar

2 tablespoons reduced-sodium soy sauce

1 tablespoon honey

1/2 teaspoon ground ginger

3 cups shredded cabbage

1 cup cut-up cooked chicken

8 medium green onions, sliced (1/2 cup)

1/2 cup shredded carrot

1. Heat oven to 350°F. In ungreased shallow pan, spread sesame seed. Bake 8 to 10 minutes, stirring occasionally, until golden brown and aromatic. Set aside.

2. In 2-quart saucepan, heat water to boiling. Break up ramen noodles before opening pouch. Remove seasoning packet from pouch. Add ramen noodles to boiling water. Cook 2 to 3 minutes, stirring occasionally, until noodles are tender; drain. Rinse in cold water to cool; drain.

3. In small bowl or 1-cup measuring cup, mix reserved pineapple juice, 1/2 teaspoon seasoning from ramen seasoning packet, the vinegar, soy sauce, honey and ginger. Set aside.

4. In large bowl, mix noodles, pineapple, cabbage, chicken, onions and carrot. Stir in dressing and sesame seed.

NOTE FROM DR. R
Specific medical tests are needed at different times in a woman's life to stay well at every age. For a list of what tests to have at which age, see pages 236–237.

1 Serving: Calories 260 (Calories from Fat 70); Total Fat 8g (Saturated Fat 2g; Trans Fat 1.5g; Omega-3 0g); Cholesterol 30mg; Sodium 670mg; Total Carbohydrate 33g (Dietary Fiber 4g; Sugars 16g); Protein 14g **% Daily Value:** Potassium 12%; Vitamin A 40%; Vitamin C 45%; Calcium 6%; Iron 10%; Folic Acid 20% **Exchanges:** 1 Starch, 1 Other Carbohydrate, 1 1/2 Lean Meat, 1/2 Fat **Carbohydrate Choices:** 2

Fruity Chicken Salad with Spring Greens and Pecans

PREP TIME: 20 Minutes   **START TO FINISH:** 20 Minutes   **4 SERVINGS**

2 boneless skinless chicken breasts (4 oz each)

1 cup cut-up red grapes

2 medium stalks celery, thinly sliced (1 cup)

1/2 cup dried cherries

1/4 cup finely chopped onion

3/4 cup fat-free honey-mustard dressing or other fat-free dressing

8 cups mixed spring greens

1/4 cup chopped pecans, toasted*

*To toast nuts, spread in ungreased shallow pan and bake at 350°F for 6 to 10 minutes, stirring occasionally, until nuts are light brown and aromatic.

1. Heat gas or charcoal grill. Place chicken on grill. Cover grill; cook over medium heat 7 to 10 minutes, turning halfway through cooking, until juice of chicken is clear when center of thickest part is cut (170°F). Cool; cut into bite-size pieces.

2. In large bowl, mix chicken, grapes, celery, cherries, onion and 1/2 cup of the dressing.

3. Divide greens among 4 plates. Top with chicken mixture; sprinkle with pecans. Drizzle each salad with 1 tablespoon dressing.

BETTY'S TIP

Dried fruits can be a good source of nutrients and should be counted in the daily number of fruit servings. In this tasty salad, you can try other types of dried fruits, such as dried cranberries, cut-up dried apricots or golden raisins.

"Most mornings, I head to the gym to get my workout done before things come up and take over my time. It's both refreshing and gets me going, at the same time." —Cheri O.

1 Serving: Calories 300 (Calories from Fat 70); Total Fat 7g (Saturated Fat 1g; Trans Fat 0g; Omega-3 0g); Cholesterol 35mg; Sodium 600mg; Total Carbohydrate 42g (Dietary Fiber 6g; Sugars 26g); Protein 16g   **% Daily Value:** Potassium 21%; Vitamin A 120%; Vitamin C 40%; Calcium 10%; Iron 15%; Folic Acid 35%   **Exchanges:** 2 Other Carbohydrate, 2 Vegetable, 2 Very Lean Meat, 1 Fat   **Carbohydrate Choices:** 3

Greek Turkey Burgers with Yogurt Sauce

PREP TIME: 20 Minutes **START TO FINISH:** 20 Minutes **4 SERVINGS**

SAUCE
1/2 cup plain fat-free yogurt
1/4 cup chopped red onion
1/4 cup chopped cucumber

BURGERS
1 lb lean ground turkey
1/2 cup plain fat-free yogurt
1 teaspoon dried oregano leaves
1/2 teaspoon garlic powder
1/2 teaspoon salt
1/2 teaspoon pepper
4 whole wheat hamburger buns

1. In small bowl, mix all sauce ingredients; refrigerate until ready to serve.

2. Set oven control to broil. In medium bowl, mix all burger ingredients except buns. Shape mixture into 4 patties, each about 1/2 inch thick and 5 inches in diameter. Place on rack in broiler pan.

3. Broil burgers with tops about 6 inches from heat 8 to 10 minutes, turning after 5 minutes, until thermometer inserted in center reads 165°F. Place burgers on buns. Serve with sauce.

NOTE FROM DR. R
If you haven't worked out before, it's a good idea to see your doctor for an evaluation before you begin exercising. You may be asked to do a treadmill test or stress test to determine an appropriate and safe level to start.

1 Serving: Calories 310 (Calories from Fat 70); Total Fat 8g (Saturated Fat 2g; Trans Fat 0.5g; Omega-3 0g); Cholesterol 75mg; Sodium 640mg; Total Carbohydrate 26g (Dietary Fiber 3g; Sugars 8g); Protein 33g **% Daily Value:** Potassium 15%; Vitamin A 0%; Vitamin C 0%; Calcium 15%; Iron 15%; Folic Acid 10% **Exchanges:** 1 Starch, 1/2 Other Carbohydrate, 4 1/2 Very Lean Meat, 1 Fat **Carbohydrate Choices:** 2

6

Great Whole Grains and Beans

Discover the heartiness and earthiness of grains and beans

Mediterranean Quinoa Salad

PREP TIME: 30 Minutes   **START TO FINISH:** 1 Hour 35 Minutes   **4 SERVINGS** (3/4 cup each)

1 cup uncooked quinoa
2 cups reduced-sodium chicken broth
1/2 cup chopped drained roasted red bell peppers (from 7-oz jar)
1/2 cup cubed provolone cheese
1/4 cup chopped Kalamata olives
2 tablespoons chopped fresh basil leaves
1 teaspoon roasted garlic (from 4-oz jar)
2 tablespoons fat-free Italian dressing

BETTY'S TIP

Quinoa is an excellent whole grain because it is a complete protein, it tastes great and it cooks in only a few minutes. You can cook it in chicken broth or vegetable broth for more flavor.

1. Rinse quinoa under cold water 1 minute; drain.

2. In 2-quart saucepan, heat quinoa and broth to boiling; reduce heat. Cover; simmer 15 to 20 minutes or until quinoa is tender; drain. Cool completely, about 45 minutes.

3. In large serving bowl, toss quinoa and remaining ingredients. Serve immediately, or refrigerate 1 to 2 hours before serving.

"I schedule social time with my friends. It's great for my mental health."   —Rita R.

1 Serving: Calories 250 (Calories from Fat 70); Total Fat 8g (Saturated Fat 3g; Trans Fat 0g; Omega-3 0g); Cholesterol 10mg; Sodium 590mg; Total Carbohydrate 33g (Dietary Fiber 3g; Sugars 5g); Protein 12g   **% Daily Value:** Potassium 14%; Vitamin A 30%; Vitamin C 70%; Calcium 15%; Iron 25%; Folic Acid 8%   **Exchanges:** 2 Starch, 1 High-Fat Meat **Carbohydrate Choices:** 2

Mushroom and Spinach Fettuccine

PREP TIME: 30 Minutes   **START TO FINISH:** 30 Minutes   **4 SERVINGS** (1 1/2 cups each)

8 oz uncooked fettuccine

3/4 cup roasted garlic–seasoned chicken broth (from 14-oz can)

2 packages (6 oz each) fresh baby button mushrooms, cut in half

6 cups loosely packed fresh spinach, chopped

1 cup cherry tomatoes, cut in half

1 1/2 teaspoons Italian seasoning

1/2 teaspoon salt

1/4 cup evaporated fat-free milk

1/4 to 1/2 cup finely shredded or shaved Parmesan cheese

1. Cook and drain fettuccine as directed on package, omitting salt.

2. Meanwhile, in 10-inch skillet, heat 1/4 cup of the broth to boiling over medium-high heat. Cook mushrooms in broth, stirring frequently, until almost all liquid is absorbed. Stir in additional 1/4 cup broth. Continue cooking mushrooms 4 to 6 minutes, stirring frequently, until tender.

3. Stir in remaining 1/4 cup broth; heat to boiling. Stir in spinach, tomatoes, Italian seasoning and salt. Cook 1 to 2 minutes, stirring constantly, until spinach is wilted. Stir in evaporated milk just until heated through.

4. Place fettuccine on large platter. Top with spinach mixture and cheese.

NOTE FROM DR. R

Spinach is packed with folic acid. All cells need folic acid to function normally, but recent studies show that many Americans don't get enough of this vital vitamin. Try whole wheat fettucine for added flavor and texture or mix half whole wheat and half regular pasta.

1 Serving: Calories 290 (Calories from Fat 45); Total Fat 5g (Saturated Fat 2g; Trans Fat 0g; Omega-3 0g); Cholesterol 55mg; Sodium 670mg; Total Carbohydrate 45g (Dietary Fiber 4g; Sugars 5g); Protein 16g   **% Daily Value:** Potassium 22%; Vitamin A 90%; Vitamin C 15%; Calcium 20%; Iron 25%; Folic Acid 50%   **Exchanges:** 2 1/2 Starch, 2 Vegetable, 1/2 High-Fat Meat   **Carbohydrate Choices:** 3

Noodles and
Peanut Sauce Salad Bowl

PREP TIME: 25 Minutes   **START TO FINISH:** 25 Minutes   **4 SERVINGS** (1 3/4 cups each)

8 oz uncooked whole wheat linguine, broken in half

2 cups fresh broccoli florets

1 cup julienne-cut carrots (from 10-oz bag)

1 medium bell pepper, cut into bite-size pieces

2 tablespoons water

2 teaspoons canola oil

1/4 cup peanut butter

2 tablespoons rice vinegar or white vinegar

2 tablespoons reduced-sodium soy sauce

1/2 teaspoon ground ginger

1/8 teaspoon ground red pepper (cayenne)

3 medium green onions, chopped (3 tablespoons)

3 tablespoons chopped fresh cilantro

NOTE FROM DR. R
Your mental health is as important as your physical health. Pay attention to what's happening in your life and how you feel about it. Sit quietly for a few minutes and think about your day—it's a way to rejuvenate your body, mind and soul.

1. Cook linguine as directed on package, adding broccoli, carrots and bell pepper during last minute of cooking; drain pasta and vegetables. Rinse with cold water until pasta and vegetables are cool; drain.

2. In small bowl, gradually beat water and oil into peanut butter with wire whisk until smooth. Beat in vinegar, soy sauce, ginger and ground red pepper.

3. In large serving bowl, stir together pasta mixture, peanut sauce, onions and cilantro until well mixed.

1 Serving: Calories 390 (Calories from Fat 90); Total Fat 10g (Saturated Fat 1.5g; Trans Fat 0g; Omega-3 0g); Cholesterol 0mg; Sodium 630mg; Total Carbohydrate 62g (Dietary Fiber 7g; Sugars 7g); Protein 15g   **% Daily Value:** Potassium 15%; Vitamin A 110%; Vitamin C 80%; Calcium 6%; Iron 20%; Folic Acid 45%   **Exchanges:** 2 Starch, 1 1/2 Other Carbohydrate, 2 Vegetable, 1/2 High-Fat Meat, 1 Fat   **Carbohydrate Choices:** 4

Noodles and Peanut Sauce Salad Bowl

Penne with Spinach and Ham

PREP TIME: 25 Minutes   **START TO FINISH:** 25 Minutes   **4 SERVINGS**

2 2/3 cups uncooked whole wheat penne pasta (8 oz)

2 teaspoons olive oil

1 medium onion, chopped (1/2 cup)

4 cloves garlic, finely chopped

1 1/2 cups grape tomatoes or halved cherry tomatoes

2/3 cup diced cooked ham

1/2 cup dry white wine or water

4 cups fresh spinach leaves

2 tablespoons finely shredded Parmesan cheese

BETTY'S TIP

By dicing the ham into small pieces, the flavor of the ham penetrates every bite without adding too much sodium. Add a mixed-fruit salad and whole-grain breadsticks to complete the meal.

1. Cook and drain pasta as directed on package, omitting salt.

2. Meanwhile, in 10-inch nonstick skillet, heat oil over medium heat. Cook onion and garlic in oil 3 to 4 minutes, stirring occasionally, until onion is tender. Stir in tomatoes, ham and wine. Cook and stir until some of the wine has evaporated.

3. Add spinach and pasta; toss gently. Sprinkle with cheese.

"Eating right and getting enough sleep do wonders for my ability to stay calm throughout the day."   —Mindy H.

1 Serving: Calories 330 (Calories from Fat 60); Total Fat 6g (Saturated Fat 2g; Trans Fat 0g; Omega-3 0g); Cholesterol 15mg; Sodium 410mg; Total Carbohydrate 51g (Dietary Fiber 5g; Sugars 4g); Protein 16g   **% Daily Value:** Potassium 15%; Vitamin A 70%; Vitamin C 15%; Calcium 10%; Iron 20%; Folic Acid 50%   **Exchanges:** 2 Starch, 1 Other Carbohydrate, 1 Vegetable, 1 Medium-Fat Meat   **Carbohydrate Choices:** 3 1/2

Mexican Bean and Pork Casserole

PREP TIME: 15 Minutes   **START TO FINISH:** 1 Hour 5 Minutes   **6 SERVINGS** (1 1/4 cups each)

1 lb ground pork
1 serrano chile, finely chopped
1 can (15 to 16 oz) pinto beans, drained, rinsed
1 package (1.25 oz) taco seasoning mix
1 can (10 oz) enchilada sauce
1/2 cup water
6 corn tortillas (6 inch), cut in half, then cut crosswise into 1-inch strips (about 2 cups)
1 cup shredded reduced-fat Monterey Jack or mozzarella cheese (4 oz)
1 medium tomato, chopped (3/4 cup)

1. Heat oven to 375°F. In 10-inch nonstick skillet, cook pork and chile over medium-high heat 5 to 7 minutes, stirring frequently, until pork is no longer pink; drain.

2. In ungreased 2-quart casserole, stir pork, beans, taco seasoning mix, enchilada sauce, water and tortilla strips until well mixed.

3. Cover; bake about 40 minutes or until thoroughly heated. Stir mixture; sprinkle with cheese. Bake uncovered 5 to 8 minutes longer or until cheese is melted. Top with tomato.

"I try to ensure that I get a good night's sleep. I truly believe being well-rested helps me stay healthy and maintain a better perspective on life."   —Karen K.

BETTY'S TIP
When you start adding beans to the equation, the health benefits start going up— protein, fiber, vitamins and minerals. For a change, try this casserole with 1 pound lean (at least 85%) ground beef or ground turkey instead of the pork.

1 Serving: Calories 390 (Calories from Fat 140); Total Fat 16g (Saturated Fat 7g; Trans Fat 0g; Omega-3 0g); Cholesterol 60mg; Sodium 680mg; Total Carbohydrate 35g (Dietary Fiber 8g; Sugars 6g); Protein 26g   **% Daily Value:** Potassium 18%; Vitamin A 25%; Vitamin C 15%; Calcium 25%; Iron 15%; Folic Acid 40%   **Exchanges:** 1 1/2 Starch, 1 Other Carbohydrate, 3 Medium-Fat Meat   **Carbohydrate Choices:** 2

Lentil-Corn Pilaf

PREP TIME: 10 Minutes   **START TO FINISH:** 30 Minutes   **4 SERVINGS** (about 1 cup each)

2 cups water
1 cup dried lentils (8 oz), sorted, rinsed
1/2 cup chopped red bell pepper
1 cup frozen (thawed) or canned (drained) whole kernel corn
2 tablespoons chopped fresh cilantro or parsley
1/2 teaspoon chili powder
1/2 teaspoon salt

BETTY'S TIP
This fiber-rich pilaf makes a terrific accompaniment to grilled chops or baked chicken. Double the serving size to make it a main dish.

1. In 2-quart saucepan, heat water to boiling. Stir in lentils and bell pepper; reduce heat. Cover; simmer 15 to 20 minutes or until lentils are tender. Drain if necessary.

2. Stir in remaining ingredients. Cook over low heat 2 to 3 minutes, stirring occasionally, until corn is tender and hot.

"Having someone clean my house was the single best thing *I did to relieve stress in my life."*   —Billie F.

1 Serving: Calories 310 (Calories from Fat 10); Total Fat 1.5g (Saturated Fat 0g; Trans Fat 0g; Omega-3 0g); Cholesterol 0mg; Sodium 410mg; Total Carbohydrate 54g (Dietary Fiber 14g; Sugars 4g); Protein 20g   **% Daily Value:** Potassium 27%; Vitamin A 20%; Vitamin C 45%; Calcium 4%; Iron 40%; Folic Acid 100%   **Exchanges:** 3 Starch, 1/2 Other Carbohydrate, 1 1/2 Very Lean Meat   **Carbohydrate Choices:** 3 1/2

Lentil-Corn Pilaf

Slow Cooker Mediterranean Minestrone Casserole

PREP TIME: 20 Minutes   **START TO FINISH:** 6 Hours 40 Minutes   **5 SERVINGS** (about 1 1/2 cups each)

3 medium carrots, sliced (1 1/2 cups)

1 medium onion, chopped (1/2 cup)

1 cup water

2 teaspoons sugar

1 1/2 teaspoons Italian seasoning

1/4 teaspoon pepper

1 can (28 oz) diced tomatoes, undrained

1 can (15 to 16 oz) garbanzo beans, drained, rinsed

1 can (6 oz) no-salt-added tomato paste

2 cloves garlic, finely chopped

1 1/2 cups frozen cut green beans (from 1-lb bag), thawed

1 cup uncooked elbow macaroni (3 1/2 oz)

1/2 cup shredded Parmesan cheese (2 oz)

NOTE FROM DR. R

Eating plenty of fruits and vegetables every day is an important part of wellness. Choose from a variety of those that are bright and colorful. They are a treasure trove of vitamins and phytonutrients.

1. In 3- to 4-quart slow cooker, mix all ingredients except green beans, macaroni and cheese.

2. Cover; cook on Low heat setting 6 to 8 hours.

3. About 20 minutes before serving, stir in green beans and macaroni. Increase heat setting to High. Cover; cook about 20 minutes or until beans and macaroni are tender. Sprinkle with cheese.

"When I'm feeling the need for some quick exercise or to clear my head of stressful thoughts, I put on lively music and dance around my house."   —Anne O.

1 Serving: Calories 370 (Calories from Fat 50); Total Fat 6g (Saturated Fat 2g; Trans Fat 0g; Omega-3 0g); Cholesterol 10mg; Sodium 440mg; Total Carbohydrate 63g (Dietary Fiber 12g; Sugars 14g); Protein 17g   **% Daily Value:** Potassium 21%; Vitamin A 100%; Vitamin C 20%; Calcium 25%; Iron 30%; Folic Acid 50%   **Exchanges:** 3 Starch, 1 Other Carbohydrate, 1 Vegetable, 1 Lean Meat   **Carbohydrate Choices:** 4

Kasha Tabbouleh

PREP TIME: 20 Minutes   **START TO FINISH:** 2 Hours 20 Minutes   **4 SERVINGS** (1 1/2 cups each)

2 cups water

1 cup uncooked buckwheat kernels or groats (kasha)

1 1/2 cups finely chopped fresh parsley

1 1/2 cups chopped seeded tomatoes (about 2 medium)

1/3 cup chopped onion (about 1 medium)

1/4 cup chopped fresh or 2 teaspoons dried mint leaves

1 small cucumber, peeled, chopped (3/4 cup)

1 can (15 to 16 oz) garbanzo beans, drained, rinsed

1/4 cup lemon juice

1 tablespoon honey

2 teaspoons Dijon mustard

2 teaspoons grated lemon peel

1/2 teaspoon salt

1/4 teaspoon pepper

4 lettuce leaves

BETTY'S TIP

Besides being a whole grain, kasha contains many important vitamins and minerals. This is a colorful, flavorful salad that is easy to make, and leftovers can be stored for a couple of days in the refrigerator.

1. In 2-quart saucepan, heat water to boiling. Stir in buckwheat kernels. Heat to boiling; reduce heat. Cover; simmer about 25 minutes or until water is absorbed and buckwheat is tender. Cover; refrigerate 25 minutes to cool.

2. In large glass or plastic bowl, mix buckwheat, parsley, tomatoes, onion, mint, cucumber and beans.

3. In small bowl, mix remaining ingredients except lettuce; toss with buckwheat mixture. Cover; refrigerate at least 1 hour. Serve on lettuce.

---

1 Serving: Calories 320 (Calories from Fat 35); Total Fat 3.5g (Saturated Fat 0.5g; Trans Fat 0g; Omega-3 0g); Cholesterol 0mg; Sodium 390mg; Total Carbohydrate 58g (Dietary Fiber 11g; Sugars 9g); Protein 13g   **% Daily Value:** Potassium 21%; Vitamin A 50%; Vitamin C 40%; Calcium 10%; Iron 30%; Folic Acid 60%   **Exchanges:** 3 1/2 Starch, 1 Vegetable **Carbohydrate Choices:** 4

Savory Slow-Cooked Grains

PREP TIME: 25 Minutes **START TO FINISH:** 4 Hours 55 Minutes **11 SERVINGS** (1 1/2 cups each)

1 cup uncooked brown rice

1/2 cup uncooked wild rice

1/2 cup uncooked green lentils

3 cups coarsely chopped fresh mushrooms (8 oz)

1 cup coarsely chopped carrots (2 medium)

3/4 cup chopped green onions (12 medium)

1 container (32 oz) roasted vegetable stock or chicken broth (4 cups)

2 tablespoons tamari sauce

2 tablespoons dry sherry, if desired

2 tablespoons butter or margarine, melted

1/2 teaspoon dried thyme leaves

1/2 teaspoon garlic salt

1/4 cup chopped walnuts, toasted (page 162)

1/3 cup finely chopped parsley

BETTY'S TIP

If you're looking to add more grains to your dinners, this recipe is a great one to start with. Using a slow cooker is a terrific way to prepare grains, because some take a while to cook. The carrots add color and extra crunch to this wonderful side or main dish.

1. In 3 1/2- to 4-quart slow cooker, mix all ingredients except walnuts and parsley.

2. Cover; cook on Low heat setting 4 hours 30 minutes to 5 hours 30 minutes or until grains are tender. Stir before serving. Sprinkle with walnuts and parsley.

"I combine brown and white rice because brown rice takes a little time to get used to." —Sheila B.

1 Serving: Calories 180 (Calories from Fat 40); Total Fat 4.5g (Saturated Fat 1.5g; Trans Fat 0g; Omega-3 0g); Cholesterol 5mg; Sodium 440mg; Total Carbohydrate 29g (Dietary Fiber 5g; Sugars 3g); Protein 6g **% Daily Value:** Potassium 9%; Vitamin A 40%; Vitamin C 4%; Calcium 4%; Iron 10%; Folic Acid 15% **Exchanges:** 2 Starch, 1 Fat **Carbohydrate Choices:** 2

Red Harvest Quinoa

PREP TIME: 20 Minutes   **START TO FINISH:** 40 Minutes   **8 SERVINGS** (1/2 cup each)

1 cup uncooked red or white quinoa

1 tablespoon butter or margarine

1/4 cup chopped red onion

1/3 cup chopped celery

1/2 cup coarsely chopped baking apple

1 1/2 cups roasted vegetable stock (from 32-oz container) or chicken broth

1/2 cup orange juice

1/2 cup dried cranberries

1 jar (1 3/4 oz) pine nuts (about 1/3 cup), toasted (page 162)

1/4 cup shredded Parmesan cheese (1 oz)

1/4 teaspoon salt

2 tablespoons finely chopped parsley

1. Rinse quinoa under cold water 1 minute; drain well.

2. In 2-quart saucepan, melt butter over medium heat. Cook onion, celery, apple and quinoa in butter 5 minutes, stirring occasionally.

3. Stir in vegetable stock and orange juice. Heat to boiling; reduce heat. Cover; simmer 15 to 20 minutes or until all liquid is absorbed and quinoa is tender. Fluff with fork.

4. Stir in cranberries, nuts, cheese and salt. Sprinkle with parsley.

"I play fetch with my dog. Her joy is infectious."   —Heidi L.

NOTE FROM DR. R
Once you get used to eating grains, you'll want to serve them often. Quinoa is high in protein, low in fat and cooks quickly, making it a great grain to use. The cranberry, orange and apple are reminiscent of fall and heartier eating. If you'd like to reduce the saturated fat, use canola oil instead of butter.

1 Serving: Calories 190 (Calories from Fat 70); Total Fat 8g (Saturated Fat 2g; Trans Fat 0g; Omega-3 0g); Cholesterol 5mg; Sodium 340mg; Total Carbohydrate 26g (Dietary Fiber 2g; Sugars 10g); Protein 5g   **% Daily Value:** Potassium 8%; Vitamin A 8%; Vitamin C 6%; Calcium 6%; Iron 15%; Folic Acid 6%   **Exchanges:** 1 1/2 Starch, 1 1/2 Fat
Carbohydrate Choices: 2

Farmers' Market Barley Risotto

PREP TIME: 1 Hour 15 Minutes **START TO FINISH:** 1 Hour 15 Minutes **4 SERVINGS** (1 1/2 cups each)

1 tablespoon olive oil
1 medium onion, chopped (1/2 cup)
1 medium bell pepper, coarsely chopped (1 cup)
2 cups chopped fresh mushrooms (4 oz)
1 cup frozen whole kernel corn (from 1-lb bag)
1 cup uncooked medium pearled barley
1/4 cup dry white wine or chicken broth
2 cups roasted vegetable stock or chicken broth
3 cups water
1 1/2 cups grape tomatoes, cut in half (if large, cut into quarters)
2/3 cup shredded Parmesan cheese
3 tablespoons chopped fresh or 1 teaspoon dried basil leaves
1/2 teaspoon pepper

NOTE FROM DR. R
Risotto is traditionally made by stirring small amounts of broth into rice throughout the cook time to get the chewy texture. This recipe uses barley instead of rice. Barley is high in soluble fiber and may have the same cholesterol-lowering properties as oats.

1. In 4-quart Dutch oven, heat oil over medium heat. Cook onion, bell pepper, mushrooms and corn in oil about 5 minutes, stirring frequently, until onion is crisp-tender. Add barley, stirring about 1 minute to coat.

2. Stir in wine and 1/2 cup of the vegetable stock. Cook 5 minutes, stirring frequently, until liquid is almost absorbed. Repeat with remaining stock and 3 cups water, adding 1/2 to 3/4 cup of stock or water at a time and stirring frequently, until absorbed.

3. Stir in tomatoes, 1/3 cup of the cheese, the basil and pepper. Cook until thoroughly heated. Sprinkle with remaining 1/3 cup cheese.

1 Serving: Calories 360 (Calories from Fat 70); Total Fat 8g (Saturated Fat 3g; Trans Fat 0g; Omega-3 0g); Cholesterol 10mg; Sodium 740mg; Total Carbohydrate 57g (Dietary Fiber 11g; Sugars 8g); Protein 13g **% Daily Value:** Potassium 19%; Vitamin A 50%; Vitamin C 70%; Calcium 20%; Iron 15%; Folic Acid 15% **Exchanges:** 3 1/2 Starch, 1 Vegetable, 1 Fat **Carbohydrate Choices:** 4

Farmers' Market Barley Risotto

Tarragon-Couscous Salad

PREP TIME: 20 Minutes   **START TO FINISH:** 40 Minutes   **8 SERVINGS** (1/2 cup each)

3 cups water
1/2 cup dried red lentils, sorted, rinsed
2 teaspoons olive oil
1/4 teaspoon salt
3/4 cup uncooked couscous
3 tablespoons olive oil
3 tablespoons seasoned rice vinegar
1 teaspoon Dijon mustard
1 clove garlic, finely chopped
1/2 cup finely chopped carrot (about 1 medium)
4 medium green onions, finely chopped (1/4 cup)
1/4 cup chopped walnuts, toasted (page 162)
2 tablespoons chopped fresh parsley
1 tablespoon chopped fresh or 1 teaspoon crushed dried tarragon leaves

BETTY'S TIP
This dish contains the freshness of a farmers' market. Tarragon is a nice touch with mild-tasting couscous, but cut back a bit if it is not your favorite flavor. Or you can double the amount of parsley and leave out the tarragon. Try whole wheat couscous for a more grainy look and texture.

1. In 1-quart saucepan, heat 2 cups of the water to boiling. Stir in lentils; reduce heat to low. Cook 10 to 12 minutes or until just tender. Drain; cool 15 minutes.

2. Meanwhile, in 1-quart saucepan, heat remaining 1 cup water, 2 teaspoons oil and the salt to boiling. Stir in couscous; remove from heat. Cover; let stand 5 minutes. Fluff couscous lightly with fork. Cool 10 minutes.

3. Meanwhile, in medium bowl, beat 3 tablespoons oil, the vinegar, mustard and garlic with wire whisk until blended. Stir in carrot, onions, walnuts, parsley and tarragon. Stir in lentils and couscous. Serve immediately or refrigerate until serving.

1 Serving: Calories 190 (Calories from Fat 80); Total Fat 9g (Saturated Fat 1g; Trans Fat 0g; Omega-3 0g); Cholesterol 0mg; Sodium 100mg; Total Carbohydrate 21g (Dietary Fiber 3g; Sugars 1g); Protein 6g   **% Daily Value:** Potassium 6%; Vitamin A 20%; Vitamin C 6%; Calcium 2%; Iron 8%; Folic Acid 20%   **Exchanges:** 1 1/2 Starch, 1 1/2 Fat
Carbohydrate Choices: 1 1/2

Tofu Stroganoff on Wild Rice

PREP TIME: 35 Minutes   **START TO FINISH:** 1 Hour 25 Minutes   **6 SERVINGS** (about 1 cup stroganoff and 1 cup wild rice)

2 cups uncooked wild rice

5 cups water

2 packages (1 lb each) firm reduced-fat tofu, drained

1/4 cup reduced-fat sour cream

1 tablespoon tomato paste or ketchup

2 cloves garlic, chopped

1 teaspoon reduced-sodium soy sauce

1/2 teaspoon salt

1/8 teaspoon ground red pepper (cayenne)

1 tablespoon olive oil

1 tablespoon butter or margarine

3 small onions, finely chopped (1 1/2 cups)

2 tablespoons reduced-sodium soy sauce

4 cups sliced baby portabella mushrooms (8 oz)

1/4 cup finely chopped fresh parsley

Freshly ground pepper to taste

1. In 3-quart saucepan, heat wild rice and water to boiling; reduce heat to low. Cover; simmer 40 to 50 minutes.

2. Meanwhile, in blender or food processor, place 1 package of tofu, the sour cream, tomato paste, garlic, 1 teaspoon soy sauce, the salt and red pepper. Cover; blend on high 1 to 2 minutes, stopping blender frequently to scrape sides, until smooth; set aside.

3. Cut remaining package of tofu into 1-inch cubes. In 12-inch skillet, heat oil over medium heat. Cook cubed tofu in oil about 10 minutes, stirring occasionally, until tofu starts to turn light golden brown; remove from skillet and set aside.

4. Add butter to skillet. Cook onions in butter 4 to 5 minutes, stirring occasionally, until softened. Stir in 2 tablespoons soy sauce and the mushrooms. Cook 3 to 4 minutes, stirring occasionally, until mushrooms are tender.

5. Stir tofu cubes and sauce into mushroom mixture. Cook 5 to 8 minutes, stirring occasionally, until thoroughly heated. Serve over wild rice. Sprinkle with parsley and pepper.

NOTE FROM DR. R
This stroganoff is a nice alternative to the typical meat and pasta one. Tofu is an excellent source of cholesterol-free, high-quality protein. Soy contains polyunsaturated fats, fiber and calcium—a super food!

1 Serving: Calories 370 (Calories from Fat 60); Total Fat 7g (Saturated Fat 2.5g; Trans Fat 0g; Omega-3 0g); Cholesterol 10mg; Sodium 590mg; Total Carbohydrate 55g (Dietary Fiber 5g; Sugars 7g); Protein 21g   **% Daily Value:** Potassium 17%; Vitamin A 8%; Vitamin C 6%; Calcium 10%; Iron 20%; Folic Acid 30%   **Exchanges:** 3 Starch, 1/2 Other Carbohydrate, 1 1/2 Lean Meat   **Carbohydrate Choices:** 3 1/2

Exercise to Stay Healthy

Want a magic potion for feeling good all your life, no matter what your age? Exercise is it! The good, old-fashioned, sweat-inducing kind. Even light intensity exercise allows the release of endorphins (the body's painkillers) in your body, reducing feelings of tension and anxiety.

Exercise benefits your life by:

➤ Strengthening your cardiovascular and respiratory systems

➤ Keeping your bones and muscles strong

➤ Managing your weight

➤ Easing depression and managing stress and pain

➤ Helping you sleep better

➤ Reducing your risk of certain types of cancer

➤ Preventing and managing diabetes

➤ Increasing your energy

What kind of exercise is best for you? Probably a combination of several. Pick ones that you enjoy so you will stick with them. Common exercises and their descriptions follow:

Warm-up and cool-down: A proper warm-up allows for a gradual increase in blood flow, body temperature and heart rate. Your workout will be more efficient if you warm up. End your exercise session with a cool-down, a slower pace with smaller movements. This allows your heart rate to lower and your muscles to ease into a slower pace, decreasing the risk of muscle soreness and injury.

Aerobic: Continuous, rhythmic exercises, like walking briskly, jumping rope, dancing, jogging, running or cycling. Make your workout intense enough to feel like you're working but not so strenuous that you can't pass the "talk test," being able to have a conversation with someone during the activity.

Strength training: Important for women because it helps:

➤ Develop and maintain strong bones

➤ Maintain muscle

➤ Control body fat

➤ Reduce risk of injury

➤ Improve sense of well-being

Stretching: Follow each workout with a few minutes of stretching. Move into each stretch with slow, controlled, pain-free motion. Once you feel mild resistance from the targeted muscle, hold that position for at least 15 to 30 seconds. Repeat this process for each major muscle group to ensure uniform, full body benefits.

Pilates: Developed by Joseph Pilates in 1945, these core-strengthening exercises complement other types of exercise. Pilates is designed to stretch, strengthen and balance the body. It builds strength, creates a sleek toned body, teaches good body awareness and improves posture. Pilates also improves flexibility and may alleviate back pain because it strengthens the back muscles.

Yoga: The practice of balancing mind, body and spirit by deep breathing, Yoga postures stretch, strengthen and tone. Regular practice enhances health and well-being. Yoga is ideally practiced under the guidance of a certified instructor.

EXERCISE ADVICE DID YOU KNOW THAT THREE 10-MINUTE BRISK WALKS OR OTHER EXERCISE ARE AS EFFECTIVE FOR IMPROVING FITNESS AS A SINGLE 30-MINUTE SESSION?

GET ENOUGH LIQUID BEFORE, DURING AND AFTER YOUR WORKOUTS. WATER IS THE BEST DRINK AND THE KEY IS TO REPLENISH YOUR LIQUID LEVEL. A GOOD RULE OF THUMB IS TO TAKE IN 6 TO 8 OUNCES EVERY 20 MINUTES WHILE EXERCISING.

PHYSICAL ACTIVITY PYRAMID

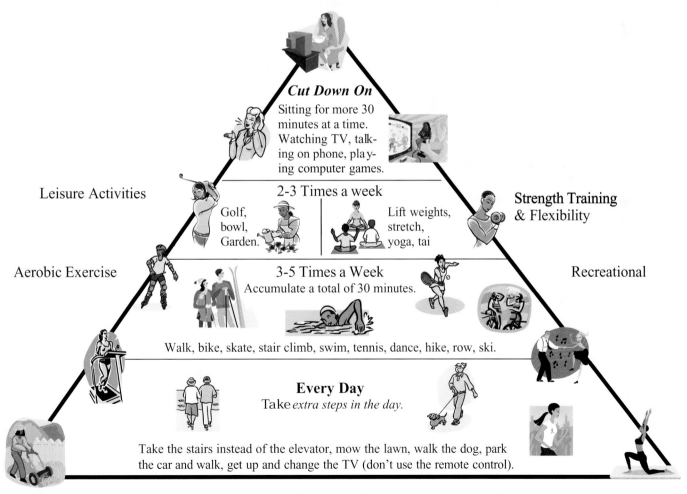

Cut Down On
Sitting for more 30 minutes at a time. Watching TV, talking on phone, playing computer games.

Leisure Activities

2-3 Times a week

Golf, bowl, Garden.

Lift weights, stretch, yoga, tai

Strength Training & Flexibility

Aerobic Exercise

3-5 Times a Week
Accumulate a total of 30 minutes.

Recreational

Walk, bike, skate, stair climb, swim, tennis, dance, hike, row, ski.

Every Day
Take *extra steps in the day.*

Take the stairs instead of the elevator, mow the lawn, walk the dog, park the car and walk, get up and change the TV (don't use the remote control).

Red Pepper Polenta with Gorgonzola

PREP TIME: 45 Minutes   **START TO FINISH:** 1 Hour   **8 SERVINGS**

2 teaspoons olive oil
2 cloves garlic, finely chopped
1/2 cup coarsely chopped red bell pepper
2 cups roasted vegetable stock (from 32-oz container) or chicken broth
1 cup fat-free (skim) milk
1 cup uncooked corn grits or cornmeal
1/2 teaspoon salt
1/2 cup crumbled Gorgonzola cheese (2 oz)

BETTY'S TIP
You can use cornmeal for a softer polenta, but be sure to stir it in slowly to avoid lumps.

1. In 2-quart saucepan, heat oil over medium heat. Cook garlic and bell pepper in oil about 2 minutes, stirring occasionally, until bell pepper is crisp-tender.

2. Stir in vegetable stock and milk; heat to boiling. Gradually stir in grits and salt; reduce heat to low. Simmer uncovered about 30 minutes, stirring frequently, until slightly thickened.

3. Spray 10-inch pie plate with cooking spray. Pour polenta into pie plate. Sprinkle with cheese. Let stand about 10 minutes or until cheese is melted and polenta is firm enough to cut. Cut into 8 wedges.

"I know that my weight is going to ebb and flow at times, but if I keep up my healthy habits, I will go back to my balance weight."
—Amity D.

1 Serving: Calories 120 (Calories from Fat 30); Total Fat 3.5g (Saturated Fat 1.5g; Trans Fat 0g; Omega-3 0g); Cholesterol 5mg; Sodium 510mg; Total Carbohydrate 19g (Dietary Fiber 0g; Sugars 3g); Protein 4g   **% Daily Value:** Potassium 4%; Vitamin A 15%; Vitamin C 15%; Calcium 8%; Iron 4%; Folic Acid 8%   **Exchanges:** 1 Starch, 1/2 Fat   **Carbohydrate Choices:** 1

Tofu Stir-Fry with Black Bean Sauce

PREP TIME: 25 Minutes   **START TO FINISH:** 1 Hour 25 Minutes   **5 SERVINGS** (about 1 cup tofu mixture and 1 cup rice each)

3 cups water

1 1/2 cups uncooked brown basmati rice

1 tablespoon olive oil

1 large onion, thinly sliced (1 cup)

4 cups chopped fresh broccoli

1 medium red bell pepper, cut into 1/2-inch slices, slices cut in half (about 1 cup)

1/3 cup black bean garlic sauce (from 7-oz jar)

2 tablespoons soy sauce

1 tablespoon chili garlic sauce (from 6.5-oz jar)

1 package (12.3 oz) firm reduced-fat tofu, cut into 3/4-inch cubes (2 cups)

1/3 cup chopped fresh cilantro

1/4 cup honey-roasted or regular sunflower nuts

BETTY'S TIP

The sauce with this stir-fry has an excellent, high-profile flavor and gets its dark color from the black bean sauce, soy sauce and chili garlic sauce.

1. In 2-quart saucepan, heat water to boiling. Stir in rice; reduce heat to low. Cover; simmer 45 to 50 minutes or until water is absorbed.

2. Meanwhile, in 12-inch heavy skillet, heat oil over medium-high heat. Cook onion in oil about 2 minutes, stirring occasionally, until crisp-tender. Add broccoli and bell pepper; stir-fry about 2 minutes or until almost crisp-tender.

3. In small bowl, mix black bean sauce, soy sauce and chili garlic sauce. Stir sauce into vegetable mixture to coat.

4. Add tofu to vegetable mixture; stir-fry 2 to 3 minutes or until thoroughly heated. Stir in cilantro. Sprinkle with nuts before serving. Serve over rice.

1 Serving: Calories 340 (Calories from Fat 90); Total Fat 10g (Saturated Fat 1.5g; Trans Fat 0g; Omega-3 0g); Cholesterol 0mg; Sodium 540mg; Total Carbohydrate 48g (Dietary Fiber 9g; Sugars 4g); Protein 14g   **% Daily Value:** Potassium 12%; Vitamin A 25%; Vitamin C 45%; Calcium 15%; Iron 15%; Folic Acid 25%   **Exchanges:** 3 Starch, 1 Vegetable, 1/2 Medium-Fat Meat, 1 Fat   **Carbohydrate Choices:** 3

Mushroom-Pepper
Whole Wheat Sandwiches

PREP TIME: 30 Minutes   **START TO FINISH:** 30 Minutes   **4 SANDWICHES**

4 medium fresh portabella mushroom caps (3 1/2 to 4 inch)
4 slices red onion, 1/2 inch thick
2 tablespoons reduced-fat mayonnaise or salad dressing
2 teaspoons reduced-fat balsamic vinaigrette
8 slices whole wheat bread
4 slices (3/4 oz each) reduced-fat mozzarella cheese
8 strips (2 × 1 inch) roasted red bell pepper (from 7-oz jar), patted dry
8 large basil leaves

1. Heat closed medium-size contact grill for 5 minutes.

2. Place mushrooms on grill. Close grill; cook 4 to 5 minutes or until slightly softened. Remove mushrooms from grill. Place onion on grill. Close grill; cook 4 to 5 minutes or until slightly softened. Remove onion from grill.

3. In small bowl, mix mayonnaise and vinaigrette; spread over bread slices. Top 4 bread slices with mushrooms, cheese, onion, bell pepper and basil. Top with remaining bread, mayonnaise sides down.

4. Place 2 sandwiches on grill. Close grill; cook 2 to 3 minutes or until sandwiches are golden brown and toasted. Repeat with remaining 2 sandwiches.

"Exercise with a friend. If I didn't know that Billie would call me if I didn't show up at exercise class, there are many mornings I would roll over and go back to sleep."   —Stacy P.

1 Sandwich: Calories 260 (Calories from Fat 80); Total Fat 9g (Saturated Fat 3g; Trans Fat 0.5g; Omega-3 0g); Cholesterol 10mg; Sodium 440mg; Total Carbohydrate 32g (Dietary Fiber 5g; Sugars 10g); Protein 14g   **% Daily Value:** Potassium 11%; Vitamin A 40%; Vitamin C 40%; Calcium 20%; Iron 15%; Folic Acid 10%   **Exchanges:** 2 Starch, 1 Medium-Fat Meat, 1/2 Fat **Carbohydrate Choices:** 2

Mushroom-Pepper Whole Wheat Sandwiches

Sensational

7

Salads and Vegetables

Indulge in the color and crunch of

a simple salad or vegetable

Sesame Green Beans

PREP TIME: 10 Minutes **START TO FINISH:** 25 Minutes **4 SERVINGS** (1 cup each)

1 lb fresh green beans
2 teaspoons sesame seed
1 tablespoon rice vinegar
1 tablespoon reduced-sodium soy sauce
1 teaspoon sugar
1/2 teaspoon crushed red pepper flakes

BETTY'S TIP
Toasting the sesame seed adds a lot of flavor without adding calories and fat. The seed continues to brown even after you take them off the burner, so remove the skillet from the heat just as the seed begins to turn golden brown.

1. In 2-quart saucepan, heat 1 inch water to boiling. Add beans. Boil uncovered 5 minutes. Cover; boil 3 to 5 minutes longer or until crisp-tender.

2. Meanwhile, in ungreased 8-inch skillet, heat sesame seed over medium-low heat 5 to 7 minutes, stirring frequently until browning begins, then stirring constantly until golden brown. Stir in remaining ingredients; cook until thoroughly heated.

3. Drain beans. Pour sauce over beans; toss until evenly coated.

1 Serving: Calories 50 (Calories from Fat 10); Total Fat 1g (Saturated Fat 0g; Trans Fat 0g; Omega-3 0g); Cholesterol 0mg; Sodium 140mg; Total Carbohydrate 9g (Dietary Fiber 3g; Sugars 4g); Protein 2g **% Daily Value:** Potassium 4%; Vitamin A 15%; Vitamin C 4%; Calcium 6%; Iron 6%; Folic Acid 6% **Exchanges:** 1/2 Other Carbohydrate, 1 Vegetable **Carbohydrate Choices:** 1/2

Sesame Green Beans

Greens with Fruit and Cheese

PREP TIME: 15 Minutes   **START TO FINISH:** 15 Minutes   **8 SERVINGS** (about 1 1/4 cups each)

SHERRY VINAIGRETTE
1/4 cup dry sherry or apple juice
2 tablespoons raspberry, balsamic or red wine vinegar
1 tablespoon sugar
1 teaspoon toasted sesame oil

SALAD
8 cups bite-size pieces mixed salad greens
1 medium pear, thinly sliced
1 1/2 cups sliced strawberries
1 small red onion, thinly sliced
1/4 cup finely crumbled blue cheese (1 oz)

1. In tightly covered container, shake all vinaigrette ingredients until sugar is dissolved.

2. On 8 salad plates, arrange salad greens, pear, strawberries and onion. Pour vinaigrette over salads. Sprinkle with cheese.

BETTY'S TIP

This salad is a delicious combination of flavors, colors and textures, plus it's high in vitamins A and C, important vitamins for overall health. If you can't find toasted sesame oil, you can use canola oil and sprinkle the salad with toasted sesame seed.

"I admire my cats because they show me how to relax."   —Natalie C.

1 Serving: Calories 70 (Calories from Fat 15); Total Fat 2g (Saturated Fat 1g; Trans Fat 0g; Omega-3 0g); Cholesterol 0mg; Sodium 65mg; Total Carbohydrate 11g (Dietary Fiber 3g; Sugars 6g); Protein 2g   **% Daily Value:** Potassium 8%; Vitamin A 60%; Vitamin C 50%; Calcium 6%; Iron 4%; Folic Acid 20%   **Exchanges:** 1/2 Other Carbohydrate, 1 Vegetable, 1/2 Fat   **Carbohydrate Choices:** 1

Citrus Salad with Poppy Seed Dressing

PREP TIME: 10 Minutes **START TO FINISH:** 10 Minutes **4 SERVINGS** (1/2 cup each)

2 tablespoons honey
1 teaspoon grated lemon peel
4 teaspoons lemon juice
1/2 teaspoon poppy seed
3 clementines or tangerines, peeled, sectioned
1 red grapefruit, peeled, sectioned
1 kiwifruit, peeled, sliced and slices cut in half

1. In small bowl, mix honey, lemon peel, lemon juice and poppy seed.

2. Remove membrane from clementine and grapefruit sections if desired. Cut each section into bite-size pieces.

3. In small serving bowl, mix clementines, grapefruit, kiwifruit and honey mixture.

NOTE FROM DR. R
Because this recipe is so high in vitamin C, it's wise to team it with a lean meat such as beef or chicken or with beans that contain iron. Vitamin C helps the iron in food be absorbed more easily.

"I schedule time with a friend for a chat session over lunch or dinner." —Brenda S.

1 Serving: Calories 110 (Calories from Fat 0); Total Fat 0g (Saturated Fat 0g; Trans Fat 0g; Omega-3 0g); Cholesterol 0mg; Sodium 0mg; Total Carbohydrate 26g (Dietary Fiber 3g; Sugars 20g); Protein 1g **% Daily Value:** Potassium 7%; Vitamin A 25%; Vitamin C 100%; Calcium 4%; Iron 0%; Folic Acid 6% **Exchanges:** 1/2 Starch, 1 Fruit **Carbohydrate Choices:** 2

Pineapple-Topped
Sweet Potatoes

PREP TIME: 5 Minutes   **START TO FINISH:** 1 Hour 15 Minutes   **4 SERVINGS**

2 medium dark-orange sweet potatoes
1/4 cup drained crushed pineapple in juice (from 8-oz can)
2 tablespoons sunflower nuts
2 tablespoons packed brown sugar

NOTE FROM DR. R
To beat stress, sit down for at least 15 minutes, close your eyes and focus on your breathing. Or take a walk and observe what's going on around you. Spending a few minutes each day relaxing can reduce stress.

1. Heat oven to 375°F. Scrub potatoes; prick all over with fork. Place in shallow baking pan or pie pan (do not use glass). Bake 55 to 65 minutes or until tender.

2. Set oven control to broil. Cut potatoes lengthwise in half. Mash cut sides slightly with fork. Spoon pineapple over cut sides of potatoes. Top with sunflower nuts and brown sugar.

3. Broil with tops 4 to 6 inches from heat 2 to 3 minutes or until brown sugar is bubbly.

1 Serving: Calories 110 (Calories from Fat 20); Total Fat 2.5g (Saturated Fat 0g; Trans Fat 0g; Omega-3 0g); Cholesterol 0mg; Sodium 25mg; Total Carbohydrate 21g (Dietary Fiber 3g; Sugars 13g); Protein 2g   **% Daily Value:** Potassium 10%; Vitamin A 220%; Vitamin C 10%; Calcium 4%; Iron 4%; Folic Acid 4%   **Exchanges:** 1 Starch, 1/2 Other Carbohydrate **Carbohydrate Choices:** 1 1/2

Italian Cauliflower

PREP TIME: 10 Minutes **START TO FINISH:** 10 Minutes **6 SERVINGS** (1/2 cup each)

4 cups fresh cauliflowerets

2 tablespoons water

2 teaspoons olive oil

2 tablespoons Italian-style dry bread crumbs

1 teaspoon dried basil leaves

1 tablespoon chopped fresh parsley

1. In medium microwavable bowl, place cauliflower and water. Cover with microwavable plastic wrap, folding back one edge 1/4 inch to vent steam. Microwave on High about 6 minutes, stirring once after 3 minutes, until tender; drain.

2. Meanwhile, in 7-inch skillet, heat oil over medium heat. Stir in bread crumbs and basil. Cook 1 to 2 minutes, stirring frequently, until bread crumbs are toasted. Stir in parsley. Sprinkle over cauliflower.

NOTE FROM DR. R
Instead of using the scale to measure whether you've lost or gained weight, go by how much energy you have, how well your clothes fit and how well you feel overall.

"There's something about volunteering—whether it's being an advocate for affordable housing or serving a meal at a shelter—that keeps me grounded and lifts my spirits." —Margaret R.

1 Serving: Calories 45 (Calories from Fat 15); Total Fat 1.5g (Saturated Fat 0g; Trans Fat 0g; Omega-3 0g); Cholesterol 0mg; Sodium 55mg; Total Carbohydrate 5g (Dietary Fiber 2g; Sugars 2g); Protein 2g **% Daily Value:** Potassium 6%; Vitamin A 0%; Vitamin C 25%; Calcium 2%; Iron 2%; Folic Acid 10% **Exchanges:** 1 Vegetable, 1/2 Fat **Carbohydrate Choices:** 1/2

Sweet-Sour Red Cabbage

PREP TIME: 40 Minutes   **START TO FINISH:** 40 Minutes   **8 SERVINGS** (1/2 cup each)

1 medium head red cabbage (1 1/2 lb), thinly sliced
4 slices bacon, diced
1 small onion, sliced
1/4 cup packed brown sugar
2 tablespoons all-purpose flour
1/4 cup water
3 tablespoons white vinegar
1/4 teaspoon salt
1/8 teaspoon pepper

NOTE FROM DR. R
Cabbage, a member of the cruciferous family of vegetables, is a good source of vitamin C and fiber. Vegetables also contain antioxidants, which may protect against some cancers.

1. In 10-inch skillet, heat 1 inch water to boiling. Add cabbage; heat to boiling. Boil uncovered about 15 minutes, stirring occasionally, until tender; drain and set aside. Wipe out and dry skillet with paper towel.

2. In same skillet, cook bacon over medium heat 4 minutes, stirring occasionally. Stir in onion. Cook 2 to 4 minutes, stirring occasionally, until bacon is crisp. Remove bacon and onion with slotted spoon; drain on paper towels. Drain fat, reserving 1 tablespoon in skillet.

3. Stir brown sugar and flour into bacon fat in skillet. Stir in water, vinegar, salt and pepper until well mixed.

4. Stir in cabbage, bacon and onion. Cook over medium heat 1 to 2 minutes, stirring occasionally, until hot.

"I like to walk at lunch to get some fresh air and exercise."

—Sharon M.

1 Serving: Calories 110 (Calories from Fat 30); Total Fat 3.5g (Saturated Fat 1g; Trans Fat 0g; Omega-3 0g); Cholesterol 5mg; Sodium 190mg; Total Carbohydrate 16g (Dietary Fiber 2g; Sugars 10g); Protein 3g   **% Daily Value:** Potassium 8%; Vitamin A 20%; Vitamin C 40%; Calcium 4%; Iron 6%; Folic Acid 4%   **Exchanges:** 1/2 Other Carbohydrate, 1 Vegetable, 1 Fat **Carbohydrate Choices:** 1

Sweet-Sour Red Cabbage

Roasted New Potatoes with Oregano

PREP TIME: 10 Minutes   **START TO FINISH:** 45 Minutes   **4 SERVINGS**

10 to 12 small red potatoes (about 1 1/2 lb), cut in half
1 tablespoon chopped fresh or 1 teaspoon dried oregano leaves
2 teaspoons olive oil
1/4 teaspoon salt
1/4 teaspoon pepper

BETTY'S TIP
Potatoes are high in potassium. Nutritionists suggest balancing potassium-rich vegetables and fruits with the amount of sodium you eat.

1. Heat oven to 400°F. Line 15 × 10 × 1-inch pan with foil; spray with cooking spray.

2. In medium bowl, toss all ingredients. Spread in single layer in pan.

3. Roast uncovered 30 to 35 minutes, turning after 15 minutes, until potatoes are tender.

"Planning really reduces stress the most for me. If I have meals planned and groceries purchased for the week, I don't have to worry about dinnertime all week." —Libby P.

1 Serving: Calories 150 (Calories from Fat 20); Total Fat 2.5g (Saturated Fat 0g; Trans Fat 0g; Omega-3 0g); Cholesterol 0mg; Sodium 160mg; Total Carbohydrate 29g (Dietary Fiber 3g; Sugars 2g); Protein 3g   **% Daily Value:** Potassium 21%; Vitamin A 0%; Vitamin C 10%; Calcium 2%; Iron 10%; Folic Acid 10%   **Exchanges:** 2 Starch   **Carbohydrate Choices:** 2

Asparagus-Pepper Stir-Fry

PREP TIME: 25 Minutes   **START TO FINISH:** 25 Minutes   **4 SERVINGS**

1 bunch (1 lb) asparagus
1 teaspoon canola oil
1 medium red, yellow or orange bell pepper, cut in 3/4-inch pieces
2 cloves garlic, finely chopped
1 tablespoon orange juice
1 tablespoon reduced-sodium soy sauce
1/2 teaspoon ground ginger

1. Break off tough ends of asparagus as far down as stalks snap easily. Wash asparagus; cut into 1-inch pieces.

2. In 10-inch nonstick skillet or wok, heat oil over medium heat. Add asparagus, bell pepper and garlic; stir-fry 3 to 4 minutes or until crisp-tender.

3. In small bowl, mix orange juice, soy sauce and ginger; stir into asparagus mixture. Cook and stir 15 to 30 seconds or until vegetables are coated.

"I find it very calming to sit in my rocker and look out the window at the trees and squirrels in my backyard for a few minutes every day."* —Cheri O.

BETTY'S TIP
When selecting vegetables, looks do count! Choosing produce that's rich in color often means that it's rich in vitamins, like this great-tasting salad that's high in vitamins A and C and folic acid.

1 Serving: Calories 40 (Calories from Fat 15); Total Fat 1.5g (Saturated Fat 0g; Trans Fat 0g; Omega-3 0g); Cholesterol 0mg; Sodium 135mg; Total Carbohydrate 4g (Dietary Fiber 2g; Sugars 3g); Protein 2g   **% Daily Value:** Potassium 5%; Vitamin A 30%; Vitamin C 60%; Calcium 0%; Iron 4%; Folic Acid 20%   **Exchanges:** 1 Vegetable, 1/2 Fat   **Carbohydrate Choices:** 0

Strawberry-Orange–Poppy Seed Salad

PREP TIME: 20 Minutes   **START TO FINISH:** 20 Minutes   **4 SERVINGS**

1/4 cup frozen orange juice concentrate

2 teaspoons honey

1 teaspoon Dijon mustard

1/2 teaspoon poppy seed

4 cups mixed salad greens

1 cup sliced strawberries

1 orange, peeled, cut into bite-size pieces

NOTE FROM DR. R
This beautiful salad is very high in folic acid. Folic acid is needed throughout life, but it is extremely important for women to get adequate amounts before and during pregnancy so their babies' brains and spinal cords develop properly.

1. In 1-cup measuring cup, mix orange juice concentrate, honey, mustard and poppy seed with fork or wire whisk.

2. Among 4 salad plates, arrange salad greens. Top with strawberries and orange pieces. Drizzle with dressing.

1 Serving: Calories 90 (Calories from Fat 5); Total Fat 0.5g (Saturated Fat 0g; Trans Fat 0g; Omega-3 0g); Cholesterol 0mg; Sodium 50mg; Total Carbohydrate 19g (Dietary Fiber 3g; Sugars 15g); Protein 2g   **% Daily Value:** Potassium 12%; Vitamin A 60%; Vitamin C 130%; Calcium 6%; Iron 6%; Folic Acid 30%   **Exchanges:** 1 Fruit, 1 Vegetable **Carbohydrate Choices:** 1

Minted Peas with Peppers

PREP TIME: 15 Minutes   **START TO FINISH:** 15 Minutes   **4 SERVINGS** (1/2 cup each)

2 cups frozen sweet peas (from 1-lb bag)
1/2 medium yellow, red or orange bell pepper, chopped (1/2 cup)
2 teaspoons no-trans-fat vegetable oil spread
1 teaspoon chopped fresh mint leaves
1/2 teaspoon lemon-pepper seasoning

1. In 1-quart microwavable dish, place peas and bell pepper. Cover; microwave on High 5 to 6 minutes, stirring once, until peas are tender.

2. Stir in remaining ingredients.

NOTE FROM DR. R
Water is an important nutrient. Eight to 10 glasses of water and other liquids daily are recommended. Milk, herbal teas and other liquids also help keep you hydrated.

1 Serving: Calories 70 (Calories from Fat 15); Total Fat 1.5g (Saturated Fat 0g; Trans Fat 0g; Omega-3 0g); Cholesterol 0mg; Sodium 105mg; Total Carbohydrate 10g (Dietary Fiber 2g; Sugars 4g); Protein 3g   **% Daily Value:** Potassium 3%; Vitamin A 30%; Vitamin C 35%; Calcium 0%; Iron 6%; Folic Acid 10%   **Exchanges:** 1/2 Other Carbohydrate, 1 Vegetable, 1/2 Fat   **Carbohydrate Choices:** 1/2

Keep Hormones in Balance

Hormones are vital chemical substances produced by the body that influence almost every cell, function and organ. They regulate our growth, development, tissue and sexual function, the way our bodies use food, the way we react to emergencies and even our moods. Hormones act as messengers to energize, stabilize and nurture tissues. These natural chemicals signal your body to make certain changes and adjustments at specific times in your life:

At puberty, **estrogen** increases to begin developing female sex organs that regulate menstrual periods and cause changes in the breasts.

Progesterone maintains menstrual cycles, an important function during the childbearing years because the shedding of the uterine lining each month reduces the risk of endometrial cancer.

Estrogen regulates various metabolic processes, including bone growth and cholesterol levels.

During the reproductive years, the pituitary gland in the brain generates **follicle-stimulating** and **luteinizing** hormones that cause a new egg to mature and be released each month.

Progesterone plays a key role in sexual desire throughout life.

During pregnancy, **progesterone** increases to promote the survival and development of the embryo and fetus and to prevent the lining of the uterus from being shed to form the placenta.

Progesterone encourages the growth of milk-producing glands in the breasts during the end of pregnancy, making it possible to breast-feed your infant.

Progesterone and **estrogen** levels fluctuate and decrease as you enter peri-menopause (the years prior to menopause when menstruation ends) and reach menopause.

Estrogen circulates in the bloodstream and binds to estrogen receptors on cells in targeted tissues, affecting not only the breast and uterus, but also the brain, bone, liver, heart and other tissues.

Estrogen helps prevent bone loss and works together with calcium and other hormones and minerals to help build bones.

Estrogen helps protect against plaque buildup in your arteries by helping to raise HDL (good) cholesterol, which helps remove LDL (bad) cholesterol. After menopause, your risk for developing coronary artery disease (CAD) increases. CAD is a condition in which the arteries that take blood to the heart become narrowed or blocked by plaque.

When Hormones are Out of Balance

High progesterone levels may be partly responsible for symptoms of premenstrual syndrome (PMS), such as breast tenderness, feeling bloated and mood swings right before menstruation.

Low estrogen levels have been linked to osteoporosis and increased risk of cardiovascular disease, as well as menopausal symptoms such as hot flashes and mood swings.

Hormones and Headaches

The relationship between female hormones and headaches or migraines is still unclear. Women may have menstrual-related headaches around the time of their menstrual period, perhaps caused by the body's fluctuation of estrogen and progesterone levels. Triggers may be oral contraceptives, hormone replacement therapy and even pregnancy. Yet, some women who suffer from migraines say these things improve their condition or make the attacks disappear completely. After menopause, when estrogen and other hormone levels decline, women who previously suffered from migraines during their reproductive years may find that their headaches subside completely.

MENOPAUSE HORMONE THERAPY

THE U.S. FOOD AND DRUG ADMINISTRATION (FDA) ADVISES DOCTORS TO PRESCRIBE MENOPAUSAL HORMONE THERAPIES (HT) AT THE LOWEST POSSIBLE DOSE AND FOR THE SHORTEST POSSIBLE LENGTH OF TIME TO ACHIEVE TREATMENT GOALS. THIS RECOMMENDATION WAS MADE AFTER FINDINGS FROM MAJOR STUDIES OF POSTMENOPAUSAL WOMEN, CONDUCTED AS PART OF THE LANDMARK FEDERAL WOMEN'S HEALTH INITIATIVE (WHI), WERE RELEASED IN JULY 2002 AND MARCH 2004. THE STUDIES, DESIGNED IN PART TO EVALUATE THE BENEFITS OF USING HT TO PREVENT HEART DISEASE OR KEEP IT FROM GETTING WORSE, CONCLUDED THAT HT DOES NOT PREVENT HEART DISEASE.

WOMEN WHO TAKE HORMONE THERAPY CONTAINING ESTROGEN TO PREVENT OSTEOPOROSIS SHOULD DISCUSS THEIR PERSONAL RISKS FOR HEART DISEASE AND BREAST AND UTERINE CANCER WITH THEIR PHYSICIAN. ALTERNATIVE PREVENTIVE MEDICINE IS AVAILABLE.

IF YOU TAKE HORMONE THERAPY OR ESTROGEN THERAPY NOW, TALK TO YOUR DOCTOR BEFORE STOPPING IT. FOR WOMEN WHO USE IT TO RELIEVE MENOPAUSAL SYMPTOMS, STOPPING SOME HORMONE THERAPY MEDICINE ABRUPTLY MAY MAKE THE SYMPTOMS OF MENOPAUSE TEMPORARILY WORSE. TAPERING OFF MAY BE HELPFUL. THERE ARE OTHER MEDICINES THAT MAY HELP WITH HOT FLASHES. TALK TO YOUR DOCTOR ABOUT OPTIONS SPECIFIC TO YOUR NEEDS.

Cucumber-Mango Salad

PREP TIME: 20 Minutes **START TO FINISH:** 20 Minutes **4 SERVINGS** (1/2 cup each)

1 small cucumber
1 medium mango
1/4 teaspoon grated lime peel
1 tablespoon lime juice
1 1/2 teaspoons sugar
1/4 teaspoon ground cumin
Dash salt
4 leaves Bibb lettuce

BETTY'S TIP
Leaving the skin on the cucumber gives the salad a brighter color and increases the fiber. This refreshing and colorful salad is perfect with grilled fish, roasted chicken or any sandwich.

1. Cut cucumber lengthwise in half; scoop out seeds. Chop cucumber (about 1 cup).

2. Score skin of mango lengthwise into fourths with knife; peel skin. Cut peeled mango lengthwise close to both sides of seed. Chop mango into 1/2-inch cubes.

3. In small bowl, mix lime peel, lime juice, sugar, cumin and salt. Stir in cucumber and mango. Spoon into lettuce leaves.

1 Serving: Calories 50 (Calories from Fat 0); Total Fat 0g (Saturated Fat 0g; Trans Fat 0g; Omega-3 0g); Cholesterol 0mg; Sodium 40mg; Total Carbohydrate 12g (Dietary Fiber 2g; Sugars 9g); Protein 0g **% Daily Value:** Potassium 5%; Vitamin A 15%; Vitamin C 30%; Calcium 0%; Iron 2%; Folic Acid 4% **Exchanges:** 1/2 Fruit, 1/2 Other Carbohydrate **Carbohydrate Choices:** 1

VITAMIN A   VITAMIN C   IRON   FOLIC ACID   POTASSIUM   FIBER

Corn Salad in Tomato Cups

PREP TIME: 30 Minutes   **START TO FINISH:** 30 Minutes   **6 SERVINGS**

1 cup frozen whole kernel corn (from 1-lb bag)

1 can (15 to 16 oz) pinto beans, drained, rinsed

1/3 cup reduced-fat sour cream

1/4 cup chopped red onion

3 tablespoons shredded reduced-fat Cheddar cheese

2 tablespoons chopped fresh parsley

1 teaspoon salt-free seasoning blend

6 medium tomatoes

1. Cook corn as directed on bag. Rinse in cold water until cool; drain.

2. In medium bowl, mix corn and remaining ingredients except tomatoes.

3. Cut about 1/2-inch slice off top of each tomato. With grapefruit spoon or teaspoon, hollow out tomatoes, leaving shell of outer flesh intact. Fill tomatoes with corn mixture.

BETTY'S TIP

You can add a lot of flavor without adding sodium with seasoning blends that combine herbs and spices including onion, black pepper, parsley, celery seed, basil, bay leaves, cayenne, cumin and mustard.

1 Serving: Calories 170 (Calories from Fat 25); Total Fat 3g (Saturated Fat 1.5g; Trans Fat 0g; Omega-3 0g); Cholesterol 5mg; Sodium 55mg; Total Carbohydrate 27g (Dietary Fiber 7g; Sugars 5g); Protein 9g   **% Daily Value:** Potassium 16%; Vitamin A 25%; Vitamin C 30%; Calcium 8%; Iron 10%; Folic Acid 35%   **Exchanges:** 1 1/2 Starch, 1 Vegetable, 1/2 Very Lean Meat, 1/2 Fat   **Carbohydrate Choices:** 2

Roasted Asparagus–Berry Salad with Pecans

PREP TIME: 10 Minutes   **START TO FINISH:** 30 Minutes   **4 SERVINGS**

1 bunch (1 lb) asparagus
Cooking spray
1/4 cup chopped pecans
1 cup sliced strawberries
4 cups mixed salad greens
1/4 cup fat-free raspberry vinaigrette
Cracked pepper, if desired

BETTY'S TIP
Roasting the asparagus and pecans adds a terrific flavor to this sensational salad. For a refreshing twist, try fresh raspberries instead of the strawberries and sliced almonds instead of the pecans.

1. Heat oven to 400°F. Line 15 × 10 × 1-inch pan with foil; spray with cooking spray.

2. Break off tough ends of asparagus as far down as stalks snap easily. Wash asparagus; cut into 1-inch pieces. Place in single layer in pan; spray with cooking spray. Place pecans in shallow pan.

3. Bake pecans 5 to 6 minutes, stirring occasionally, until golden brown and aromatic; bake asparagus 10 to 12 minutes or until crisp-tender. Cool 8 to 10 minutes or until room temperature.

4. In medium bowl, toss asparagus, pecans, strawberries, greens and vinaigrette. Sprinkle with pepper.

"I take the scenic route home from work every day. It gives me time to appreciate nature's beauty and leave the stress of the workday behind."   —Ellen F.

1 Serving: Calories 120 (Calories from Fat 60); Total Fat 6g (Saturated Fat 0.5g; Trans Fat 0g; Omega-3 0g); Cholesterol 0mg; Sodium 50mg; Total Carbohydrate 12g (Dietary Fiber 4g; Sugars 6g); Protein 3g   **% Daily Value:** Potassium 10%; Vitamin A 60%; Vitamin C 80%; Calcium 4%; Iron 8%; Folic Acid 40%   **Exchanges:** 1/2 Other Carbohydrate, 1 1/2 Vegetable, 1 Fat   **Carbohydrate Choices:** 1

BLT Potato Salad

PREP TIME: 20 Minutes   **START TO FINISH:** 45 Minutes   **4 SERVINGS** (1 cup each)

4 small new red potatoes (about 12 oz), cut into 1/2-inch cubes
1/4 cup fat-free mayonnaise or salad dressing
1 teaspoon Dijon mustard
2 teaspoons chopped fresh or 1/2 teaspoon dried dill weed
1/2 teaspoon salt
1/8 teaspoon pepper
1/2 cup grape tomatoes or halved cherry tomatoes
1 1/2 cups bite-size pieces romaine lettuce
2 slices bacon, cooked, crumbled

1. In 2-quart saucepan, place potatoes. Add enough water to cover. Heat to boiling; reduce heat to low. Cover; cook 10 to 15 minutes or until potatoes are tender. Drain. Cool about 10 minutes.

2. Meanwhile, in medium bowl, mix mayonnaise, mustard, dill weed, salt and pepper. Stir in potatoes, tomatoes and lettuce. Sprinkle bacon over salad just before serving.

BETTY'S TIP
Save time and add fiber by leaving the skins on the potatoes in this quick salad. Leave out the salt if you are watching your sodium. To make it ahead of time, just cook and chill 4 to 5 hours before serving.

1 Serving: Calories 110 (Calories from Fat 20); Total Fat 2.5g (Saturated Fat 1g; Trans Fat 0g; Omega-3 0g); Cholesterol 5mg; Sodium 550mg; Total Carbohydrate 19g (Dietary Fiber 3g; Sugars 3g); Protein 3g   **% Daily Value:** Potassium 18%; Vitamin A 30%; Vitamin C 30%; Calcium 2%; Iron 10%; Folic Acid 10%   **Exchanges:** 1 Starch, 1/2 Fat
Carbohydrate Choices: 1

Mixed Greens with Fruit and Raspberry Dressing

PREP TIME: 5 Minutes **START TO FINISH:** 5 Minutes **4 SERVINGS**

2 cups mixed salad greens
1 can (8 oz) pineapple tidbits, drained
1 cup raspberries
2 medium bananas, sliced
2 medium green onions, sliced (2 tablespoons)
1/2 cup fat-free raspberry vinaigrette

BETTY'S TIP
This is a terrific salad to customize to your taste. Try blueberries instead of raspberries or cut-up fresh mango instead of pineapple. Make it a main-dish salad by topping with grilled chicken breast or leftover roast beef strips.

Among 4 salad plates, divide all ingredients except vinaigrette. Drizzle with vinaigrette.

"I keep a pen and paper by my bed so that when I wake up in the middle of the night worrying, I can jot the thought down and deal with it in the morning. Then I can relax and get back to sleep." —Nancy J.

1 Serving: Calories 160 (Calories from Fat 5); Total Fat 0.5g (Saturated Fat 0g; Trans Fat 0g; Omega-3 0g); Cholesterol 0mg; Sodium 290mg; Total Carbohydrate 38g (Dietary Fiber 6g; Sugars 22g); Protein 2g   **% Daily Value:** Potassium 13%; Vitamin A 30%; Vitamin C 40%; Calcium 4%; Iron 6%; Folic Acid 15%   **Exchanges:** 2 Fruit, 1 Vegetable **Carbohydrate Choices:** 2 1/2

Orange-Almond Salad
in Lettuce Cups

PREP TIME: 10 Minutes   **START TO FINISH:** 10 Minutes   **4 SERVINGS**

1/4 cup orange juice
2 tablespoons honey
1/2 teaspoon Dijon mustard
12 Bibb lettuce leaves
2 medium oranges, divided into segments, cut into thirds
1/4 cup chopped smoked almonds

1. In small bowl, mix orange juice, honey and mustard with fork.

2. On each of 4 salad plates, arrange 3 lettuce leaves. Fill lettuce leaves with orange pieces and almonds. Drizzle with orange juice mixture.

NOTE FROM DR. R
Nuts are actually quite good for your health. Almonds contain fiber, a type of fat that is good for your heart and vitamin E, which may help prevent plaque buildup inside your arteries.

1 Serving: Calories 130 (Calories from Fat 40); Total Fat 4.5g (Saturated Fat 0g; Trans Fat 0g; Omega-3 0g); Cholesterol 0mg; Sodium 45mg; Total Carbohydrate 20g (Dietary Fiber 3g; Sugars 16g); Protein 3g   **% Daily Value:** Potassium 8%; Vitamin A 20%; Vitamin C 70%; Calcium 6%; Iron 4%; Folic Acid 10%   **Exchanges:** 1 Fruit, 1 Vegetable, 1 Fat
Carbohydrate Choices: 1

Broccoli, Feta and Tomato Salad

PREP TIME: 10 Minutes   **START TO FINISH:** 10 Minutes   **4 SERVINGS** (about 1/2 cup each)

4 cups water

2 cups fresh broccoli florets

2 small plum (Roma) tomatoes, chopped (2/3 cup)

1/4 cup reduced-fat feta cheese

2 tablespoons fat-free balsamic vinaigrette

2 teaspoons chopped fresh or 1 teaspoon dried oregano leaves

1. In 2-quart saucepan, heat water to boiling over high heat. Add broccoli; cook 10 to 20 seconds or until broccoli is bright green. Drain broccoli; rinse in cold water until cool.

2. In small serving bowl, mix broccoli and remaining ingredients.

BETTY'S TIP

Blanching the broccoli, by cooking it in a small amount of water for a very short time, brings out the bright green color and saves nutrients. Chopped red onion and bell pepper make colorful and crunchy additions to this salad.

"As a young woman, I am focusing on long-term health, developing habits that I can keep for the rest of my life." —Amity D.

1 Serving: Calories 45 (Calories from Fat 10); Total Fat 1.5g (Saturated Fat 1g; Trans Fat 0g; Omega-3 0g); Cholesterol 0mg; Sodium 240mg; Total Carbohydrate 5g (Dietary Fiber 2g; Sugars 2g); Protein 3g   **% Daily Value:** Potassium 4%; Vitamin A 15%; Vitamin C 35%; Calcium 4%; Iron 2%; Folic Acid 8%   **Exchanges:** 1 Vegetable, 1/2 Fat   **Carbohydrate Choices:** 1/2

Broccoli, Feta and Tomato Salad

Herb-Roasted Root Vegetables

PREP TIME: 15 Minutes **START TO FINISH:** 1 Hour 10 Minutes **6 SERVINGS** (1/2 cup each)

2 medium turnips, peeled, cut into 1-inch pieces (3 cups)

2 medium parsnips, peeled, cut into 1/2-inch pieces (1 1/2 cups)

1 medium red onion, cut into 1-inch wedges (1 cup)

1 cup ready-to-eat baby-cut carrots

Cooking spray

2 teaspoons Italian seasoning

1/2 teaspoon coarse salt

BETTY'S TIP

Roasting is a great way to cook vegetables; it brings out the natural flavor and sweetness of vegetables without adding extra calories.

1. Heat oven to 425°F. Spray 15 × 10 × 1-inch pan with cooking spray. Arrange vegetables in single layer in pan. Spray with cooking spray (2 or 3 seconds). Sprinkle with Italian seasoning and salt.

2. Roast uncovered 45 to 55 minutes, stirring once, until vegetables are tender.

"I planted a vegetable garden in pots on my deck this summer. We now have fresh vegetables within a few steps, and they taste so much better than the vegetables you buy." —Jeanne A.

1 Serving: Calories 70 (Calories from Fat 0); Total Fat 0.5g (Saturated Fat 0g; Trans Fat 0g; Omega-3 0g); Cholesterol 0mg; Sodium 230mg; Total Carbohydrate 14g (Dietary Fiber 4g; Sugars 5g); Protein 1g **% Daily Value:** Potassium 10%; Vitamin A 50%; Vitamin C 15%; Calcium 6%; Iron 4%; Folic Acid 8% **Exchanges:** 1 Starch **Carbohydrate Choices:** 1

Herb-Roasted Root Vegetables

8

Dazzle Yourself
with Dessert

*Satisfy your sweet tooth with a
luscious light dessert or treat*

Blueberry-Rhubarb Crisp

PREP TIME: 20 Minutes   **START TO FINISH:** 1 Hour 30 Minutes   **6 SERVINGS**

3/4 cup packed brown sugar

1/3 cup all-purpose flour

1 teaspoon grated lemon peel

1 teaspoon ground cinnamon

1/4 teaspoon ground nutmeg

4 cups chopped fresh rhubarb

1 cup fresh blueberries

1 cup Honey Nut Clusters® cereal, slightly crushed

1/4 cup chopped pecans

BETTY'S TIP
This crisp that tastes and looks terrific also has lots of fruit, fiber, vitamins and minerals. If the blueberries you're using are rather tart, add 1 tablespoon additional brown sugar.

1. Heat oven to 375°F. Spray bottom and sides of 8-inch square glass baking dish with cooking spray.

2. In large bowl, mix brown sugar, flour, lemon peel, cinnamon and nutmeg. Stir in rhubarb and blueberries. Spoon into baking dish. Sprinkle with crushed cereal and pecans.

3. Bake uncovered 30 to 40 minutes or until rhubarb is tender when pierced with a fork. Let stand 30 minutes before serving.

"I bought a bike last year, and I take routes that get me quickly out of the city and into the country. I love the smell of the fresh summer air blowing over the fields."   —Jeanne A.

1 Serving: Calories 230 (Calories from Fat 35); Total Fat 4g (Saturated Fat 0g; Trans Fat 0g; Omega-3 0g); Cholesterol 0mg; Sodium 60mg; Total Carbohydrate 46g (Dietary Fiber 3g; Sugars 33g); Protein 3g   **% Daily Value:** Potassium 10%; Vitamin A 2%; Vitamin C 6%; Calcium 20%; Iron 10%; Folic Acid 8%   **Exchanges:** 1 Starch, 1 Fruit, 1 Other Carbohydrate, 1/2 Fat   **Carbohydrate Choices:** 3

Melon Float with Lime and Mint

PREP TIME: 15 Minutes   **START TO FINISH:** 1 Hour 15 Minutes   **4 SERVINGS**

1/2 cup sugar

1/3 cup water

1 tablespoon chopped fresh mint leaves

1 tablespoon grated lime peel

1 1/2 cups honeydew melon balls

1 1/2 cups cantaloupe balls

1 1/2 cups (12 oz) club soda, chilled

1. In 1-quart saucepan, heat sugar, water, mint and lime peel to boiling; reduce heat. Simmer uncovered about 5 minutes or until sugar is dissolved.

2. In heatproof medium bowl, place honeydew and cantaloupe balls; pour hot syrup through strainer over melon, removing lime peel and mint. Cover; refrigerate at least 1 hour or until chilled.

3. To serve, divide melon balls and syrup among 4 parfait glasses or dessert dishes. Top with club soda.

NOTE FROM DR. R
Take the time to do things that make you feel good. Use your best dishes once in a while, even if it's not a holiday. Garnish parfait glasses with lime peel and a mint leaf.

1 Serving: Calories 150 (Calories from Fat 0); Total Fat 0g (Saturated Fat 0g; Trans Fat 0g; Omega-3 0g); Cholesterol 0mg; Sodium 40mg; Total Carbohydrate 36g (Dietary Fiber 1g; Sugars 35g); Protein 0g   **% Daily Value:** Potassium 9%; Vitamin A 40%; Vitamin C 60%; Calcium 0%; Iron 0%; Folic Acid 6%   **Exchanges:** 1 Fruit, 1 1/2 Other Carbohydrate **Carbohydrate Choices:** 2 1/2

Crunchy Pears

PREP TIME: 15 Minutes **START TO FINISH:** 1 Hour **4 SERVINGS**

4 firm ripe large pears
1/4 cup orange juice
1/4 cup peach or apricot preserves
1/4 cup vanilla wafer crumbs
1/4 cup finely chopped almonds
1 container (6 oz) orange low-fat yogurt (2/3 cup)
Ground cinnamon, if desired

NOTE FROM DR. R
Pears are high in fiber, so they make a good choice for a snack or dessert. The good things in nuts can help lower cholesterol, may prevent plaque buildup in the arteries and help keep bones and muscles—including the heart—strong.

1. Move oven rack to lowest position. Heat oven to 350°F. Spray 9-inch glass pie plate with cooking spray. Carefully peel pears, leaving stems attached; place on large plate. In small bowl, mix orange juice and preserves; brush evenly over pears.

2. In another small bowl, mix wafer crumbs and almonds. Sprinkle crumb mixture evenly over pears; press in gently. Stand pears upright in pie plate. Mix yogurt and remaining preserves mixture from plate; refrigerate.

3. Bake pears 35 to 45 minutes or until tender when pierced with fork (baking time may vary due to size of pears). Serve warm with yogurt sauce; sprinkle with cinnamon.

"My dog helps connect me to my neighborhood. When I walk her, I not only get exercise, I also get to talk to my neighbors and meet new people." —Anne O.

1 Serving: Calories 300 (Calories from Fat 60); Total Fat 7g (Saturated Fat 1g; Trans Fat 0g; Omega-3 0g); Cholesterol 0mg; Sodium 55mg; Total Carbohydrate 55g (Dietary Fiber 7g; Sugars 37g); Protein 5g **% Daily Value:** Potassium 12%; Vitamin A 4%; Vitamin C 15%; Calcium 10%; Iron 6%; Folic Acid 8% **Exchanges:** 1/2 Starch, 1 Fruit, 2 Other Carbohydrate, 1/2 High-Fat Meat, 1/2 Fat **Carbohydrate Choices:** 3 1/2

Crème Brûlée with Raspberries

PREP TIME: 25 Minutes **START TO FINISH:** 25 Minutes **4 SERVINGS**

1 cup raspberries
1/3 cup granulated sugar
2 tablespoons cornstarch
1/4 teaspoon salt
2 cups fat-free (skim) milk, soymilk or fat-free half-and-half
1/2 teaspoon vanilla
4 teaspoons packed brown sugar

1. Among 4 (10-oz) custard cups or ramekins, divide raspberries evenly. In 2-quart saucepan, mix granulated sugar, cornstarch and salt. Stir in milk. Heat to boiling over medium heat, stirring frequently. Stir in vanilla. Spoon over raspberries.

2. Set oven control to broil. Sprinkle 1 teaspoon brown sugar over mixture in each custard cup. Broil with tops 4 to 6 inches from heat 2 to 3 minutes or just until brown sugar is melted. Serve immediately. Store covered in refrigerator.

BETTY'S TIP
This popular restaurant dessert isn't just low-fat, it's also quick and easy. The raspberries give it fiber, and the milk gives it calcium, a great combination. Here's to your health!

"I substitute lower-fat ingredients for regular full-fat ingredients. My favorite product is fat-free half-and-half. I use it in pasta sauces and, every once in a while, on my cereal. It's so good!" —Lori F.

1 Serving: Calories 160 (Calories from Fat 0); Total Fat 0g (Saturated Fat 0g; Trans Fat 0g; Omega-3 0g); Cholesterol 0mg; Sodium 200mg; Total Carbohydrate 35g (Dietary Fiber 2g; Sugars 29g); Protein 5g   **% Daily Value:** Potassium 7%; Vitamin A 6%; Vitamin C 6%; Calcium 15%; Iron 2%; Folic Acid 4%   **Exchanges:** 2 Other Carbohydrate, 1/2 Skim Milk
Carbohydrate Choices: 2

Dreamy Orange Cream

PREP TIME: 5 Minutes   **START TO FINISH:** 10 Minutes   **4 SERVINGS** (1/2 cup each)

1 box (4-serving size) vanilla instant pudding and pie filling mix
1 cup orange juice
1 cup frozen (thawed) fat-free whipped topping
1 pouch (2 bars) crunchy granola bars (from 8.9-oz box), crushed
1 can (15 oz) mandarin orange segments, drained

1. In medium bowl, beat pudding mix and orange juice with wire whisk 2 minutes. Refrigerate 5 minutes. Fold in whipped topping.

2. Into 4 dessert dishes, divide pudding mixture. Top with crushed granola bars and orange segments.

BETTY'S TIP
This dessert will remind you of creamy orange ice cream pops. Make the orange cream up to a day ahead. Just before serving, top with crushed granola bars and mandarin orange segments.

1 Servings: Calories 230 (Calories from Fat 20); Total Fat 2.5g (Saturated Fat 1.5g; Trans Fat 0g; Omega-3 0g); Cholesterol 0mg; Sodium 390mg; Total Carbohydrate 50g (Dietary Fiber 2g; Sugars 37g); Protein 2g   **% Daily Value:** Potassium 8%; Vitamin A 25%; Vitamin C 80%; Calcium 2%; Iron 4%; Folic Acid 4%   **Exchanges:** 1 Starch, 1/2 Fruit, 2 Other Carbohydrate **Carbohydrate Choices:** 3

Dreamy Orange Cream

Frosty Mocha

PREP TIME: 10 Minutes **START TO FINISH:** 10 Minutes **4 SERVINGS**

1 cup water
2 tablespoons instant coffee granules
1/2 cup chocolate-flavor syrup
2 1/2 cups vanilla fat-free no-sugar-added ice cream
2 cups ice cubes

1. In blender, place water, coffee granules and chocolate syrup. Cover; blend on high speed until well blended.

2. Add ice cream. Cover; blend on high speed until smooth. Add ice cubes. Cover; blend on high speed until ice is crushed. Pour into 4 serving glasses.

BETTY'S TIP
Now you can make your own frosty coffee drinks at home. For a caramel-coffee version, substitute 1/2 cup fat-free caramel syrup for the chocolate syrup. Garnish servings with a sprinkling of chocolate-covered coffee beans.

"Bubble baths with the lights off and lots of candles are a great way to get rid of the stresses of the day." —Kelly T.

1 Servings: Calories 170 (Calories from Fat 0); Total Fat 0g (Saturated Fat 0g; Trans Fat 0g; Omega-3 0g); Cholesterol 0mg; Sodium 115mg; Total Carbohydrate 37g (Dietary Fiber 0g; Sugars 28g); Protein 4g **% Daily Value:** Potassium 9%; Vitamin A 10%; Vitamin C 0%; Calcium 15%; Iron 0%; Folic Acid 0% **Exchanges:** 2 Other Carbohydrate, 1/2 Skim Milk **Carbohydrate Choices:** 2 1/2

Chocolate Soufflé Cakes

PREP TIME: 20 Minutes **START TO FINISH:** 1 Hour 5 Minutes **8 SERVINGS**

1 oz sweet baking chocolate

1 tablespoon butter or margarine, melted

1 teaspoon instant espresso coffee granules

2 egg whites

2 eggs, separated

1 container (8 oz) vanilla low-fat yogurt

1/2 cup granulated sugar

1/4 cup packed brown sugar

1/4 cup all-purpose flour

1/4 cup unsweetened baking cocoa

1/4 teaspoon ground cinnamon

1/4 cup chocolate-flavored syrup

4 teaspoons powdered sugar

1/2 teaspoon instant espresso coffee granules

Frozen (thawed) fat-free whipped topping, if desired

1. Heat oven to 375°F. Spray bottoms only of 8 jumbo muffin cups, 3 3/4 × 1 7/8 inches, with cooking spray. In 1-quart saucepan, heat chocolate, butter and 1 teaspoon espresso granules over low heat, stirring constantly, until melted and smooth; cool slightly.

2. In medium bowl, beat 4 egg whites with electric mixer on high speed until stiff peaks form; set aside.

3. In another medium bowl, beat 2 egg yolks and yogurt on medium speed until blended. Gradually beat in granulated sugar, brown sugar and chocolate mixture. Stir in flour, cocoa and cinnamon just until blended. Fold in egg whites. Spoon into muffin cups.

4. Bake 20 to 22 minutes or until firm to the touch. Cool 5 minutes (centers of cakes will sink slightly). Remove from muffin cups to wire rack. Cool 15 minutes.

5. In 1-quart saucepan, heat chocolate syrup, powdered sugar and 1/2 teaspoon espresso granules over low heat, stirring constantly, until smooth.

6. Place cakes on individual plates. Drizzle with chocolate sauce. Serve with whipped topping.

NOTE FROM DR. R
Instead of doing just one kind of exercise, find several activities you like and vary your workouts, depending on your mood and your schedule.

BETTY'S TIP
Want an easy dress-up for this dessert? Try a sprinkling of baking cocoa, ground cinnamon or powdered sugar. If you don't have the jumbo muffin cups, try using large size (10 ounce) custard cups.

1 Serving: Calories 220 (Calories from Fat 50); Total Fat 6g (Saturated Fat 3g; Trans Fat 0g; Omega-3 0g); Cholesterol 60mg; Sodium 70mg; Total Carbohydrate 37g (Dietary Fiber 2g; Sugars 29g); Protein 6g **% Daily Value:** Potassium 6%; Vitamin A 2%; Vitamin C 0%; Calcium 8%; Iron 10%; Folic Acid 4% **Exchanges:** 1/2 Starch, 2 Other Carbohydrate, 1/2 Medium-Fat Meat, 1/2 Fat **Carbohydrate Choices:** 2 1/2

Dark Chocolate Fondue

PREP TIME: 30 Minutes **START TO FINISH:** 30 Minutes **16 SERVINGS** (2 tablespoons fondue and 1/2 cup fruit each)

8 cups assorted fresh fruit (sliced kiwifruit, sliced bananas, strawberries, Bing cherries, cut-up pineapple, dried apricot halves, green grapes)

1 can (14 oz) fat-free sweetened condensed milk (not evaporated)

1 cup semisweet chocolate chips (6 oz)

1/4 cup dark chocolate syrup

1/4 cup boiling water

2 teaspoons instant espresso coffee granules

1 teaspoon vanilla

NOTE FROM DR R
Dark chocolate contains phytonutrients that are good for your health. A bit of chocolate, as in this recipe, especially when served with fruits, is a tremendous way to get many nutrients. For an extra-chilly treat, freeze the fruit. When the frozen fruit hits the warm chocolate, it makes a wonderful cover.

1. Prepare fruits; set aside.

2. In 2-quart saucepan, cook milk, chocolate chips and chocolate syrup over low heat 5 to 8 minutes, stirring frequently, until chips are melted.

3. In small bowl, stir boiling water and coffee granules until granules are dissolved. Stir into chocolate mixture. Cook over low heat 5 minutes, stirring frequently. Stir in vanilla. Remove from heat; pour into fondue pot.

4. Using fondue forks, dip fruit into chocolate mixture.

"Chocolate, in small doses (and large ones at times), is a great treat and stress reliever, plus it's good for me." —Lynn V.

1 Serving: Calories 210 (Calories from Fat 30); Total Fat 3.5g (Saturated Fat 2g; Trans Fat 0g; Omega-3 0g); Cholesterol 0mg; Sodium 30mg; Total Carbohydrate 41g (Dietary Fiber 3g; Sugars 35g); Protein 3g **% Daily Value:** Potassium 11%; Vitamin A 6%; Vitamin C 40%; Calcium 8%; Iron 6%; Folic Acid 4% **Exchanges:** 1 Starch, 1 Fruit, 1/2 Other Carbohydrate, 1/2 Fat **Carbohydrate Choices:** 3

Dark Chocolate Fondue

Stay Mentally Healthy

Need a problem solved? Work out for 25 minutes! **Physical exercise** may be as healthy for your mind as it is for your body. This was the finding of a 1997 study at Middlesex University in England; participants scored higher on a creativity test after a 25-minute aerobic workout. Additionally, physiological changes in our bodies, enhanced by exercise, such as increases in metabolism, cardiac activity and oxygen flow to the brain, also appear to heighten our creativity and memory. Physical exercise also paves the way to mental relaxation; it helps clear our minds and lets our creative thoughts flow more freely.

Use It or Lose It

The advice we follow for physical exercise is also true for mental exercise. **Mental exercises** help strengthen mental acuity and have beneficial effects for people of all ages. The decline in specific mental abilities associated with aging—memory loss, problem-solving blocks or sluggish thinking—are not inevitable as you age. Using your brain to learn a new language, solve crossword puzzles, master a new hobby or engage in a friendly debate stimulates blood flow and strengthens the connections between nerve cells in the brain. A study from Washington University in St. Louis found that memorizing techniques encourage the brain to work more efficiently and may reduce age-related memory loss. The Memory Clinic at UCLA recommends trying to visualize a picture in your mind to help you remember a person's name or a street name. Or instead of trying to verbally remember, write it down and study it for a few minutes.

Create a Mentally Fit Lifestyle

To keep your mental skills as sharp as possible:

Become involved in an organization, a club or a friendship that gets you out and interacting with others.

Overcome monotony and routine in your daily life. Monotony generates mental (and emotional) lethargy and resignation.

Try something new. Take a class on a topic you've always been interested in, take up a new hobby, sign up to learn a new skill or craft, learn a new language, meet and interact with new people.

Schedule daily interactions and talk to others to keep up with the world around you.

Find an exercise that works for you. Take a brisk walk outside, dance to a favorite song. It's never too late to start exercising, and if we don't use our muscles, we lose them.

Spend time volunteering to help someone in need; it in turn adds to your own healthy self-esteem and bright outlook.

Other healthy lifestyle behaviors also play a role in mental acuity:

Eating foods rich in antioxidants (vitamins C and E and beta-carotene) and B vitamins may enhance memory.

Eating fish may slow the deterioration of brain function with age.

Getting enough sleep has been shown to help memory and concentration.

MEMORY WORRIES IF YOU'RE LIKE MOST WOMEN, YOU'LL EXPERIENCE SOME FORGETFULNESS FROM TIME TO TIME. NOT TO WORRY. SOME LAPSES IN MEMORY ARE INEVITABLE AS WE AGE. BUT IF IT STARTS TO DISRUPT YOUR FAMILY LIFE, IT'S TIME TO TALK TO YOUR DOCTOR. ALSO REVIEW ANY MEDICATIONS YOU TAKE WITH YOUR DOCTOR. SOME COMBINATIONS MAY AFFECT MEMORY, AND SWITCHING TO A DIFFERENT DOSE OR DRUG MAY TAKE CARE OF THE PROBLEM. SIMPLY MODIFYING YOUR DIET AND MAKING SURE YOU ARE GETTING ENOUGH SLEEP MAY ALSO HELP.

Frozen Strawberry Cheesecake

PREP TIME: 25 Minutes   **START TO FINISH:** 6 Hours 15 Minutes   **10 SERVINGS**

CRUST

2 tablespoons butter or margarine, melted

1/4 cup old-fashioned oats

1/4 cup finely chopped walnuts

3 tablespoons ground flaxseed or flaxseed meal

2 tablespoons shredded coconut

2 tablespoons all-purpose flour

1/8 teaspoon ground cinnamon

Dash salt

FILLING

1 box (3.4 oz) instant cheesecake pudding and pie filling mix

1 cup cold 2% milk

2 cups vanilla reduced-fat ice cream, softened

1 cup chopped fresh strawberries (5 oz)

1 pint (2 cups) strawberry sorbet, softened

5 fresh strawberries, cut in half, if desired

1. Heat oven to 350°F. In medium bowl, mix all crust ingredients. Press in bottom and up side of 9-inch glass pie plate. Bake about 10 minutes or until golden brown. Cool completely, about 30 minutes.

2. In large bowl, beat pudding mix and milk with wire whisk until smooth. Gently stir in ice cream with wire whisk until smooth. Stir in chopped strawberries. Pour mixture into cooled crust. Freeze 2 to 3 hours or until firm.

3. Spread sorbet evenly over ice cream. Freeze 2 hours. Remove from freezer 10 minutes before serving. Cut into wedges. Garnish each wedge with strawberry half.

"I savor my morning walk and use it to reflect and start the day *on the right foot, plus it's invigorating."* —Lynn V.

1 Serving: Calories 230 (Calories from Fat 70); Total Fat 8g (Saturated Fat 3.5g; Trans Fat 0g; Omega-3 0.5g); Cholesterol 15mg; Sodium 210mg; Total Carbohydrate 36g (Dietary Fiber 2g; Sugars 27g); Protein 4g   **% Daily Value:** Potassium 5%; Vitamin A 4%; Vitamin C 8%; Calcium 8%; Iron 4%; Folic Acid 4%   **Exchanges:** 1 Starch, 1 1/2 Other Carbohydrate, 1 1/2 Fat **Carbohydrate Choices:** 2 1/2

Frozen Strawberry Cheesecake

Chewy Barley-Nut Cookies

PREP TIME: 45 Minutes   **START TO FINISH:** 45 Minutes   **2 DOZEN COOKIES**

1/3 cup canola oil

1/2 cup granulated sugar

1/4 cup packed brown sugar

1/4 cup reduced-fat mayonnaise or salad dressing

1 teaspoon vanilla

1 egg or 2 egg whites

2 cups barley flakes or 2 cups plus 2 tablespoons old-fashioned oats

3/4 cup all-purpose flour

1/2 teaspoon baking soda

1/2 teaspoon salt

1/4 teaspoon ground cinnamon

1/3 cup "heart-healthy" mixed nuts (peanuts, almonds, pistachios, pecans, hazelnuts)

NOTE FROM DR. R
Women do not get enough of several nutrients: folic acid, iron, calcium and magnesium. By eating more fruits, vegetables, lean meats and whole grains as well as having an overall low-fat diet, you can get those nutrients from the foods you eat.

1. Heat oven to 350°F. Spray cookie sheet with cooking spray.

2. In medium bowl, mix oil, sugars, mayonnaise, vanilla and egg with spoon. Stir in barley flakes, flour, baking soda, salt and cinnamon. Stir in nuts.

3. Drop dough by rounded measuring tablespoonfuls 2 inches apart onto cookie sheet.

4. Bake 10 to 14 minutes or until edges are golden brown. Cool 2 minutes; remove from cookie sheet to wire rack.

"Singing helps me release a lot of tenseness. I sing in my car on the way to and from work and in the shower." —Cheri O.

1 Cookie: Calories 150 (Calories from Fat 50); Total Fat 5g (Saturated Fat 0.5g; Trans Fat 0g; Omega-3 0g); Cholesterol 10mg; Sodium 95mg; Total Carbohydrate 23g (Dietary Fiber 3g; Sugars 7g); Protein 3g   **% Daily Value:** Potassium 2%; Vitamin A 0%; Vitamin C 0%; Calcium 0%; Iron 4%; Folic Acid 2%   **Exchanges:** 1 Starch, 1/2 Other Carbohydrate, 1 Fat
Carbohydrate Choices: 1 1/2

Cranberry-Orange Oatmeal Cookies

PREP TIME: 1 Hour **START TO FINISH:** 1 Hour **3 DOZEN COOKIES**

1/3 cup canola oil

1/2 cup granulated sugar

1/4 cup packed brown sugar

1 teaspoon vanilla

1 egg or 2 egg whites

2 cups old-fashioned or quick-cooking oats

2/3 cup all-purpose flour

1/2 teaspoon baking soda

1/2 teaspoon salt

1 teaspoon ground ginger

1/2 teaspoon ground allspice

1/2 cup orange-flavored dried cranberries

1/4 cup chopped walnuts

1. Heat oven to 350°F. Spray cookie sheet with cooking spray.

2. In large bowl, mix oil, sugars, vanilla and egg with spoon. Stir in oats, flour, baking soda, salt, ginger and allspice. Stir in cranberries and walnuts.

3. Drop dough by rounded teaspoonfuls 2 inches apart onto cookie sheet.

4. Bake 9 to 13 minutes or until edges turn golden brown. Cool 1 minute; remove from cookie sheet to wire rack.

NOTE FROM DR. R Recognize the importance of relationships throughout your life and take the time to nurture them. Go for a walk and talk with a friend, call your gal pals, have a girls night out or catch up on a little chit-chat during lunch.

"I rarely watch TV, but there's one show that I just love to watch once a week. I go in my bedroom, lock the door and have a half-hour of complete indulgent time just for myself!" —Kelly T.

1 Cookie: Calories 70 (Calories from Fat 25); Total Fat 3g (Saturated Fat 0g; Trans Fat 0g; Omega-3 0g); Cholesterol 5mg; Sodium 55mg; Total Carbohydrate 11g (Dietary Fiber 0g; Sugars 6g); Protein 1g **% Daily Value:** Potassium 1%; Vitamin A 0%; Vitamin C 0%; Calcium 0%; Iron 2%; Folic Acid 0% **Exchanges:** 1/2 Starch, 1/2 Fat **Carbohydrate Choices:** 1

Blueberry Barley Pudding

PREP TIME: 20 Minutes **START TO FINISH:** 3 Hours **6 SERVINGS**

2 cups water

Dash salt

1 cup uncooked quick-cooking barley

1/2 cup vanilla low-fat yogurt

3 tablespoons maple-flavored syrup

1 cup frozen (thawed) reduced-fat whipped topping

1/3 cup chopped walnuts, toasted (page 162)

1/4 teaspoon ground cinnamon

1/2 cup fresh or frozen blueberries, thawed and drained

Additional chopped walnuts, if desired

Dash ground cinnamon

BETTY'S TIP

Remember rice pudding? Well, this is even better, with more texture and chewiness, plus the goodness of barley. Instead of the blueberries, try raspberries or other fresh fruits in this creamy pudding.

1. In 2-quart saucepan, heat water and salt to boiling. Stir in barley; reduce heat. Cover; simmer 10 to 12 minutes or until tender. Cool completely, about 30 minutes.

2. In medium bowl, mix yogurt and maple syrup. Gently stir in whipped topping. Stir in barley, 1/3 cup walnuts and 1/4 teaspoon cinnamon. Cover; refrigerate 2 hours. Stir in blueberries.

3. Sprinkle pudding with additional walnuts and dash cinnamon before serving.

1 Serving: Calories 240 (Calories from Fat 60); Total Fat 6g (Saturated Fat 2g; Trans Fat 0g; Omega-3 0.5g); Cholesterol 0mg; Sodium 50mg; Total Carbohydrate 40g (Dietary Fiber 6g; Sugars 12g); Protein 6g **% Daily Value:** Potassium 6%; Vitamin A 0%; Vitamin C 0%; Calcium 6%; Iron 6%; Folic Acid 4% **Exchanges:** 2 Starch, 1/2 Other Carbohydrate, 1 Fat **Carbohydrate Choices:** 2 1/2

Blueberry Barley Pudding

Top Health Concerns

As women, our first tendency is to put our spouse or kids' needs and concerns ahead of our own. Unknowingly, we may be risking our own health.

You can lower your risk of heart disease, stroke, diabetes and cancer by making a few major lifestyle changes. See the table on page 235 to make changes.

Heart Disease and Stroke

Because you can't see it, you may not realize the importance of maintaining a healthy heart and healthy circulation. Heart disease and stroke kill more women than any other disease or cause of death.

Obesity

Health experts are concerned about the rising rate of obesity in the U.S. Obesity, when basal metabolic rate (BMI) is greater than 30, can lead to disability and poor health. (See BMI chart, page 240.) Women who are obese are more likely to develop long-term diseases like high blood pressure, high blood cholesterol, type 2 diabetes, heart disease and stroke, gallbladder disease and arthritis. Cancers of the breast, endometrium and colon are more common in women who are overweight.

Losing weight can help you manage your cholesterol levels, blood sugar and blood pressure. Losing just 5% to 10% of your weight, for example, 10 to 20 pounds if you weigh 200 pounds, can improve your health.

Diabetes

Type 2 diabetes is on the rise among women because a growing number of American women are obese, a strong risk factor for diabetes. Diabetes increases the chances that a woman will develop heart disease. Pregnant women with diabetes must be followed closely by their doctor to help manage diabetes-related complications.

Cancer

The American Cancer Society estimates that about one-third of all cancer deaths may be due to poor nutrition, physical inactivity, overweight and obesity. Also add the cancers linked to tobacco use. Now, consider cancers that can be detected by early screening (for example, cervical cancer through PAP smears) or prevented (skin cancer, with use of sunscreen). It is easy to see how the risk of cancer can be lessened tremendously by stopping smoking, eating healthy, managing your weight and being physically active every day.

Breast cancer affects more women than any other type of cancer (although the death rate from lung cancer is higher). Some breast cancer risk factors—genetics, family history, age—cannot be changed, but others can be lessened through simple lifestyle changes.

Screening for colon cancer through a routine colonoscopy and removal of precancerous areas has made a big difference in the number of women who develop and die from the third most common cancer among women, after breast and lung cancers. As with breast cancer, lifestyle factors loom large.

Osteoporosis

Osteoporosis, a disease of weakened bones, affects twice as many women as men. It is more common in the years after menopause because of changes in a woman's hormones with the fastest bone loss in the first years after menopause. Women who build strong bones at a younger age by eating wisely and getting regular physical activity may lessen bone loss later in life.

Alzheimer's

Women with Alzheimer's disease gradually lose their memory of people, events and daily tasks. Risk of Alzheimer's goes up as a woman gets older. Staying active—both physically and mentally—may help prevent Alzheimer's. Scientists are studying how lifestyle may affect this crippling disease.

	Top risk factors	Eat more of	Eat less of	Adopt a healthy lifestyle
Heart disease and stroke	• Family history • Age (post-menopause) • Obesity • High blood pressure • High blood cholesterol • High blood sugar	• Fruits and vegetables • Whole grains • Fish • Lean meat • Low-fat and fat-free milk and yogurt	• Full-fat dairy foods • High-fat meats • Foods high in fat • Saturated fat • Cholesterol • Salty and high-sodium foods • Fried foods • Commercial baked goods	• Stop smoking • Be active • Take time for yourself • Maintain healthy weight
Cancer	• Family history • Genetics • Increasing age • Tobacco use • Alcohol • High meat diet • Too few fruits and vegetables • Physical inactivity • Sun exposure	Fruits and vegetables; whole grains; fish, poultry, beans	• Red meat • High-fat meats • Processed meats • Refined grains and sugars	• Maintain healthy weight • Stop smoking • Do moderate to vigorous activity at least 5 days a week • Breastfeed • Avoid regular alcohol use
Osteoporosis	• Female • Thin body • Family history • Post-menopausal • Caucasian or Asian • Diet low in calcium and vitamin D • Inactivity • Cigarette smoking	Calcium- and vitamin D–rich foods: low-fat and fat-free milk and yogurt; calcium- and vitamin D–fortified juice, soy products, and breakfast cereals; leafy greens; canned fish with bones	Alcohol	Do weight-bearing physical activities like walking, gardening, stair climbing, dancing; do not smoke
Diabetes	African American, Latina, Native American, Asian American, Pacific Islander; overweight/obese; increasing age; family history; physical inactivity; delivered a baby over 9 pounds	Vegetables; whole grains; fruits; non-fat dairy products; beans; lean meats, poultry and fish	Low-nutrient, high-carbohydrate foods	Get 30 minutes daily of moderate physical activity; if overweight, reduce weight by 5% to 10%
Alzheimer's and Dementia	Age; obesity; high blood pressure; high cholesterol; diet high in saturated fat and cholesterol	Monounsaturated oils like olive and canola oil; dark green vegetables; berries; salmon and other higher-fat fish; nuts	Foods high in saturated fat and cholesterol; fried foods	Involvement in intellectual, social and physical activities
Obesity	Eating too many calories; physical inactivity	Fruits and vegetables; low-fat and fat-free dairy; lean meats; legumes; whole grains		Weight loss of 5% to 10%; daily physical activity

Recommended Screenings and Immunizations for Women at Average Risk for Most Diseases

These charts are guidelines only. Your doctor will personalize the timing of each test and immunization to meet your health care needs.

Screening Tests	Ages 18-39	Ages 40-49	Ages 50-64	Ages 65 and Older
General Health: Full checkup, including weight and height	Discuss with your doctor or nurse	Discuss with your doctor or nurse	Discuss with your doctor or nurse	Discuss with your doctor or nurse
Thyroid test (TSH)	Start at age 35, then every 5 years	Every 5 years	Every 5 years	Every 5 years
Heart Health: Blood pressure test	At least every 2 years	At least every 2 years	At least every 2 years	At least every 2 years
Cholesterol test	Start at age 20, discuss with your doctor or nurse.	Discuss with your doctor or nurse	Discuss with your doctor or nurse	Discuss with your doctor or nurse
Bone Health: Bone mineral density test		Discuss with your doctor or nurse	Discuss with your doctor or nurse	Get a bone mineral density test at least once. Talk to your doctor or nurse about repeat testing.
Diabetes: Blood sugar test	Discuss with your doctor or nurse	Start at age 45, then every 3 years	Every 3 years	Every 3 years
Breast Health: Mammogram (x-ray of breast)		Every 1-2 years. Discuss with your doctor or nurse	Every 1-2 years. Discuss with your doctor or nurse	Every 1-2 years. Discuss with your doctor or nurse
Reproductive Health: Pap test & pelvic exam	Every 1-3 years if you have been sexually active or are older than 21	Every 1-3 years	Every 1-3 years	Discuss with your doctor or nurse
Chlamydia test	If sexually active, yearly until age 25. Ages 26-39, if you are at high risk for Chlamydia or other STDs, you may need this test.	If you are at high risk for Chlamydia or other sexually transmitted diseases (STDs) you may need this test	If you are at high risk for Chlamydia or other sexually transmitted diseases (STDs) you may need this test	If you are at high risk for Chlamydia or other sexually transmitted diseases (STDs) you may need this test
Sexually Transmitted Disease (STD) tests	Both partners should get tested for STDs, including HIV, before initiating sexual intercourse.	Both partners should get tested for STDs, including HIV, before initiating sexual intercourse	Both partners should get tested for STDs, including HIV, before initiating sexual intercourse	Both partners should get tested for STDs, including HIV, before initiating sexual intercourse

Colorectal Health: Fecal occult blood tests			Yearly	Yearly
Flexible Sigmoidoscopy (with fecal occult blood test is preferred)			Every 5 years (if not having a colonoscopy)	Every 5 years (if not having a colonoscopy)
Double Contrast Barium Enema (DCBE)			Every 5-10 years (if not having a colonoscopy or sigmoidoscopy)	Every 5-10 years (if not having a colonoscopy or sigmoidoscopy)
Colonoscopy			Every 10 years	Every 10 years
Rectal exam	Discuss with your doctor or nurse	Discuss with your doctor or nurse	Every 5-10 years with each screening (sigmoidoscopy, colonoscopy, or DCBE)	Every 5-10 years with each screening (sigmoidoscopy, colonoscopy, or DCBE)
Eye and Ear Health: Eye exam	Get your eyes checked if you have problems or visual changes	Every 2-4 years	Every 2-4 years	Every 1-2 years
Hearing test	Starting at age 18, then every 10 years	Every 10 years	Discuss with your doctor or nurse	Discuss with your doctor or nurse
Skin Health: Mole exam	Monthly mole self-exam: by a doctor every 3 years, starting at age 20	Monthly mole self-exam: by a doctor every year	Monthly mole self-exam: by a doctor every year	Monthly mole self-exam: by a doctor every year
Oral Health: Dental exam	One to two times every year	One to two times every year	One to two times every year	One to two times every year
Mental Health Screening	Discuss with your doctor or nurse	Discuss with your doctor or nurse	Discuss with your doctor or nurse	Discuss with your doctor or nurse
Immunizations: Influenza vaccine	Discuss with your doctor or nurse	Discuss with your doctor or nurse	Yearly	Yearly
Pneumococcal vaccine				One time only
Tetanus-Diphtheria Booster vaccine	Every 10 years	Every 10 years	Every 10 years	Every 10 years

Make the Most of Your Menu

Below are menus geared toward the nutrition needs of three different women. Take a look at the changes in each:

> ➤ a 30-year-old woman who is moderately active and in her child-bearing years

> ➤ a 45-year-old woman who has not yet gone through menopause

> ➤ a 65-year-old woman

If you're a **30-year-old woman**, iron and folic acid are important nutrients to pay attention to—they help maintain healthy blood and reduce the chances of delivering a baby with a neural tube birth defect.

At **age 45**, you still have an opportunity to develop good calcium habits before menopause. For the two younger women, menu choices are suggested for a household with or without children.

If you're a **65-year-old woman**, calcium and vitamin D—the bone health nutrients—are the ones to pay attention to—as well as vitamin B-12, a nutrient that is better absorbed from fortified foods, like breakfast cereal, as we age.

You can use these menus as a guide to portion sizes and food choices. Feel free to include any recipes in this cookbook in your personal eating plan.

A Guide to Food Choices

	30 years old 2,000 calories		45 years old 1,800 calories		65 years old 1,600 calories
	No children	*Children*	*No children*	*Children*	*Empty nest*
Breakfast	Raspberry-Chocolate Muffin (page 87)	Orange Pancakes with Raspberry Sauce (page 40)	Buckwheat Pancakes with Butter-Pecan Syrup (page 44)	Creamy Mango Smoothies (page 62)	Oatmeal–Tropical Fruit Muffins (page 53)
	1 cup fat-free (skim) milk	6 ounces fat-free yogurt	1 cup fat-free (skim) milk	1 whole wheat English muffin	1 cup fat-free (skim) milk
	1 cup fresh fruit salad	1/2 cup cantaloupe	1/2 cup sliced banana	2 teaspoons squeeze or soft tub margarine	1/2 cup pineapple
Meal total	*375 cal*	*415 cal*	*479 cal*	*388 cal*	*310 cal*
Lunch	Minestrone Soup (page 108)	Noodles and Peanut Sauce Salad Bowl (page 168)	2 ounces turkey breast on 2 slices whole wheat bread, lettuce and tomato	2 ounces ham, 1 ounce reduced-fat Swiss on whole grain roll, lettuce and tomato	Tilapia Florentine with 1/2 cup whole wheat couscous (page 130)
	1 medium whole-grain roll with 2 teaspoons squeeze margarine	1 cup wonton soup	Broccoli, Feta and Tomato Salad (page 210)	Sweet Potato–Pear Soup (page 113)	1 cup sliced carrots
	1 cup green salad with balsamic vinegar, 1 teaspoon olive oil	1 cup grapes	1/2 cup coleslaw	1 medium orange	1/2 cup honeydew chunks
	1 medium apple	1 cup fat-free (skim) milk	1/2 cup blueberries	6 ounces fat-free yogurt	1 cup fat-free (skim) milk
Meal total	*600 cal*	*585 cal*	*388 cal*	*547 cal*	*495 cal*
Dinner	Pork Tenderloin with Apples and Sweet Potatoes (page 146)	Grilled Italian Steak and Vegetables (page 140)	Vegetable Stew with Polenta (page 112)	Asian Chicken Roll-Ups (page 157)	Open-faced veggie burger on 1/2 wheat bun, tomato slices, ketchup
	1 cup green beans	Large green salad with 1 tablespoon reduced-fat Italian dressing	Large spinach salad with 1 tablespoon walnuts, 1 tablespoon reduced-fat Italian dressing	1 cup snow peas with 1 tablespoon sesame seeds	Mixed Greens with Fruit and Raspberry Dressing (page 208)
	1 cup egg noodles	2/3 cup brown rice		1 cup miso soup	1 cup light cranberry juice
	1 poached pear	1/2 cup pineapple	1/2 cup cranberry juice	1 cup cantaloupe	
Meal total	*710 cal*	*456 cal*	*630 cal*	*564 cal*	*400 cal*
Snack	Girlfriends' Gorp (page 86)	Cranberry-Orange Oatmeal Cookies (page 231)	Chocolate Soufflé Cakes (page 223)	Zesty Corn Dip with Veggies (page 76)	Crunchy Pears (page 218)
	4 dried apricot halves	1 cup fat-free (skim) milk	1 cup fat-free (skim) milk	1 ounce baked tortilla chips	1 cup fat-free (skim) milk
	6 ounces fat-free yogurt			1 cup fat-free (skim) milk	
Meal total	*265 cal*	*590 cal*	*300 cal*	*270 cal*	*385 cal*
Daily total	**1945 cal**	**2046 cal**	**1800 cal**	**1769 cal**	**1590 cal**

Body Mass Index

BODY MASS INDEX (BMI)

Body mass index, or BMI, is the measurement of choice for many physicians and researchers studying obesity. BMI uses a mathematical formula that takes into account both a person's height and weight. BMI equals a person's weight in kilograms divided by height in meters squared. ($BMI=kg/m^2$)

Determining Your Body Mass Index (BMI)

The table below has already done the math and metric conversions. To use the table, find the appropriate height in the left-hand column. Move across the row to the given weight. The number at the top of the column is the BMI for that height and weight.

BMI (kg/m²)	Normal							Overweight				Obese		
	19	20	21	22	23	24	25	26	27	28	29	30	35	40
Height (in.)	Weight (lb.)													
58	91	96	100	105	110	115	119	124	129	134	138	143	167	191
59	94	99	104	109	114	119	124	128	133	138	143	148	173	198
60	97	102	107	112	118	123	128	133	138	143	148	153	179	204
61	100	106	111	116	122	127	132	137	143	148	153	158	185	211
62	104	109	115	120	126	131	136	142	147	153	158	164	191	218
63	107	113	118	124	130	135	141	146	152	158	163	169	197	225
64	110	116	122	128	134	140	145	151	157	163	169	174	204	232
65	114	120	126	132	138	144	150	156	162	168	174	180	210	240
66	118	124	130	136	142	148	155	161	167	173	179	186	216	247
67	121	127	134	140	146	153	159	166	172	178	185	191	223	255
68	125	131	138	144	151	158	164	171	177	184	190	197	230	262
69	128	135	142	149	155	162	169	176	182	189	196	203	236	270
70	132	139	146	153	160	167	174	181	188	195	202	207	243	278
71	136	143	150	157	165	172	179	186	193	200	208	215	250	286
72	140	147	154	162	169	177	184	191	199	206	213	221	258	294
73	144	151	159	166	174	182	189	197	204	212	219	227	265	302
74	148	155	163	171	179	186	194	202	210	218	225	233	272	311
75	152	160	168	176	184	192	200	208	216	224	232	240	279	319
76	156	164	172	180	189	197	205	213	221	230	238	246	287	328

Body weight in pounds according to height and body mass index.

Risk of Associated Disease According to BMI and Waist Size

BMI	Waist less than or equal to 40 in. (men) or 35 in. (women)	Waist greater than 40 in. (men) or	35 in. (women)
18.5 or less	Underweight		N/A
18.5– 24.9	Normal		N/A
25.0– 29.9	Overweight	Increased	High
30.0–34.9	Obese	High	Very High
35.0–39.9	Obese	Very High	Very High
40 or greater	Extremely Obese	Extremely High	Extremely High

Adapted with permission from Bray, G.A., Gray, D.S., Obesity, Part I, Pathogenesis, West J. Med. 1988: 149: 429-41.

Federal guidelines define a BMI of 19 to 24 as normal. That means if your BMI falls within these boundaries, your weight is probably at a healthy level, and there's no health advantage to changing it. (If your BMI is less than the number 19 on the chart, you may be severely underweight; talk to your doctor about your health risks.)

If your BMI is between 25 and 29, you're considered "overweight;" if it's 30 or above, you are in the "obese" category. The higher your BMI within these ranges, the greater your risk of heart problems and other weight-related health issues—and the more you'll benefit from losing weight! Talk to your doctor about your BMI; occasionally some people are fit and muscular yet they fall into the overweight category.

PEAR OR APPLE?

Carrying excess fat is a known health risk, but *where* you carry it on your body matters, too. Studies show that people with "apple" shapes—those who tend to accumulate fat around their waists—have an increased risk of coronary heart disease, high blood pressure, stroke, diabetes and even some cancers, when compared with their "pear"-shaped counterparts—those who tend to carry fat around their hips and thighs. This connection between weight and body shape leads some health experts to feel that taking a waist measurement is important to assess health risks.

To determine whether you're carrying too much fat around your middle, place a tape measure around your waist just above your hipbones. A reading of more than 40 inches in a man, or 35 inches in a woman, is considered a health risk—especially if your BMI places you in the "overweight" range or above.

THE 10-PERCENT SOLUTION

If you're overweight, losing just a few pounds may seem like a drop in the bucket, but from your heart's point of view, it's a major improvement. Studies show that a weight loss of just 5 to 10 percent of body weight can significantly lower your blood pressure, improve cholesterol readings, and, if you are diabetic, improve your ability to control your diabetes.

What does 5 to 10 percent amount to? If you weigh 160 pounds now, it's a weight loss of just 8 to 16 pounds.

The Wellness Kitchen

Having a wide variety of ingredients in your pantry offers you flexibility for preparing fresh, easy and great-tasting recipes.

Bakery: Deliver B vitamins, fiber, antioxidants and phytonutrients (in whole-grain products)

Whole-grain breads, English muffins, pitas, corn and/or flour tortillas.

Beans, Legumes, Nuts, Seeds: Deliver fiber, good fats

Canellini, kidney, chili, soy beans

Brown legumes, split green and yellow peas, black-eyed peas

Almonds, peanuts, walnuts, sunflower seeds, pumpkin seeds

Canned and Bottled Goods: Deliver nutrients, depending on choice, in a time-saving way

Reduced-sodium broths, reduced-sodium tomato soup, canned beans

Canned tomatoes, bean dip, canned fruits (in water or fruit juice)

Condiments and spreads: Little nutrition value

Light cream cheese, reduced-fat or fat-free sour cream, tub margarine, light butter, honey, jams and preserves

Dairy: Deliver calcium and vitamin D for healthy bones

Fat-free (skim) or low-fat (1%) milk, fat-free yogurt, flavored reduced-fat yogurt, reduced-fat cheese

Fish/Meats/Poultry/Fish: Deliver protein and iron

Lean beef, pork and lamb cuts ("loin"), skinless chicken and turkey, all types of shellfish and fish, especially fatty types (salmon, tuna, shrimp), lean cold cuts (sliced roast turkey or beef), low-fat sausages

Frozen Foods: Delivers healthy food whenever you need it

Soy burgers and crumbles (look for low-fat brands), frozen juice

Low-fat frozen yogurt or reduced-fat ice cream, whole-fruit freezer pops

Fruits: Deliver vitamins A and C, folic acid, potassium

Orchard fruits: Apples and pears, avocados

Bananas, kiwis

Grapes: Red grapes, green grapes, purple grapes

Berries: Blackberries, blueberries, raspberries, strawberries

Citrus: Oranges, grapefruits, lemons, limes, tangerines

Dried: Apricots, cherries, cranberries, dates, figs, plums, raisins

Melons: Cantaloupes, honeydews, watermelons

Orange and red fruits: Apricots, mangoes, papayas, persimmons

Grains: Deliver antioxidants, phytonutrients, B vitamins

Barley, wheat, quinoa, oats, whole-grain cereals and pasta, oatmeal

Oils and Dressings/Sauces: Deliver vitamin E

Canola oil, olive oil, natural peanut butter, low-fat or fat-free salad dressings, sherry-, balsamic- and/or flavored vinegars, reduced-sodium marinara sauce, salsa

Snacks: Deliver calories, extra nutrients (depending on choice)

Whole-grain crackers or flatbreads, rice crackers, whole wheat pretzels

Plain popcorn or low-fat microwave popcorn, fig bars, graham crackers

Vegetables: Deliver vitamins A and C, folic acid, potassium

Broccoli, cabbage, carrots, cucumbers, garlic, onions, potatoes

Salad greens (any variety), spinach, sweet potatoes

Glossary of Health Terms

Listed below are definitions of the terms used in this cookbook.

Antioxidant: Substance that inhibits oxidation in plant and animal cells. Antioxidants include vitamin C, vitamin E and beta-carotene and are found in fruits and vegetables; they may be important in preventing cholesterol from damaging your arteries.

Beta-carotene: A plant pigment found in dark green and orange vegetables and fruits. In the body, beta-carotene is converted into an active form of vitamin A. It is an antioxidant that helps protect cells from damage.

Body Mass Index (BMI): A method of measurement used to determine whether a person is obese, taking weight and height into account.

Cardiovascular Disease: The catch-all term for diseases of the heart and blood vessels.

Cholesterol: A fatlike substance found in animal fat that is important for cell structures, hormones and nerve coverings. LDL (low-density lipoprotein), or "bad" cholesterol, increases the risk of heart disease. HDL (high-density lipoprotein), or "good" cholesterol, protects against heart disease.

Circulatory System: The organs that move blood through the body, including the heart, lungs, arteries and veins.

Coronary Heart Disease (CHD): A buildup of fatty, cholesterol-filled deposits in the coronary arteries that block the normal flow of blood and can cause a heart attack. In America, this is the most common heart disease.

Diabetes: A disease that occurs when the body is not able to use glucose (a form of sugar produced from the digestion of carbohydrate foods) for energy, either at all, or properly.

Elemental Calcium: The actual amount of calcium in a calcium supplement.

Fat: A necessary nutrient, fat helps build new cells, shuttles vitamins through the body and makes particular hormones that regulate blood pressure.

Fiber: The material in plant foods that the body does not digest; it passes through to be eliminated.

Folic Acid (Folate): An important nutrient found in leafy green vegetables, citrus fruits and legumes. Folic acid protects the heart by helping to lower the body's levels of homocysteine, produced when the body breaks down proteins.

Heart Attack: A disabling or life-threatening condition that occurs when blood flow to the heart is cut off.

High Blood Pressure (Hypertension): When the force of a heartbeat pushes blood into your arteries, it exerts pressure on the walls of the blood vessels. Blood pressure is classified as "high" when it is equal to or greater than 140/90 millimeters of mercury.

High-Density Lipoprotein (HDL): "Good" cholesterol, HDL carries cholesterol to the liver where it is broken down and removed from the body. The higher your HDL, the lower your risk of cholesterol building up in your arteries, and the lower your risk of developing coronary heart disease.

Insoluble Fiber: Fiber that doesn't dissolve in water; it helps add bulk to stools and keeps the bowels moving regularly. It is found primarily in whole-grain cereals and breads, bran and in the skins of fruits and vegetables.

Isoflavones: Hormone-like substances, found in plant sources such as soybeans, that may have heart-protective and cancer-preventive effects.

Lipoprotein: The combination of the lipids and protein in your blood.

Low-Density Lipoprotein (LDL): "Bad" cholesterol, LDL carries cholesterol through the bloodstream to your cells. The higher your LDL, the higher your risk of cholesterol building up in your arteries, and the greater your risk of developing coronary heart disease.

Meditation: A quiet form of contemplation and mindfulness used to establish a sense of peace, inner calm and relaxation.

Monounsaturated Fat: "Good" fats found in canola oil, olive oil, nuts and avocados. Liquid at room temperature, these fats tend to raise heart-healthy HDL cholesterol while lowering "bad" LDL cholesterol.

Nutrients: Substances used by the body to build, repair and maintain cells. Protein, carbohydrates, fats, water, vitamins and minerals all are examples of essential nutrients.

Obese: The medical designation for people who have a body mass index (BMI) of 30 or above.

Omega-3 Fatty Acids: Unsaturated fats, found in fatty fish such as salmon, herring, mackerel, sardines, bluefish, pompano and albacore tuna and in plant sources such as flaxseed and walnuts.

Overweight: The medical designation for people who have a body mass index (BMI) of 25 to 29.

Phytonutrients: Nutrients found in plant foods that help strengthen our bodies' defenses against diseases, especially heart disease and cancer.

Protein: This nutrient helps the body build new cells. In addition, proteins work with hormones and enzymes to help the body function and generate infection-fighting antibodies.

Polyunsaturated Fat: "Good" fats, liquid at room temperature, found in corn, soybean, sunflower and other salad oils.

QiChong: A self-healing art that combines movement, meditation and visualizations to enhance the mind/body connection and assist healing.

Saturated Fat: "Bad" fats that tend to elevate blood cholesterol levels and that are solid at room temperature. These fats are found mostly in animal foods such as meat, cheese, butter, whole milk and poultry. Other highly saturated fats are found in coconut and palm oils, as well as in cocoa butter.

Soluble Fiber: Fiber that can be dissolved in water. It helps lower cholesterol in the blood. The best sources of soluble fiber are oats, barley, rye, beans, seeds, nuts, brown rice and most fruits and vegetables.

Stroke: The sudden reduction or loss of consciousness, sensation and voluntary motion caused by a rupture or obstruction of an artery in the brain.

Tai Chi: Tai chi, as it is practiced today, can best be thought of as a moving form of yoga and meditation combined. It is slow, graceful movements and is often practiced to improve flexibility and relieve pain.

Trans Fatty Acids: Fats produced when hydrogen is added to liquid vegetable oil, turning it into a solid fat. Found in shortening, stick margarine, doughnuts and baked goods.

Triglycerides: A transportable type of fat found in the blood. Triglycerides are used as a form of energy by the body; high blood triglyceride levels add to the risk of developing heart disease.

Unsaturated Fat: "Good" fats, liquid at room temperature, that do not tend to elevate blood cholesterol levels. These fats usually come from plant sources and include olive oil, sunflower oil, corn oil, nuts and avocados.

Vitamins: A group of vital nutrients, found in small amounts in a variety of foods, that are key to cell development, controlling body functions and helping release energy from fuel sources.

Whole Grains: The entire edible part of any grain: the bran, endosperm and germ. Wheat, corn, oats and rice are the most common whole grains. Experts recommend eating at least three servings of whole grains every day.

Yoga: An ancient practice based on deep breathing, stretching and strengthening exercises that is believed to balance the mind, body and spirit.

Additional Resources

Web Sites

Overall Health

Centers for Disease Control and Prevention
www.cdc.gov

Healthier US
www.healthierus.gov

Mayo Clinic
www.mayoclinic.com

The National Women's Health Information Center (NWHIC), U.S. Department of Health and Human Services
www.4women.gov

National Women's Health Resource Center
www.healthywomen.org

The Office on Women's Health, U.S. Department of Health and Human Services
www.4woman.gov/owh

U.S. Department of Health and Human Services
www.hhs.gov

WISEWOMAN™—Well-Integrated Screening and Evaluation for Women Across the Nation, Centers for Disease Control and Prevention
www.cdc.gov/wisewoman

Cancer

American Cancer Society
www.cancer.org

American Institute for Cancer Research
www.aicr.org

Fitness

Federal Recreation Resources
www.recreation.gov

Melpomene Institute
www.melpomene.org

The President's Council on Physical Fitness and Sports
www.fitness.gov

Heart Health

American College of Cardiology
www.acc.org

American Heart Association
www.americanheart.org

National Heart, Lung, and Blood Institute
www.nhlbi.nih.gov

Heart Health (continued)

Texas Heart Institute
www.texasheartinstitute.org

WomenHeart: The National Coalition for Women with
Heart Disease
www.womenheart.org

Menopause Health

The North American Menopause Society
www.menopause.org

Nutrition and Healthy Eating Web Sites

American Dietetic Association
http://www.eatright.org

Beltsville Human Nutrition Research Center
www.barc.usda.gov/bhnrc

Consumer Corner, U.S. Department of Agriculture Food
and Nutrition Information Center
www.nal.usda.gov/fnic/consumersite

International Food Information Council
www.ific.org

MyPyramid.gov, U.S. Department of Agriculture
www.mypyramid.gov

Osteoporosis

Osteoporosis and Related Bone Diseases—National
Resource Center, National Institutes of Health
www.osteo.org

Pregnancy Health

BabyCenter
www.babycenter.com

Food Safety for Moms-to-Be, U.S. Food and Drug
Administration, Center for Food Safety and Applied
Nutrition
www.cfsan.fda.gov/~pregnant/pregnant.html

Weight Management

WIN: Weight-control Information Network
http://win.niddk.nih.gov

Books

*American Dietetic Association's Complete Food and
Nutrition Guide*, 2nd Edition, Roberta Larson Duyff,
MS, RD, FADA, CFCS, John Wiley & Sons, Inc., 2002

*Strong Women Eat Well: Nutritional Strategies for a
Healthy Body and Mind*, Miriam E. Nelson and Judy
Knipe, Putnam Publishing Group, 2001

*Women's Bodies, Women's Wisdom: Creating Physical
and Emotional Health and Healing*, Christiane
Northrup, MD, Bantam Books, 1998

Helpful Nutrition and Cooking Information

Nutrition Guidelines

We provide nutrition information for each recipe that includes calories, fat, cholesterol, sodium, carbohydrate, fiber and protein. Individual food choices can be based on this information.

RECOMMENDED INTAKE FOR A DAILY DIET OF 2,000 CALORIES AS SET BY THE FOOD AND DRUG ADMINISTRATION

Total Fat	Less than 65g
Saturated Fat	Less than 20g
Cholesterol	Less than 300mg
Sodium	Less than 2,400mg
Total Carbohydrate	300g
Dietary Fiber	25g

CRITERIA USED FOR CALCULATING NUTRITION INFORMATION

➤ The first ingredient was used wherever a choice is given (such as 1/3 cup sour cream or plain yogurt).

➤ The first ingredient amount was used wherever a range is given (such as 3- to 3 1/2–pound cut-up broiler-fryer chicken).

➤ The first serving number was used wherever a range is given (such as 4 to 6 servings).

➤ "If desired" ingredients and recipe variations were not included (such as sprinkle with brown sugar, if desired).

➤ Only the amount of a marinade or frying oil that is estimated to be absorbed by the food during preparation or cooking was calculated.

INGREDIENTS USED IN RECIPE TESTING AND NUTRITION CALCULATIONS

➤ Ingredients used for testing represent those that the majority of consumers use in their homes: large eggs, 2% milk, 80%-lean ground beef, canned ready-to-use chicken broth and vegetable oil spread containing not less than 65% fat.

➤ Fat-free, low-fat or low-sodium products were not used, unless otherwise indicated.

➤ Solid vegetable shortening (not butter, margarine, nonstick cooking sprays or vegetable oil spread as they can cause sticking problems) was used to grease pans, unless otherwise indicated.

EQUIPMENT USED IN RECIPE TESTING

We use equipment for testing that the majority of consumers use in their homes. If a specific piece of equipment (such as a wire whisk) is necessary for recipe success, it is listed in the recipe.

➤ Cookware and bakeware without nonstick coatings were used, unless otherwise indicated.

➤ No dark-colored, black or insulated bakeware was used.

➤ When a pan is specified in a recipe, a metal pan was used; a baking dish or pie plate means ovenproof glass was used.

➤ An electric hand mixer was used for mixing only when mixer speeds are specified in the recipe directions. When a mixer speed is not given, a spoon or fork was used.

COOKING TERMS GLOSSARY

Beat: Mix ingredients vigorously with spoon, fork, wire whisk, hand beater or electric mixer until smooth and uniform.

Boil: Heat liquid until bubbles rise continuously and break on the surface and steam is given off. For rolling boil, the bubbles form rapidly.

Chop: Cut into coarse or fine irregular pieces with a knife, food chopper, blender or food processor.

Cube: Cut into squares 1/2 inch or larger.

Dice: Cut into squares smaller than 1/2 inch.

Grate: Cut into tiny particles using small rough holes of grater (citrus peel or chocolate).

Grease: Rub the inside surface of a pan with shortening, using pastry brush, piece of waxed paper or paper towel, to prevent food from sticking during baking (as for some casseroles).

Julienne: Cut into thin, matchlike strips, using knife or food processor (vegetables, fruits, meats).

Mix: Combine ingredients in any way that distributes them evenly.

Sauté: Cook foods in hot oil or margarine over medium-high heat with frequent tossing and turning motion.

Shred: Cut into long thin pieces by rubbing food across the holes of a shredder, as for cheese, or by using a knife to slice very thinly, as for cabbage.

Simmer: Cook in liquid just below the boiling point on top of the stove; usually after reducing heat from a boil. Bubbles will rise slowly and break just below the surface.

Stir: Mix ingredients until uniform consistency. Stir once in a while for stirring occasionally, often for stirring frequently and continuously for stirring constantly.

Toss: Tumble ingredients (such as green salad) lightly with a lifting motion, usually to coat evenly or mix with another food.

Metric Conversion Guide

VOLUME

U.S. Units	Canadian Metric	Australian Metric
1/4 teaspoon	1 mL	1 ml
1/2 teaspoon	2 mL	2 ml
1 teaspoon	5 mL	5 ml
1 tablespoon	15 mL	20 ml
1/4 cup	50 mL	60 ml
1/3 cup	75 mL	80 ml
1/2 cup	125 mL	125 ml
2/3 cup	150 mL	170 ml
3/4 cup	175 mL	190 ml
1 cup	250 mL	250 ml
1 quart	1 liter	1 liter
1 1/2 quarts	1.5 liters	1.5 liters
2 quarts	2 liters	2 liters
2 1/2 quarts	2.5 liters	2.5 liters
3 quarts	3 liters	3 liters
4 quarts	4 liters	4 liters

WEIGHT

U.S. Units	Canadian Metric	Australian Metric
1 ounce	30 grams	30 grams
2 ounces	55 grams	60 grams
3 ounces	85 grams	90 grams
4 ounces (1/4 pound)	115 grams	125 grams
8 ounces (1/2 pound)	225 grams	225 grams
16 ounces (1 pound)	455 grams	500 grams
1 pound	455 grams	1/2 kilogram

Note: The recipes in this cookbook have not been developed or tested using metric measures. When converting recipes to metric, some variations in quality may be noted.

MEASUREMENTS

Inches	Centimeters
1	2.5
2	5.0
3	7.5
4	10.0
5	12.5
6	15.0
7	17.5
8	20.5
9	23.0
10	25.5
11	28.0
12	30.5
13	33.0

TEMPERATURES

Fahrenheit	Celsius
32°	0°
212°	100°
250°	120°
275°	140°
300°	150°
325°	160°
350°	180°
375°	190°
400°	200°
425°	220°
450°	230°
475°	240°
500°	260°

University of California, San Francisco National Center of Excellence in Women's Health

The UCSF National Center of Excellence in Women's Health is one of the original six institutions awarded this designation by the U.S. Department of Health and Human Service's Office of Women's Health. The center is part of the University of California at San Francisco and of UCSF Medical Center, which is consistently ranked among the top 10 hospitals in the nation by *U.S. News & World Report*.

The UCSF National Center of Excellence in Women's Health has developed a new model to transform the traditional academic medical center from a fragmented set of activities into a dynamic and multidisciplinary health care system focused on the needs of women of all ages.

It is advancing the field of women's health by:

➤ Providing comprehensive and state-of-the-art health care for women

➤ Promoting an extensive women's health research agenda

➤ Building partnerships and linkages with community groups and organizations

➤ Educating tomorrow's health care providers about the principles of women's health through professional education programs

➤ Paving the way for women to hold key leadership positions in our institution.

Women's Health

UCSF Women's Health is continuously developing relationships with specialty women's health programs to meet each woman's specific health care needs. Specialty clinics are available in the fields of:

➤ Breast Care

➤ Continence

➤ Dysphasia

➤ Fertility

➤ Fibroids

➤ HIV

➤ Mental Health

➤ Prenatal Genetics

Specialty Care

UCSF Women's Health also provides a seamless link with other UCSF Medical Center specialty and sub-specialty programs that provide services tailored to the specific needs of women and children, including:

UCSF Children's Hospital—One of the nation's top-ranked children's hospitals.

Comprehensive Cancer Center—UCSF Medical Center has the only federally designated Comprehensive Cancer Center in Northern California treating all forms of adult and childhood cancers.

Fetal Treatment Center—The Fetal Treatment Center is a world leader in diagnosing and treating birth defects, using advanced therapies including fetal surgery.

Heart and Vascular Center—The UCSF Heart and Vascular Center pulls together specialists from a variety of disciplines to provide coordinated, seamless care for adults suffering from diseases of the heart and circulatory system. Our doctors have experience and special expertise in treating heart conditions in women of all ages.

Neurosciences—UCSF has the largest brain tumor treatment program in the country and is known for excellence in neurological surgery.

Transplant Center—UCSF doctors perform liver, pancreas, heart, lung and intestinal transplants. We pioneered using living donors for kidney and liver transplants.

To Learn More

To learn more about the UCSF National Center of Excellence in Women's Health and UCSF Medical Center programs for women, please visit www.ucsf.edu/coe/ or www.ucsfhealth.org. Rita Redberg, M.D.

Index

Pages with illustrations in *italics*.

Complete your cookbook library with these *Betty Crocker* titles

Betty Crocker Baking for Today
Betty Crocker Basics
Betty Crocker's Best Bread Machine Cookbook
Betty Crocker's Best Chicken Cookbook
Betty Crocker's Best Christmas Cookbook
Betty Crocker's Best of Baking
Betty Crocker's Best of Healthy and Hearty Cooking
Betty Crocker's Best-Loved Recipes
Betty Crocker's Bisquick® Cookbook
Betty Crocker Bisquick® II Cookbook
Betty Crocker Bisquick® Impossibly Easy Pies
Betty Crocker Celebrate!
Betty Crocker's Complete Thanksgiving Cookbook
Betty Crocker's Cook Book for Boys and Girls
Betty Crocker's Cook It Quick
Betty Crocker Cookbook, 10th Edition — *The* **BIG RED** *Cookbook*®
Betty Crocker's Cookbook, Bridal Edition
Betty Crocker's Cookie Book
Betty Crocker's Cooking Basics
Betty Crocker's Cooking for Two
Betty Crocker's Cooky Book, Facsimile Edition
Betty Crocker Decorating Cakes and Cupcakes
Betty Crocker's Diabetes Cookbook
Betty Crocker Dinner Made Easy with Rotisserie Chicken
Betty Crocker Easy Family Dinners
Betty Crocker's Easy Slow Cooker Dinners
Betty Crocker's Eat and Lose Weight
Betty Crocker's Entertaining Basics
Betty Crocker's Flavors of Home
Betty Crocker 4-Ingredient Dinners
Betty Crocker Grilling Made Easy
Betty Crocker Healthy Heart Cookbook
Betty Crocker's Healthy New Choices
Betty Crocker's Indian Home Cooking
Betty Crocker's Italian Cooking
Betty Crocker's Kids Cook!
Betty Crocker's Kitchen Library
Betty Crocker's Living with Cancer Cookbook
Betty Crocker Low-Carb Lifestyle Cookbook
Betty Crocker's Low-Fat, Low-Cholesterol Cooking Today
Betty Crocker More Slow Cooker Recipes
Betty Crocker's New Cake Decorating
Betty Crocker's New Chinese Cookbook
Betty Crocker One-Dish Meals
Betty Crocker's A Passion for Pasta
Betty Crocker's Picture Cook Book, Facsimile Edition
Betty Crocker's Quick & Easy Cookbook
Betty Crocker's Slow Cooker Cookbook
Betty Crocker's Ultimate Cake Mix Cookbook
Betty Crocker's Vegetarian Cooking
Betty Crocker Win at Weight Loss Cookbook
Cocina Betty Crocker